Social Capital and Collective Action in Pakistani Rural Development

Shaheen Rafi Khan · Shahrukh Rafi Khan

Social Capital and Collective Action in Pakistani Rural Development

palgrave
macmillan

Shaheen Rafi Khan
Sustainable Development Policy Institute
Islamabad, Pakistan

Shahrukh Rafi Khan
Department of Economics
Mount Holyoke College
South Hadley, MA, USA

ISBN 978-3-030-71449-9 ISBN 978-3-030-71450-5 (eBook)
https://doi.org/10.1007/978-3-030-71450-5

Cover illustration: kenkuza_shutterstock.com

This Palgrave Macmillan imprint is published by the registered company Springer Nature Switzerland AG
The registered company address is: Gewerbestrasse 11, 6330 Cham, Switzerland

Dedicated to the hardworking people who so generously shared their stories

Acknowledgments

Many contributed to assist us in the fieldwork resulting in the various chapters of this book. For Chapters 3 and 4 we wish to thank Shoaib Sultan Khan for the opportunity to evaluate LSOs. This is an exciting institutional initiative, a continued testimony to his innovative approach to socially relevant development.

Needless to say, we would not have made much headway without the active cooperation of the communities. We can never thank them enough for their patience, warmth, and hospitality. This applies across the board for all our empirical work. The word "vulnerability" has been overused to the point of exhaustion by development professionals; our field exposure highlighted another wonderful attribute that the rural poor possess, namely, the "resilience" that takes the edge off such vulnerability. Thanks are also due to the LSO elected officials and support staff who, as the focal points, provided logistical assistance, institutional insights, and local knowledge.

Many RSP professionals contributed to this report. In particular, we would like to thank Shandana Khan, Khaleel Tetlay, Muhammad Ali Azizi, and Nida Khan for their support through the various stages of the study. Their constructive input during formulation, implementation, and revision of the study was immeasurably valuable. It would be remiss of us not to acknowledge the senior RSP senior staff for organizing and participating in group discussions, and in extending logistic support to our survey teams.

We would like to thank the survey teams for implementing the field research. In particular, we acknowledge the high professional standards of the Gilgit–Baltistan, Thar, and Baluchistan teams.

For Chapter 5, thanks are due to the field team including Fatimah Aslam, Rashid Bashir, Abdul Fatah, Asif Mahmood, Khalid Pervez, and Noreen Saher. In particular, I would like to thank Sajid Kazmi who led the field team and his dedication and hard work produced what we considered to be high-quality data sets. Thanks are also due to Mozaffar Qizalbash, Haris Gazdar, Asif Mahmood, and Tariq Banuri for useful comments. For Chapter 6, we would like to thank Moeed Yusuf, Shahbaz Bokhari, Riaz Ahmed, and Richard Matthews.

Finally, thanks are due to Mount Holyoke College for providing research support to one of the authors who has a Research Associate affiliation with the College.

Contents

Abbreviations

ADP	Aurat Development Program
AJK	Azad Jammu and Kashmir
AKRSP	Agha Khan Rural Support Program
AMP	*Anjuman Mozareen Punjab*
APRPRP	Andhra Pradesh Rural Poverty Reduction Project
BAC	Border Area Committee
BoR	Board of Revenue
CBOs	Community-Based Organizations
CIF	Community Investment Fund
CO	Community Organization
CPEC	China-Pakistan Economic Corridor
DPIP	District Poverty Initiatives Project
EB	Executive Body
EDOR	Executive District Officer of Revenue
EEZ	Exclusive Economic Zone
EPSEM	Equal Probability of Selection
ERRA	Earthquake Relief and Rehabilitation Agency
EU	European Union
FAO	Food and Agriculture Organization
FATA	Federally Administered Tribal Areas

FC	Forestry Commission
FCS	Fishermen's Cooperative Society
FD	Forest Department
FFC	Fauji Fertilizer Corporation
FGD	Focus Group Discussion(s)
FPS	Forest Protection Societies
GB	General Body
GBAO	Gorno-Badakhshan Autonomous Oblast
GI	Galvanized Iron
GO	Government Organization
HDP	High-Density Polyethylene
hhs	Households
HIC	High Income Countries
HRW	Human Rights Watch
IDA	International Development Association
ILO	International Labor Organization
IMF	International Monetary Fund
JCO	Junior Commissioned Officer
JFM	Joint Forest Management Committee
KPK	Khyber Pakhtunkhwa
L/LMIC	Low/Low Middle Income Countries
LDO	Local Development Organization
LGRDD	Local Government and Rural Development Department
LSO	Local Support Organization
MAF	Million-Acre Feet
MMS	Mandil Mahila Samkhyas
MOU	Memorandum of Understanding
MSDSP	Mountain Societies Development Support Program
NCO	Non-Commissioned Officer
NGO	Non-Government Organization
NOC	No-Objection Certificate
NRM	Natural Resource Management
NRSP	National Rural Support Program
NWFP	North Western Frontier Province
O&M	Operation and Maintenance
PD	Participatory Development
PFF	Pakistan Fisherfolk Forum
PHED	Public Health Engineering Department
PHKN	Pakistan Hoslamand Khwateen Network

PIT	Project Implementation Team
PPI	Productive Physical Infrastructure
PPS	Probability Proportionate to Size
RSP	Rural Support Program
RSPN	Rural Support Program Network
RWSS	Rural Water Supply Schemes
SAFI	Sarhad Awami Forestry Program
SAPAP	South Asia Poverty Alleviation Program
SDPI	Sustainable Development Policy Institute
SERP	Society for Eradication of Rural Poverty
SHG	Self Help Group
SUDVO	Social Union for Development of Village Organizations
TGLP	Tajikistan Governance and Livelihoods Program
UC	Union Council
UNDP	United Nations Development Program
VDO	Village Development Organization
VO	Village Organization
WCOM	Water Committee
WWF	World Wildlife Fund
YWSPFK	Youth Welfare Society for the Protection of Forest Kalkot

List of Figures

List of Tables

Part I

Introduction and Conceptual Framework

1

Introduction

This book distinguishes between indigenous and constructed social capital and the associated spontaneous and induced collective action for rural development and natural resource preservation. The importance of social capital and collective action come into focus when juxtaposed against top-down development and growth models traditionally in vogue in Pakistan. Their record is poor, with an attendant litany of misgovernance, waste, and poor delivery. Pakistan's record of growth-oriented, anti-poor economic policies, degrading infrastructure, inadequate social services, lack of livelihood opportunities, and environmental degradation bear witness to the country's failure as a development laboratory.

In particular, the elitist thrust of development is underscored by pervasive multidimensional poverty, which officially stands at 19%, almost seventy years after the country's formation.[1] Generally, Pakistan fares poorly on most global indicators across the gender, social, political, human rights, and governance spectrums. While there is no clear evidence yet linking poverty to religious extremism, the possibility is a forewarning that the costs of neglected or skewed development could be very high.

S. R. Khan and S. R. Khan, *Social Capital and Collective Action in Pakistani Rural Development*, https://doi.org/10.1007/978-3-030-71450-5_1

The government is aware of alternative development choices. While Pakistan continues to pursue the elitist model, currently spearheaded by IMF-led structural adjustment and the China-Pak Economic Corridor (CPEC), it has attempted to mitigate adverse distributional impacts. The remedial path adopted by the government reconfigures existing paradigms to make them more efficient and accountable, with the expectation that trickle-down effects will occur. "Unleashing the private sector potential" and "good governance" are neoliberal terms that have gained currency with policymakers.

While rectifying the shortcomings of conventional approaches to development at the macro level is important (for example, with the political economy of development or new development approaches),[2] the focus in this book is to delineate broader development paths at the meso and micro level. In this context, the case studies in this book highlight two themes. First, cost-effective, community-centric, and empirically grounded initiatives can lead to positive broad-spectrum development outcomes; economic, social, and environmental, primarily through induced collective action. In addition, spontaneous collective action encompasses resource preservation, development outcomes as well as resistance to the excesses engendered by conventional development.

In the last four decades several poverty alleviation initiatives, including participatory development have been tried.[3] The basic concept of participatory development, discussed in detail in Chapter 2, is that if communities take responsibility for meeting their needs via collective action (spontaneous or induced), the results will be sustainable. The reasoning is that such participation can tap local knowledge. Further, it can give communities a sense of ownership and involvement, leading to sound project construction, operation, and maintenance. This process is associated not only with greater efficiency, but also with greater democratization and community empowerment.

As documented and discussed in Chapter 2, critics have picked holes in participatory development on methodological and technocratic grounds. Radical critics have sought to go beyond such criticisms to a more fundamental critique. They view participatory development and other similar initiatives as mechanisms to diminish the role of the state in delivering social services and furthering human development. Additionally, they argue that such initiatives conceal and reinforce oppression at the micro level while obscuring and sustaining macro-level inequality and injustice.

To an extent we do concede the value of these criticisms. The World Bank and partner organizations (e.g., multilateral aid agencies, regional development banks, and bilateral aid agencies) have picked up many of these poverty alleviation initiatives, which originated in academia or from the work of indigenous development practitioners.[4] Progressives claim that the primary, if unstated, mission of these organizations is to promote and preserve a market-based socio-economic system with a neoliberal agenda. To impart credibility to such an agenda, they sugar coat it with an overlay of participatory development initiatives, ostensibly aiming to sustainably reduce poverty and inequality.

Multilateral and bilateral donor agencies adopt a project-based, sector-specific, approach to participatory development. Once donor funding ceases, the projects tend to collapse as contingent counterpart funding dries up as well. When donor-created community organizations survive they essentially become departmental constructs, covertly promoting a neoliberal agenda while masquerading as community benefactors.[5] Social critics are thus weary of international financial organizations championing poverty alleviation initiatives that emerge from civil society on grounds that they inevitably become a trojan horse for a neoliberal agenda.

If the capitalist system is mostly an arbitrary misery-generating machine (blind to equity or social justice), the question of what to replace it with is one with which many have struggled. On this issue, radical critics of poverty alleviation initiatives are silent. While we do not aspire to present holistic answers to this question the thrust of this book is to present case studies which suggest that alternatives based on social mobilization and collective action are promising. More promising are social movements as a broader form of collective action.

Ultimately, strengthening social democracies is one major objective of social activism and social movements. In L/LMICs, social movements are not as well organized, coherent, or sustained as they are in HICs. They can also confront brutal repression. For these among other reasons, social movements, such as the Arab Spring, dissipate before realizing their potential with regard to social benefits. However, it could be argued the Arab Spring countries were neophytes when it came to instituting democratic traditions and, in the absence of viable institutions, were unable to cope with the freedoms the Arab Spring unleashed.

Pakistan falls in an intermediate category. While far from being an ideal democracy, one that is able to mitigate the effects of capitalist excesses, its institutions, the judiciary, and the media, have matured and on several occasions shown the ability to resist authoritarian dictates. It is in this spirit that this book presents alternative development options with the concurrent expectation that as democratic institutions find their footing so will community-grounded development and social initiatives.

Some of our case studies focus on spontaneous collective action aimed at mitigating the anti-poor effects of statist policies. These case studies demonstrate both advocacy for policy reform, social movements and, in the extreme, armed resistance. We also explore a hybrid form of collective action in that the spontaneous collective action is given more effective and sustainable shape by an outside organization with experience of induced collective action.

To sum up, radical social change may be ideal, but, in practice, the positives outweigh the negatives—not even taking into consideration the social dislocation and violence that might result from moving toward it. Enhancing social democracy by supporting social movements is currently the most feasible option. However, given the difficulties in realizing this option in L/LMICs, our view is that progressives could support various poverty alleviation initiatives, such as participatory development, as an interim pragmatic option at the meso and micro level.

This book is grounded in the wider contextual literature on social capital and collective action. Exploring alternative community-centric paths to development, especially those attuned with sustainability imperatives, is part of a global search for solutions. Such solutions negate top-down monocratic remedies. The empirical case studies in this book embrace sector, thematic and institutional dimensions with a national scope, i.e., a broad spatial spread.

This book has three parts apart from the concluding chapter. Part I includes this introduction and Chapter 2 that elaborates on our conceptualization of social capital and collective action. We distinguish between indigenous and constructed social capital and the corresponding spontaneous and induced forms of collective action. In addition, we explore a mixed or hybrid form of collective action which is initiated and sustained at the grassroots level but which is facilitated by capacity-building development NGOs.

We discuss the conditions under which social capital-related collective action may come about, assuming a positive association of social capital and collective action. However, such an assumption needs verification and we provide evidence regarding the association of social capital and collective action based on research conducted in Africa, Asia, and South America (Chapter 2). This review enables us to contextualize our conceptualization and to benchmark the case studies presented in the rest of the book which add to the existing body of reviewed evidence.

Part II contains three chapters that pertain to induced collective action. Rural development NGOs, referred to as Rural Support Programs (RSPs) in Pakistan, are often trapped into indefinite support for grassroots organizations they help create. Chapter 4 explores an exit strategy whereby such NGOs help establish multitier apex organizations *of* the people, rather than *for* the people, referred to as Local Support Organizations (LSOs), that are able to replace them.

This enables the RSPs to move on to other communities or to address their resource constraints as donor funding becomes tighter. Based on extensive fieldwork, our findings suggest that LSOs have the ability to mobilize successfully for ambitious collective action for community betterment. The projects tackled were much needed, ambitious in scale, and demonstrated a surprising level of innovation in finding solutions to difficult problems.

Observation of processes demonstrated the LSOs' ability to bring about cultural change that empowered communities, women, and the poorest of the poor and enabled them to engage in collective action. In our assessment, a third of the LSOs become institutionally and financially sustainable, an impressive achievement given the short time they had been in existence. There appeared to be two prevailing strategies on how to proceed. One view can be characterized by a "sink or swim" approach. An alternative was a more nurturing strategy, and this is the one we endorse to ensure a higher success rate.

Some LSOs referred to above are exclusively run by women. Our focus in Chapter 4 is on the impact of the RSP-exit strategy on rural women LSOs. Our major survey-based findings are that women have fared well, been more effective in running the LSOs than men, and despite confronting a conservative culture, have effectively filled spaces vacated by men.

In Chapter 5 we explore the effectiveness of RSP social capital construction method in delivering rural water supply compared to two public sector line department initiatives, i.e., those of the Local Government and Rural Development Department (LGRDD) and Public Health Engineering Department (PHED). Our findings were based on field reports written by trained field teams and on analyses of data generated from focus group meetings, household interviews, interviews with the project field staff, and technical evaluations by engineers.

Our findings based on the field reports (which we privileged) show that the National Rural Support Program (NRSP) schemes stuck much more closely to the project rules and implementation procedures specified in the project documents. They had a much higher success rate in sustainable delivery and their schemes were also more cost-effective. NRSP staff managed to mobilize communities in three different provinces under very different social, economic, and technological conditions. The accomplishment was particularly noteworthy in Sindh where the communities were highly differentiated by ethnicity and income. This represented a strong endorsement of their approach to social capital construction. The results of technical, community, and household data analysis, for the most part, confirmed the evaluations of the field teams contained in the field reports.

In Part III we explore spontaneous and hybrid forms of collective starting with community attempts to protect resource rights in forestry. British colonial rule arrogated community rights and responsibilities to manage forest resources. Following partition from India, Pakistan's Forest Department continues to retain an enforcement mindset. Communities reacted to the deprivation of their rights and entitlements by raiding forest resources—albeit on a much smaller scale than the timber contractors (referred to locally as the timber mafia).

Chapter 6 documents two forms of collective action. One arose spontaneously as a reaction to social injustice (denied and delayed royalties that were due to locals) and led to violent conflict. The other embodied the social resentment into an organizational form, i.e., the Sarhad Awami Forestry Ittehad (SAFI) and sustained collective action for forestry sector reforms. SAFI as a membership organization, registered in 2008, lobbies to reinstate peoples' rights and for community-based forest management.

We view SAFI's efforts as a mixed or hybrid form of collective action since it has sought and benefited from the capacity-building of a development NGO. In this regard it differs from the purely spontaneous collective action or the development NGO induced collective action where the NGO drives the collective action.

The Pakistan Fisherfolk Forum (PFF), a community-based civil society organization, was established in May 1998. Its aim is to safeguard the socio-economic well-being and resource rights of indigenous fisherfolk. Community resource rights have traditionally been the key to sustainable fisheries management, their attenuation underscored by the rapid depletion of freshwater and marine fisheries. The PFF advocacy campaigns target exploitative contractor practices, illegal acquisition of open resources, habitat-destroying fishing nets, and fishing policies dictated by commercial needs.

Chapter 8 documents the allocation of the commons to senior military officers. Starting from social acceptance when the military was viewed as a guardian and defender, social attitudes among the peasantry turned to resentment as the resource capture became increasingly predatory. This chapter documents how this social resentment bred collective action with stunning success given the power asymmetry between the military and peasantry. The key lesson from this chapter is that when the collective action assumes organizational form, based on linking social capital, the ability to sustain the collective action over decades is much more likely and that spontaneous collective action can dissipate otherwise.

Chapter 9 explores why spontaneous collective action based on indigenous social capital may not be enough to mitigate the negative impacts of disasters. This chapter contains two case studies of community coping.

The first case study pertains to coping with the impact of an earthquake and the second case study to coping with the fallout of COVID-19.

On October 8, 2005 an earthquake registering 7.6 on the Richter scale struck northeast Pakistan. The impact was intense, killing at least 73,000 people, injuring another 70,000, and leaving 2.8 million without shelter at the onset of winter and thus susceptible to further harm. Understandably, much initial attention to this earthquake centered on official relief and rehabilitation. But within this focus, scant attention was paid to the broken interface of social and institutional dimensions that made people vulnerable to such extreme damage in the first place. Also, instead of traditional institutional networks leveraging official relief and rehabilitation packages, the latter were subject to capture by the Khans. In contrast, social processes (customs, traditions, practices) based on indigenous social capital were able to provide some measure of mutual relief for the most vulnerable.

Another case study showed that autonomous social capital that drove successful indigenous collective action with initiatives in education, health, and infrastructure was ineffective when it came to coping with COVID-19. Local institutions (norms, cultural practices) that reinforce autonomous social capital were at odds with the need to contain infection rates. An attempt to draw in a national organization adept at induced collective action had little success in overcoming entrenched cultural practices.

We view this book as making a two-fold contribution: first, in providing a conceptual classification of different forms of social capital and associated collective action; second, in providing a body of case study material on this issue. This case study material, in an updated context, is based on fieldwork we did jointly or separately over the past few decades. While most of the fieldwork for this book was done a while back, we believe the lessons learnt remain as relevant now and when we did the field research.

Notes

1. Government of Pakistan/UNDP, p. 15, Multidimensional Poverty Index, https://www.undp.org/content/dam/pakistan/docs/MPI/Multidimensional%20Poverty%20in%20Pakistan.pdf, consulted 10/6/2019. The same report (p. 4) indicates the poverty based on the national poverty line for 2014–2015 to be 25.5%, 18.2 urban and 35.6 rural. This highlights the importance of rural development.
2. For a review of alternative approaches to economic development, refer to Khan (2020).
3. Others include microcredit, conditional, and unconditional cash transfers and the graduation model. Refer to Khan (2020, Chapter 4 for details.
4. The work of Akhtar Hameed Khan and Shoaib Sultan being two notable examples from Pakistan.
5. Also, when there is government buy-in, as in the case of the Rural Support Program (RSP) initiatives (Chapters 3–5) which the Pakistan Muslim League government of Nawaz Sharif extended across the country, such buy-ins can cease with a change in government. The Pakistan Tareek-e-Insaf government of Imran Khan elected in 2018 abruptly ended support for RSPs. A potentially promising effort fell victim to political vicissitudes. Further, inverting this premise, and abstracting from the political aspect, raises the question as to why there is not more official take-up of home-grown initiatives.

Reference

Khan, S.R. 2020. *Development Economics: A Critical Introduction*. New York: Routledge.

2

Social Capital-Driven Collective Action

Introduction

In this chapter we first elaborate on our conceptualization of social capital and the associated spontaneous, induced or mixed (hybrid) forms of collective action. Next, we discuss the conditions under which collective action may come about. Induced collective action or participatory development has been subject to harsh criticism over the last three decades. This criticism is reviewed and a case made for induced collective action. The title of this chapter implicitly assumes a positive association of social capital and collective action. However, such an assumption needs verification and we provide evidence regarding the association of social capital and collective action based on research conducted in Africa, Asia, and South America.

S. R. Khan and S. R. Khan, *Social Capital and Collective Action in Pakistani Rural Development*, https://doi.org/10.1007/978-3-030-71450-5_2

Social Capital

In rural development, social capital can lead to collective action when communities mobilize or are mobilized for collective or joint action.[1] Social capital is defined for this book as the mutual trust and social interactions that enable communities to cooperate and engage in collective action for mutual benefit.

This definition is similar to Woolcock's (2002, p. 22) definition of social capital as norms and networks that facilitate collective action. Woolcock also provided a useful categorization of social capital into bonding (between close family members, friends, and neighbors), bridging (horizontal associations between more distant associates and colleagues or between communities) and linking (vertical linkages to people, associations, and organizations beyond the community with influence or power). All three forms of social capital come into play in this book.

Uphoff (2000, p. 221) provided another useful classification for empirical work and distinguished between cognitive and structural social capital. Cognitive social capital is manifested as shared norms, values, attitudes, and beliefs in the domain of civic culture and the dynamic factors include trust, solidarity, cooperation, and generosity. Structural social capital is manifested as roles and rules, procedures, precedents, networks, and interpersonal relations in the domain of social organizations and the dynamic factors are horizontal and vertical linkages. Cognitive social capital is internal and pertains to how people think whereas structural social capital is external and more visible. Cognitive social capital inclines individuals toward collective action while structural social capital facilitates collective action.

The two classifications appear to intersect. For example, cognitive social capital could be associated with bonding and even bridging social capital while linking social capital is associated with structural social capital. Further, one could argue that cognitive-bonding/bridging is conducive to spontaneous collective action while the linking-structural social capital is more associated with induced collective action. However, classifications are not hard and fast in that cognitive /bonding social capital can be viewed as a precondition for structural/linking social capital.

We view social capital to be manifested in social interactions via networks and even trust that resides in the individual acquires meaning in a social context. This view of social capital is distinct from Bourdieu's (1986) view of social capital in the sense of contacts and networks that could be seen as an asset for self-enhancement by elites, most likely in a zero-sum game.

Forms of Collective Action

Collective action is defined as working jointly and voluntarily for a common goal yielding mutual benefits. Collective action could be *spontaneous* such that rural communities organize themselves for it. In Pakistan, the defining features and institutional expressions of such collective action include traditional village events, mutual aid, participatory decision-making, and dispute resolution. We explore various examples in this book of spontaneous collective action seemingly driven by social capital. The social capital takes the form of norms (including sanctions), rules, and procedures for networks and formal or informal organizations to function effectively for a positive and mutually beneficial cause.

More recently, collective action in Pakistan, and more generally across South Asia and beyond, has been induced by constructed organizational forms, such as community, village, and union council level organizations.[2] This form of induced collective action has been referred to in the literature as participatory development.

Usually an external agent, such as a development NGO often with donor assistance, taps social capital to mobilize communities. The organizational forms catalyzed by development NGOs can be viewed as constructed social capital. Thus, one can distinguish between preexisting, indigenous or informal social capital, and formal or constructed social capital. When external agencies tap such preexisting social capital to build community organizations, the process can be referred to as the formalization of social capital. A broader definition of social capital, therefore, includes both the informal norms and networks that make the organizations possible and also the organizations themselves. In turn, this formalized social capital can facilitate collective action which is referred to as induced, distinguished from spontaneous collective action based on indigenous or informal social capital.[3]

We also observed a mixed form of collective action during our field work on forestry as described in Chapter 6. In this case, social resentment boiled over, led to collective action in the form of violent conflict and, subsequently, precipitated negotiations. This collective action dissipated after the negotiations but reemerged since the underlying social injustice was not addressed but temporarily deflected by these negotiations. A grassroots organization emerged in one locality, with the capacity-building assistance of a development NGO, to harness the social resentment for ongoing collective action. This differs from induced collective action driven by a rural development NGO since the organizational impetus emerged and remained at the grassroots level.

Recall that authentic cognitive/bonding (informal) social capital is a prerequisite for structural/linking social capital. That would also apply to outside agency attempts to construct or formalize social capital. For example, joint forest management committees (JFMs) foisted on communities by the forest department and designed to manipulate them, are essentially hollow shells masquerading as constructed social capital (Chapter 6).[4]

Collective action is heterogeneous and therefore different conditions apply for different kinds of collective action. We consider three kinds of social capital-driven collective action in this book, two spontaneous and one induced. The spontaneous forms of collective action include the protection of natural resource rights (Chapters 6–8) and mitigating the impact of natural disasters (Chapter 9). The induced form of collective action pertains to rural development initiatives.

Collective action ranges from the micro or village level on one extreme to state action on the other extreme. Thus, the broadest national manifestation of collective action is taxation in return for public service delivery by the state. Even broader is global collective action whereby nation states agree to engage in resolving collective problems, for example, such as those resulting from climate change. The 2016 Paris Agreement is an example of an attempt at global collective action.[5]

In mainstream economics, individual action is driven by utility maximization. The calculus of evaluating benefits and costs on the margin maximizes utility for the individual or the household. To deny that individuals are driven by impulses for self-betterment seems deluded and the classic mistake of utopian socialists.

However, to deny that individuals are complex and driven by multiple motivations, some self-interested and others altruistic, seems as deluded as utopian socialists premising success of alternatives to capitalism on individuals motivated by the collective good. Nonetheless, our value judgment is to privilege motivations where the individual is able to transcend pure utility maximization and work with others for the collective good at the micro and meso levels.[6]

As stated above, social capital, among other factors, enables collective action. In this regard, one could view social capital as latent and social mobilization and collective action as the "active" manifestation of the social capital. Social capital can be viewed as a stock variable and the collective action that results as a flow variable.

The quality of the autonomous social capital could contribute to the effectiveness of the collective action. On one extreme, one could think of high-quality living social capital as embodied in the highly effective functioning of networks and organizations that yield effective collective action. On the other extreme, social capital would be revealed to be dead or defunct in non-functioning networks and organizations.[7] At any given time, the quality of social capital could vary between these extremes in given communities and could change over time. Effective collective action could be one factor in strengthening the quality of social capital and in this regard these two variables can be thought of as mutually interactive in leading to virtuous or vicious cycles.

As mentioned earlier, social capital can be "constructed." For example, development NGOs concerned with poverty alleviation may start their development work by mobilizing communities to construct social capital. Constructed social capital takes the form of community or village organizations with regular meetings, organized savings, and an agenda for collective action including building and maintaining social infrastructure

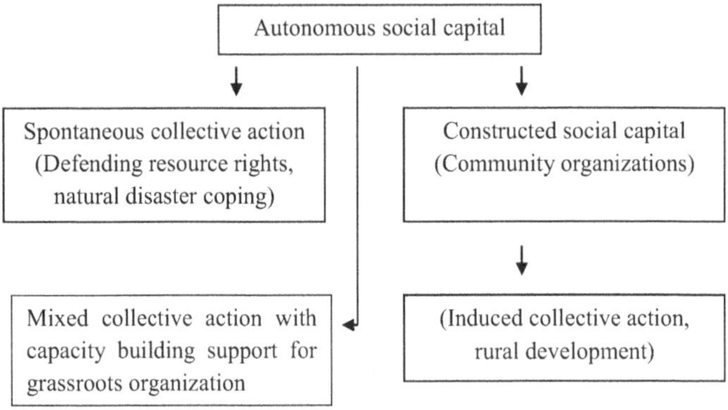

Fig. 2.1 Forms of social capital and collective action

to enhance community well-being.[8] Figure 2.1 explains our conceptualization for the alternative paths to the collective actions discussed in this book and their association with different forms of social capital.

As indicated by Fig. 2.1, this book will discuss various initiatives pertaining to social capital and collective action. These include:

a. Institutional formulations in the shape of local support organizations, which represent constructed social capital in the form of community, village, and higher tier apex organizations that induce rural development collective action. We refer to this as induced collective action.
b. People's rights movements, which aim to safeguard and sustainably use land, forest, and water resources that are essential to their livelihoods. We refer to this as spontaneous collective action.
c. Indigenous social organizations that are supported by development NGOs but where the initiative remains at the grassroots level. We refer to this as mixed or hybrid collective action.

Our focus on spontaneous, induced and mixed collective action enables us to highlight a rich set of associated issues. For example, constructed social capital may be viewed as a bridging effort for donor–civil society or public–civil society partnerships. The government can extend its mandate spatially by providing financial support. In Pakistan it had done so, for a while (see Chapter 1), in a non-intrusive manner, ensuring that the autonomy of development NGOs is not compromised. In this special case, the development NGOs tried to ensure that the driving force was that of an organization of the people rather than one constructed for the people.

Constructed social capital and the associated induced collective action can, in principle, work both ways. On the one hand, it may diminish the underlying impulses which bring communities together and hence dependency might weaken autonomous social capital and associated collective action. On the other hand, formalizing the social capital might strengthen community social capital.

People's rights movements and community responses to extreme events have both a complementary and confrontational aspect. They fill in for government lapses and do the job more efficiently and responsively. Yet, they can also confront the government for its lapses and often for its oppressive stances. It is possible to learn from both successes and failures and in Chapter 9 we explore how autonomous collective action can be undermined.

For the moment, let us assume that there is an association of social capital and collective action. More challenging is identifying the precise mechanisms that lead to this association. Even if a high level of autonomous social capital is present in communities, certain conditions would still need to be satisfied for the collective action to be forthcoming, particularly for rural development initiatives. We discuss these possible conditions below.

Conditions for Collective Action and Elite Capture

Even though joint action seems commonsensical, in practice it faces several obstacles. These include elite capture when there is extreme power asymmetry and those in power are able to appropriate most of the benefits of joint action.[9] Examples would include the construction of an irrigation channel whereby the large landlord running the village has most to gain from it given his larger landholdings. Even if the power asymmetry is not extreme, coming up with a formula for roughly even distribution of benefits and effort could be difficult. Finally, even if the latter obstacle is overcome opportunistic behavior such as free-riding, whereby some are willing to gain from the work but escape the effort by shirking or stealing (claiming more benefits than assigned) could undermine the collective action (Ostrom 1993a).

Elite capture and how it figures into and is dealt within the cases of both spontaneous and induced collective action is an important consideration. On the one hand we argue that Olson's (1971, pp. 22–33—see below) pessimistic view of the constraint to collective action pertains more to certain kinds of development initiatives in which an economic calculus is the primary concern. Where the conditions for collective action do not exist, partly due to elite capture, induced collective action may be called for. On the other hand, we argue that spontaneous collective action can arise as a counter to elite capture in cases of protecting the commons. Thus, the motivation for collective action in such cases is not solely economic.

Given the free-rider problem, Olson (1971, pp. 22–33) showed that in small groups collective action would be forthcoming if the benefit to any one individual exceeded the total project cost. If this condition is satisfied, free-riding, which undermines collective action, is no longer an issue. By contrast, Wade (1988) could be viewed as guardedly optimistic about collective action. Wade pointed out that community collective action could result from economic compulsions and externalities that require communities to work together.[10]

The problem with Olson's condition as it applies in a rural development context is that dominant village notables can capture most of the benefits leaving others in the community with little motivation to act voluntarily. We presume that action based on intimidation does not constitute collective action since there is a presumption of voluntary effort if the outcome is to be called collective action.

Sandler (2015) in a retrospective of Olson's seminal book, *The Logic of Collective Action*, explored how Olson's propositions sparked a plethora of research across the social sciences. Our concern is only with one proposition that concerns products that are rivalrous in consumption and for which exclusion is possible.[11]

Khan (1999, pp. 71–72) showed that collective action might still be forthcoming for a development rural initiative if individual benefits exceed or are equal to individual costs on the margin and if the benefits and costs are roughly equal for all individuals. These are stringent conditions and may only apply in a few cases. For example, in a water supply scheme, the participants in collective action may agree to a common tariff and an equal distribution of water supply that provides equivalent benefits that are equal to or exceed the tariff. The latter condition is deemed to be satisfied by revealed preference if the collective action is forthcoming. However, elite dominance and capture is a problem for spontaneous rural development collective action. Notables would not tolerate social organization if it excludes them and equal benefits are not likely if it includes them.

It is most likely that for this reason an outside agency is needed for inducing collective action for rural development initiatives. A rural development NGO, particularly if it has the backing of some level of government (local, state, central), will be able to frame equitable rules and ensure their implementation. Typically, such organizations, when they have government backing, find ways to bypass local notables by claiming that the development work is designed for poverty alleviation and so the more prosperous are excluded by stringent inclusion criteria if they do not self-select themselves out of the initiatives. The development-oriented collective action in Part II of this book represents this kind of induced collective action led by a development NGO. The challenge for rural development initiatives is to find a way of converting induced collective action into sustained community effort for maintenance.

The other case studies represent spontaneous collective action and these fit into the category of protecting the commons (resource rights) or mitigating the impacts of natural disasters. Protecting natural resources from depredation and raiding by local elites, particularly when resource rights are involved, is collective action sparked by outrage. Mitigating the outcome of natural disasters is collective action born of dealing with a common threat. It could be complemented by humanitarianism when that is an important part of the local culture.

Elite capture is not likely to retard the non-development categories of collective action. In natural resource protection collective action, anti-capture is the trigger for collective action. Again, since resources intended for the broader communities after disasters is often captured by elites, the social mobilization for collective action is, again, a form of resistance to such capture. In this case, the collective action is a mechanism for self-help that bypasses elites. In both cases, the motivation is not entirely economic and so marginal conditions mentioned above need not come into play.

Critique of and Case for Induced Collective Action

Participatory development[12] (PD), or induced collective action, has been severely criticized on several counts. In this section, we distinguish between "friendly criticism" and fundamental criticism. Friendly criticism in principle accepts the value of induced collective action but raises serious issues of a methodological or technocratic nature that induced collective action needs to contend with to succeed. Fundamental criticism goes beyond the methodological or technocratic criticism and questions whether induced collective action can really amount to much.[13]

The most foundational of the methodological criticism is that induced collective action presumes that an external agent (social organizer of a development NGO) can start the process by mobilizing a community. However, the very definition of a community has been contested by many scholars. Baland et al. (2006) view the concept of community in a rural development context as fictional. The argument is that what is represented as a homogeneous unit by calling it a community is really a mosaic including class, caste, gender, age, and ethnicity. We do not dispute that this is the case but demonstrate in this book that, heterogeneity notwithstanding, people who live in contiguous areas are often galvanized into collective action to safeguard their interests.

Critics of PD have picked holes in all aspects of the practice (e.g., Cleaver 1999). They think there is an overemphasis on formal constructed organizations, a neglect of local "informal" institutions and a neglect of group social dynamics that complicate what participation really means. The motivation of participation as derived from rationality is not considered in accord with existing norms and cultural practices of social networks.[14] Since much of the funding comes from donor agencies, the accountability they claim is vertical rather than to the grassroots level.

Participation is engendered within an external framework and on an external agenda and based on an external vision and values. There is no real shaping of the project by local needs and local knowledge but merely lip service to these concepts and indeed to local empowerment (Michener 1998). There is no check on elite capture at the local level and little consideration of context (Platteau and Abraham 2002; O'Meally 2014). Participation can mean different things to different actors (e.g., donors, development NGOs, state tiers) and there is little clarity on who is to be empowered and how much empowerment one project can deliver (Cleaver 2001, p. 35).

In a Thai case study, Funder (2010) views local "activists" as an intermediary between development NGOs and the community and in this role can act as gatekeepers, guiding the intervention toward a favored group. In the case study explored, activists influenced the process and project by selecting who was to be included, even if elites were avoided as specified by the project guidelines, and benefited from opportunities available. Thus, they subverted the original project goals to those that would provide more benefits to the "in-group" and even harm the poor who were from a different ethnicity, ironically the original intended project beneficiaries. This case study, however, belied the notion of the project shaping and controlling agendas at the grassroots level. However, it did highlight the importance of development NGOs being vigilant and sensitive to context.

While donors responded to the feminist movement in HICs to make participatory development gender sensitive, Mayoux's (1995) words of caution, are in a similar vein to those of Funder. "Gender inequalities in resources, time availability and power, shape the activities, priorities and organizational framework of participatory projects as much as 'top-down' development and market activities." She went on to point out that "unless these issues are addressed then in many cases 'participatory development for women' will constitute little more than a further increase in the unpaid contribution of women to development programmes from which they derive little benefit."[15]

Cleaver (2005) provided an account of why the chronically poor, possibly due to loss of family members or ill health and hence unable to contribute their labor power, may be unable to participate in collective action. Participating in associational life can entail a direct cost (joining and recurrent fees) and an opportunity cost (foregone livelihood opportunities) and hence excludes the chronically poor. In such cases, social capital induced collective action is no substitute for equity reforms ensuring entitlements and building capacities.

Many of the prominent fundamental critics are featured in a collected volume edited by Cooke and Kothari (2001) that emerged from a conference. This book became highly influential and remains a key critique of PD. The authors collectively agreed to dub participation as "the new tyranny" even if sometimes by well-meaning actors. The editors in the first chapter on the purpose of the book define the task at hand as going beyond the internal critiques of the PD orthodoxy on definitional, philosophical, technocratic, and methodological issues to a more fundamental critique.

This critique is summarized by the editors in the opening chapter framing the purpose of the book, though they concede the contributions to the edited volume are quite diverse. Based on the essence of the contributions, the editor's responses to the first two rhetorical questions they raised are that: First, yes, outsiders override legitimate decision-making processes at the grassroots level; Second, yes, PD can conceal and reinforce oppressions at the micro level and obscure and sustain macro-level inequalities and injustice. In response to the third and final question they raised, the editors did not reject PD but suggested that academics and PD practitioners should engage in honest reflection and be open to that possibility. The task at hand they suggested was to move to a more nuanced understanding of the workings of power.[16]

This conclusion is unsatisfactory for two reasons. First, it appears that the fundamental critique of PD is really a critique of the system it is introduced into and not a critique of PD per se. Hence, the fundamental critique amounts to a Marxist critique, i.e., that private property and accumulation are the cause of social injustice where ever manifested.[17] In L/LMICs, a hybrid semi-feudal/semi-capitalist/statist system usually prevails. This system, based predominantly on the private ownership of the means of production, gives some play to market forces. A Marxist critique applies to this hybrid system also (i.e., it is based on accumulation and hence can be extractive, predatory, and oppressive). The outcomes of this hybrid system are more deleterious to the public good because effective legal and social protections, like those that were instituted in high-income countries (HICs) to counter the spread of Marxist ideology, are limited. To expect poverty alleviation initiatives to somehow address system shortcomings is a big ask.

The critics are right that the concept of empowerment should be associated with structural transformation of existing power structures at the societal level, i.e., in terms of a transformation of law, property rights and social and governance institutions. However, arguing that PD is blameworthy because it depoliticizes the concept of empowerment is missing the point. The system is what it is independent of PD.

Second, the critics provide no alternative to PD, or for that matter other poverty alleviation initiatives, if they are to be rejected. A defense of PD and other poverty alleviation initiatives emerge from a clearer understanding of their limitations. If they are introduced into a semi-feudal/statist/semi-capitalist system, they can only be a pragmatic option to improve human well-being as discussed in Chapter 1.

The first best could be a social revolution if one could be assured that it would lead to a just society in all regards and also that such cataclysmic change can be attained without injustice.[18] There is little evidence so far that either assurance can be provided. While Marx diagnosed the cause of social injustice, his analysis contains the seeds of undermining a utopian alternative. The implicit human proclivity to accumulation of wealth and power that he asserted also suggests that an alternative based entirely on altruism and social harmony was unlikely.[19] The attempts at building a society without feudal and capitalist exploitation have for the most part manifested other forms of accumulation, autocracy, and repression of human freedoms, although socialist societies have invested more in gender and human development.[20]

Human history is much too brief to concede that capitalism has triumphed because it is more consistent with average human behavior. However, so far, no good alternative has emerged so the challenge is to make systems based on private ownership and markets, while they last, more just. Social democracies based on radical land, other wealth, and income redistribution are a good alternative option and this is in the realm of social activism and social movements. In L/LMICs, social movements are not as well organized, coherent, or sustained as they are in HICs. They can also confront brutal repression. For these among other reasons, social movements, such as the Arab Spring, dissipate before realizing their potential with regard to social benefits. As mentioned in the intro such outcomes are the result of weak institutions.

Given the problems with the first two options, the third option at the meso or micro level is to be willing to make the most of poverty alleviation initiatives like PD in the imperfect systems that exist in low/middle-income countries (L/MICs). However, to expect that these initiatives will rectify an imperfect system is a stretch.

If the evidence suggests that rural development NGOs engaged in PD have substantively improved lives of the most marginalized poor, it is worthy of support. In terms of the dichotomy of participation as an end in and of itself (empowerment) or a means to an end (human development of the most marginalized), the latter position is being supported here if it is an either-or choice. However, we think an eclectic mix is possible. While it would be erroneous to believe induced collective action can deliver in this regard, none the less the hybrid version of spontaneous collective action against say land or forest royalty grabs could contribute to a system change.

The issue of whether this is the best allocation of resources remains. The view adopted on this issue here is that in a development context, rational allocation of resources based on the highest social returns for development interventions is simply not practiced. In the spirit of satisficing as developmental realists, we suggest that if the intervention is cost-effective relative to others, it is worth pursuing. It certainly beats allocating resources to submarines, fighter planes, and tanks or having them disappear in capital outflows.[21]

PD is therefore defended and endorsed here, and, in this context, there are two points to note. First, progressive critics view this as a World Bank intervention which stigmatizes it for them. This is in fact not the case and PD predates the World Bank's taking it up as a development intervention. The World Bank with its enormous development research capacity is in the habit of co-opting and owning poverty alleviation interventions that originate in academia or from the experimentation of development practitioners and advocates. For example, other than PD, this has been the case with social capital, microcredit, and cash transfers.

However, vigilance is still called for. If we concede that humans are driven on average by self-interest, initiatives like PD need to be carefully monitored so that development NGO management are "doing good" as suggested by their mission statements and not empire building and lining their pockets (Karim 2011; Faraizi et al. 2011). Thus, there is room here for methodological and technocratic critiques. Having made a case for induced collective action, we turn next to a review of how social capital has been instrumental in realizing it across L/LMICs.

Social Capital and Collective Action: A Review[22]

So far, we have assumed that social capital is positively associated with collective action. In the section below we review the evidence that demonstrates that is indeed the case in particular cultural contexts. We review studies that find a positive association of social capital and collective action, with the implied causality running from the former to the later. However, as stated above, an interaction is likely such that successful collective action could reinforce social capital just as unsuccessful collective action could undermine it.

The research reviewed includes empirical studies based on the deductive method (quantitative) favored by economists as well as inductive case studies (qualitative) we set greater store by for reasons explained below. The deductive method requires the use of data sets whereby collective action and social capital are defined and measured. Following this, social capital is used as a variable among others to identify if it a significant and substantive explanatory variable for collective action. There are numerous possible problems in the empirics such as those identified by Fine (2001) and Durlauf and Fafchamps (2004) even beyond the problem of reasonable definitions and the difficulty of establishing causality.

Mosse's (2006) anthropological perspective on collective action or the lack of it in rural societies revealed how simplistic the quantitative empirical method is even beyond the criticisms of the empirics. In explaining collective action pertaining to village irrigation in South India, Mosse identified the importance of understanding the multifaceted nature of water tanks as social and cultural systems.

He argued that collective action had more to do with power, caste, hierarchy, and patronage than trust, organization, and associational life. Further, while scarcity and risk might be explanatory factors, their relevance to collective action requires an understanding of history, ecology, technology, stability of production systems, power and caste dominance. The most telling criticism was that a "-- single-moment survey cannot help but produce a statistical artifact that freezes a dynamic set of relations and permits confused causality or that quantifies social connections in ways that misrepresent their significance" (p. 719).

Other social scientists have at least one advantage over rich anthropological studies that put them at a disadvantage. This is their ability to touch on multiple sites by using large data sets rather than being confined to one or very few sites. Thus, there is the possibility, with qualifications, of establishing empirical regularities and also the magnitude and strength of associations and it is in this spirit that the cross-sectional study findings are presented below.

Empirical studies from Africa, Asia, and South America, based both on the inductive and deductive method, date back several decades and cover a number of rural development topics. These include social capital-based collective action for drinking and irrigation water, sanitation, watershed and land management, poultry, livestock, marketing, and agriculture. The findings are reported by continent and within this category organized loosely by topic. The studies summarized below present examples of the positive association of social capital and collective action.

Africa

Smale and Ruttan (1997) gave an account of Groupements Naam that were a part of transnational federation of farmers' groups that spanned the Sahel including the Yatenga in Burkino Faso. Exploring the latter region, they found that these groups had successfully undertaken costly public works in water retention infrastructure. Bising et al. (2014) showed a positive association between elements of social capital and participation in collective action in the context of addressing water and sanitation issues in the lakeshore village of Usoma, Western Kenya.

Coppock and Desta (2013) studied 16 dynamic women's collective-action groups in small settlements throughout north-central Kenya. These groups, governed by detailed by-laws, were encouraged by local development agency staff (GO or NGO). Of the 63 groups in the area that were created over the 25 years prior to the survey period, 47 were thriving. The collective action they were engaged in included microfinance, livelihood diversification, and mitigation of drought effects; they also spearheaded and funded community education and health initiatives. The authors stated that the fact that the collective action emerged and persisted in the pastoral regions studied was surprising since they have been characterized by expansive landscapes and low densities of nomadic or seminomadic peoples that are members of loosely structured social networks. Such forms of social organization are viewed as accommodating greater independence and opportunistic behavior among individuals and households, facilitating the use of patchy, variable foraging environments.

Lyon (2000) empirically explored the role of trust, norms, and informal networks among farmers in Ghana that enabled them to realize market opportunities and increased incomes. De Hann (2001) reported on the more effective transfer of information within groups in the context of a Heifer Project International initiative among the marginalized in rural Tanzania. The project was based on working with groups built on existing social networks to provide in this case more milk productive goats, the offsprings of which were to be passed on to others in the community. The groups constructed their own rules and benefited from their own learning. Social capital was instrumental in all groups in the acquisition of a goat.[23]

Reid and Salmen (2002) used the term social cohesion for social capital and in a qualitative study showed that the most important factor determining the success of external interventions in rural Mali, such as agricultural extension, was the degree of social cohesion already existing in the community prior to the intervention. They suggested various indicators of social cohesion such as common maintenance of public buildings (e.g., school or a mosque), Friday prayer attendance, village cleanliness, associational activity, and accepted leadership.

Isham (2002) explored the impact of social capital on fertilizer adoption in rural Tanzania by drawing on and extending a neoclassical model to incorporate characteristics of the social structure and then estimating it. Instead of a composite social capital index, distinct forms of social capital were separately included in the estimating equation to allow different mechanisms via which social capital characteristics like group homogeneity, participatory norms, and leadership heterogeneity might influence adoption. The main findings were that households with ethnically based and participatory social affiliations were more likely to diffuse information about new technologies and facilitate adoption.

Schroeder and Zeller (2013) researched mostly self-organized democratic mixed farmer groups engaged in rice production in Benin. In some cases, the impulse for group formation was given by external agents such as local NGOs, pastors, community workers, and/or district heads. Farming in groups, based on a gendered division of labor, helped with securing and sharing intermediate and capital inputs and securing external assistance. Their findings showed that social capital and associated collective action enhanced women's economic and social position and their personal advancement. The mutual learning and exchange of good practices that accompanied group membership and rules to thwart free-riding were noteworthy in particular.

Mabuza et al. (2012) studied spontaneously formed farmers groups in mushroom production in Swaziland. They presented quantitative empirical evidence that suggested that members from communities characterized by positive cognitive social capital were most likely to engage in voluntary collective action in an attempt to improve their livelihoods.

Mubangizi (2003) described how in rural South Africa, members paid a fee to join production groups to engage in various production activities such as poultry for broilers or egg production, pig production, or vegetable growing. The groups were run democratically and members shared the dividends of the enterprise based on rules and norms set out in the formation constitutions.

Gebremedhin et al. (2004) used the presence of local organizations in the village as a measure of social capital and showed that it had a positive and significant impact on collective action for grazing land management in the highlands of Northern Ethiopia. Bastelaer and Leathers (2006) empirically estimated the impact of various kinds of social capital on repayment rates of seed loans among 256 joint liability farmers groups in southern Zambia. They found that cognitive social capital, proxied by trust toward strangers, was strongly associated with repayment performance.

Ruben and Heras (2012) found a similar result among coffee-growing cooperatives in Ethiopia. Kihiu (2016) found that household involvement with external organizations, structural social capital, was among the variables that significantly influenced participation in collective management of pastoral resources in Southwestern Kenya.

Willy and Holm-Müller (2013) explored the impact of social capital on collective action for farm-level soil conservation in rural Kenya. They found that social participation, social support, reciprocity, and trustworthiness had a positive impact on the probability of participating in collective action while social networks had a negative impact. This finding about networks is replicated elsewhere in the literature and is explained as networks facilitating individual action and therefore undermining collective action.

Davenport and Hassan (2019) qualitatively explored the elements of social capital (particularly structural and linking) behind the success of self-organized collective action in a long-standing and effective community-based conservation and development project in South Africa.

Asia

Ostrom (1997) attributed the success of water user associations she studied in Nepal to their being built on existing social networks. The engineering was based on local knowledge and farmers were allowed to prioritize improvements. Mutual farmer exchange visits enabled learning from successful governance mechanisms. Some farmers even charged a fee to train other farmers.

Li and Li (2011) found in their empirical analysis that higher levels of social capital and greater homogeneity of cultivating crop varieties within water user groups in Hubei, China, contributed to more successful collective water management. They inferred that the reason for this was were that the higher social capital enhanced the confidence to engage in collective action and lowered the transaction costs of doing so.

Mondal (2000) referred to the work of the most prominent rural development NGOs in Bangladesh, BRAC (Bangladesh Rural Advancement Committee), and Proshika attributing their success to social capital formation. Based on a field survey of 500 members of groups created by these organizations, beneficial and harmful effects of collective actions for rural development (the former overwhelming the latter by a ratio of about 140:1) were documented. The poor and women were shown to have derived much greater benefits from such collective action (ratio of about 4:1 and 2.5:1, respectively).

Bangladesh is also credited for originating a widely replicated model of microcredit. Conventional banks avoid loans to the rural poor because of high transaction costs resulting from limited infrastructure, the lack of information and the small size of loans. Additional problems include the lack of collateral and contract enforcement difficulties. The Grameen Bank model overcame these obstacles via peer group lending, where peer groups provide support and social pressure for repayments.

The social mobilization process in building peer group organizations is very similar to that of constructing community or village organizations and for many development NGOs, microcredit is one component of a composite package used to engage, train, and attain community participation and development. The social relations and networks in poor rural communities is what many non-government programs bank on as social collateral to make loans without conventional collateral and ensure timely repayment, hence the reference to "banking on social capital."[24]

Nawaz (2018) provided qualitative evidence of a virtuous cycle where by the initial stock of social capital was banked on for a development initiative, in this case, microcredit, which in turn led to an increment in the stock of social capital and more collective action. The mechanisms in this case for the stock increment were regular meetings, networking and the building of mutual associations, and trust. The second round of spontaneous collective action included developmental activities like building village infrastructure and challenging patriarchal norms and social injustice, including child marriage, female harassment and physical abuse.

D'Silva and Pai (2003) presented case studies of social capital and collective action for joint forest management and watershed development in three Indian villages. They concluded that successful collective action depended on social context. They claimed that in tribal villages, based on culture, tradition, and the need to preserve the commons for survival there was a greater proclivity for joint action based on social capital. By contrast, in a village characterized by caste and class divisions and aspiration among the young for social mobility based on education and migration, collective action was not forthcoming.[25] Also important were trusted local leadership and a cadre of committed local government officials who were able to draw on existing social capital to train and guide in the initial phase of village institution building for collective action.[26]

Uphoff (2000) narrated his experience with a water development project in the Gal Oya region in Sri Lanka. The objective was to improve the efficiency of water management in the irrigation system. Success was attained by establishing water user associations and by mobilizing and reinforcing certain value orientations of cooperation and generosity that were available within the culture. The method of investment used was to recruit, train, and deploy young persons called Institutional Organizers (1Os) as "catalysts" for collective action and formation of organizations. Gal Oya was said by engineers and officials to be the most deteriorated and disorganized irrigation system in the country. Yet it became one of the most efficient and cooperatively managed systems fairly quickly. The efficiency of water use was doubled within two years. Fairly conservative benefit–cost calculations indicated about a 50% rate of return on this investment in social infrastructure.

Krishna and Uphoff (2002) developed a social capital index and found that it was consistently positively correlated with superior development outcomes in both watershed conservation and cooperative development activities in Rajasthan, India. They ruled out other hypothesis such as need, relative power, quality of government extension staff support, modernization or the lack thereof, literacy, and community heterogeneity that have been hypothesized in the literature as influencing collective action.

In earlier research (2001), they found that villages that had stronger predispositions and capacities for collective action, captured by the social capital index, performed better in land-use management. Krishna (2001) showed, using a similar social capital index to measure the stock of social capital, that agency in the form of informed leadership capable of linking the villages with local government and market opportunities was necessary for this stock to yield a flow of development benefits.

Cramb (2005) discussed the formation of community groups in the Philippines to facilitate the diffusion of knowledge and practice concerning land conservation. He quantitatively showed that participation in groups significantly increased the probability—by a factor of 2.7, of adoption of such practice. His qualitative analysis indicated that group formation reflected the initial stock of social capital and reinforced the preexisting bonds. In addition, land care groups were most easily formed and most sustainable in communities where bonding social capital was high.

Sapkota et. al. (2015) conducted a quantitative study across 20 community forest user groups in Central Siwalik, Nepal. They found that users' participation in crafting the rules and strong social capital which ensured the strong enforcement of rules and sanctions, were the major variables that strengthened collective action in forest fire management.

Using qualitative and quantitative research, Ido (2019) demonstrated that, despite the severe depletion of social capital due to past armed conflict in Cambodia, existing social capital helped group members organize collective action to manage community forests. Members engaged in meetings, joint patrolling, and sanctions to attain desired results.

Dahal and Adhikari (2008) provided a descriptive account of successful collective forest resource management in Kalahan, Philippines, partly due to the practice of governing forests through traditional systems of decision-making and networks of tribal communities belonging to one ethnic group. There were other contextual factors accounting for this success. In particular, a settled expatriate catalyzed bonding social capital to protect local resources from external raiding. He also facilitated bridging and linking social capital based on his contacts.

South America

Rodriguez and Pascual (2004) showed that one proxy of social capital (membership in formal associations) but not others (participation rate in committees) positively and significantly influenced the rehabilitation of scrubland for the production of cochineal (for natural dyes) in Ayacucho, Peru. Healy (2002) reviewed the impact on rural development of the replacement of the hacienda by indigenous grassroots organizations and federations in Bolivia and found a positive association. Molinas (1998) found a positive relationship of associational social capital and cooperative performance of peasant committees in Paraguay.

Winters et al. (2002) used a neoclassical economic framework and factor analysis to develop three social capital factors including cooperation, formal production arrangements, and ejido (small farmer) organizations in Mexico. These were then used in regression analysis and the findings were that ejido organizations were important determinants of participation in crop and livestock production, non-agricultural wage employment, and remittance income. Also, the lack of formal production arrangements hindered self-employment and agricultural and livestock income generation.

Hoogesteger (2013) explored how new water user organizations of smallholders, supported by the state and NGOs, developed in formerly state-managed irrigation systems in the Ecuadorian highlands since the

1990s. External agents supported democratic governance and provided technical and organizational training. In turn, these organizations managed to sustainably use the irrigation systems. Since the infrastructure served many communities, bridging social capital needed to be constructed for successful operation. Such bridging enabled the organizations to access external resources for the maintenance and improvement of the irrigation system.

Marín et. al. (2012) studied small-scale artisanal fisher organizations engaged in a coastal benthic resources co-management system in Chile. Their results showed that fisher organizations with higher levels of linking and bridging social capital performed the best.

Beitl (2014) documented that many people in coastal communities organized around social justice issues in response to environmental degradation associated with shrimp farming on the Ecuadorian coast throughout the 1990s and early 2000s. The government encouraged collective action for mangrove protection by granting 10-year mangrove concessions to local associations throughout the coast. These new common property rights called *custodias* were designed to conserve and restore degraded mangrove areas and to promote sustainable resource use and community management.

To qualify, a community or group of "ancestral users" had to first organize into an association or cooperative officially recognized by the state. As an organization, they had to submit an application package consisting of maps, the names of officers, a list of members, a copy of the association's agreement, and a management plan detailing the sustainable use of resources. Selected associations could benefit from government support in the form of credits and subsidies.

Beitl's (2014) research showed that, membership in local associations fostered a higher propensity of individuals to contribute to different kinds of collective action compared to independents. They participated in mangrove reforestation, community mariculture, workshops, and political activism related to the defense of mangroves. As a result, mangroves throughout the Ecuadorian coast moved to a path to recovery through reforestation projects, *custodias*, awareness campaigns, and other institutionalized forms of collective action. The downside was exclusion of independents, who mistrusted institutions or NGOs, from favored zones.

Cross Continent

Pretty and Ward (2001) claim that in the 1990s, there was a remarkable advance in group formation such that 408,000–478,000 groups emerged with 8.2–14.3 million members engaged in various forms of collective action in watershed, irrigation, microfinance, forest, and integrated pest management, and for farmers' research.

Westermann et al. (2005) analyze 46 randomly selected groups with at least three years working experience using a mixed composition (eight women's, six men's, and 32 mixed) across 33 rural programs in twenty countries of Africa, Asia, and Latin America. They found that women-only or mixed groups ranked higher on various dimensions of social capital such as solidarity, collaboration, and conflict resolution and that these groups demonstrated a higher capacity for self-sustaining collective action. It bears repeating here that the focus of our review is on "success stories" of social capital and collective action in rural development.

Summary

Our conceptual framework distinguishes between indigenous or informal social capital and formal or constructed social capital. Informal social capital can be manifested in grassroots organizations and can lead to spontaneous collective action. Development NGOs often build on such grassroots organizations or construct grassroots organizations from scratch—both embody social capital. We refer to constructed social capital as formal and this includes the underlying social capital that makes the organization possible and the organization itself. Collective action forthcoming from formal social capital is referred to as induced.

This book reviews both kinds of collective action, spontaneous and induced, and a review of such collective action from around the developing world is explored in this chapter. We also posit a hybrid or mixed form of collective action whereby an external agency gets involved to back-stop the spontaneous emergence of a grassroots activist organization promoting collective action for say protecting natural resource rights (Chapter 7).

Assuming that social capital is positively associated with collective action, it is possible to explore the conditions under which social capital is likely to be forthcoming. Elite capture can retard spontaneous collective action and induced collective action via the agency of development NGOs can be a way around this. We make a case for induced collective action as a pragmatic option.

While it seems commonsensical to expect social capital to positively impact collective action, evidence is nonetheless called for to verify the validity of such an assumption. We review the evidence from around the developing world to demonstrate the validity of this assumption. In the best of circumstances, there is likely to be a mutual association of social capital and collective action in a community such that the former triggers the latter which in turns enhances the social capital in the community. Such mutual associations are noted in qualitative case studies reviewed in this chapter.

Quantitative studies assume causality runs in one or the another direction and estimate the significance and magnitude of the association. However, at best such studies capture a snapshot of a dynamic association as was so aptly noted by Mosse (2006). So, given the nature of the dynamic process under study, attempting to statistically identify causality is a fool's errand.

Notwithstanding this caveat, there are some lessons evident from quantitative studies from across the developing world in addition to those demonstrated by qualitative analysis. Both informal and formal social capital can result in collective action for community benefit, spontaneous or induced. It appears that interventions by external agencies, such as development NGOs, in constructing social capital for collective action are more likely to bear fruit when they build on existing structural social capital such as preexisting community associations and networks. While it is possible to build social capital by directly initiating collective action, the more successful, though a much more painstaking strategy, is to first mobilize communities to formalize social capital. As can be expected, engaging groups in the framing of rules for responsibilities, benefits, and sanctioning deviant behavior results in more successful outcomes.

Success in either case also depends among other factors on context and this finding, along with the others, are also demonstrated by the case studies we present in this book which contribute to the existing body of evidence regarding the mutual association of social capital and collective action.

Notes

1. Elinor Ostrom has probably contributed most to an understanding of the association of social capital and collective action. In this regard, among her many works alone and with co-authors, Ostrom and Ahn (2007) is particularly noteworthy and highly cited. Ostrom (1996, pp. 1073–1087), provides references to the early literature on collective action. Ostrom (1993b) reviews examples and draws generalizations from cases across countries where collective action is successful in different situations.
2. Union Councils in Pakistan are administrative tiers below province, district and *tehsil*.
3. This distinction between spontaneous and induced collective action was made in Khan et al. (2007, Chapter 1). Mansuri and Rao (2013) make a distinction between organic (social movements, membership based organizations, unions) and induced participation (state led decentralization, community based development).
4. This criticism could in principle apply to the work of development NGOs, such as the ones we review in Chapters 3, 4, and 5. Since field staff are expected to meet targets regarding community organization/village organization (CO/VO) construction, critics charged that they use a "cookie cutter" approach to CO/VO construction compared to the work of local NGOs that painstakingly build on indigenous social capital via social mobilization. Ultimately the issue is empirical and a test of the criticism of the development NGO model, as characterized above, needs to be based on the sustainability of its constructed social capital and induced collective action that enhances community well-being. We return to this issue in Part II.

5. https://unfccc.int/process-and-meetings/the-paris-agreement/the-paris-agreement, consulted October 3, 2019.
6. This would mean accepting rules, such as greater benefits for the less well off, which do not strictly conform to the cost–benefit calculus of utility maximization for any given individual participating in a collective endeavor.
7. For example, such networks and organizations could be created with ulterior motives and do not really represent social capital but just its façade.
8. We do not delve into the mechanisms that enable social capital to lead to collective actions. Our field experience suggests that the role of leadership is critical in all kinds of collective action. In the case of induced collective action, development NGOs cultivate it by building on the skills and abilities of village activists who have the confidence of the community and who the NGOs consider most promising in this regard.
9. See Kyamusugulwa and Hilhorst (2015) for a distinction between "bad" and "good" elite capture. Their case studies suggest that it is possible to work with elites to deliver development particularly when the context is right and the incentives are aligned.
10. While cooperative behavior can enhance material benefits for the community, individualist behavior can lead to non-optimum outcomes (the Prisoners Dilemma).
11. While the good produced is rivalrous and excludable, free-riding and cheating is still possible and hence several scholars, including Ostrom (1990) have utilized game theory to analyze collective action.
12. Participatory Rural Appraisal (PRA) (say to identify needs) and Participatory Learning (say to identify local knowledge) are associated with PD but not addressed in this chapter. Critics are also not persuaded that participatory learning really happens and view local needs and local knowledge to be often shaped by project objectives (e.g., Mosse 2001).
13. This distinction was made by eds. Cooke and Kothari (2001) and their critique is addressed below.
14. This is referred to as rational choice vs. social being dichotomy in the literature.
15. Cornwall (2003) emphasized the points that women were excluded in participatory appraisals, there was no institutional mechanism to ensure voice if they were included, and no meaningful policy impact if there was voice.
16. While resource capture and anti-women biases are concerns that undermine PD, they are not intractable. In Part II, Chapters 6–8 we discuss how

spontaneous or the hybrid model of collective action can address resource capture while in Chapter 4 we discuss how induced collective action can empower women.

17. Some refer to Freire (2000) in the context of a system critique.
18. There seems to be no reasonable calculus to compare short-term injustice with long-term equity and social justice, if it could be attained, although historically some have not shied away from such a calculus.
19. There is no reason to believe that capitalists are intrinsically different from workers although some distinguish capitalist from working class consciousness. Capitalists are in the position they are for the most part because of social class they were born into, contacts, and luck though effort and ability can play a role. Marx's implicit assumption is that humans with the opportunity have the proclivity to accumulate. This is very like the neoclassical economics axiom of non-satiation.
20. A cursory look at the UNDP's Human Development Reports show this in a cross-country context and the social performance of left-leaning Indian states like West Bengal and Karela show this to be true within a large country. Not surprisingly, Kerala was also the state that performed the best in India in initially flattening the COVID-19 curve.
21. Oakley's et al. (1995, pp. 18, 26–27, 37) discussion of the costs and benefits of participatory development are still relevant.
22. Academic Search Premier, EconLit, Google Scholar and JSTOR were used for the literature search for this section with collective action, social capital and rural development as the keywords. Google Scholar returned almost 900,000 hits in October 2019. Thus, given the multi and interdisciplinary nature of the topic, the literature is immense and our review is selective. Khan et al. (2007, Chapter 2) was partly used as an earlier review.
23. An interesting observation was that based on the coercion experienced by the villagers in the Ujama Village Project, villagers were actually wary of induced collective action.
24. For many critics, microcredit did not prove to be the promised panacea. Refer to Khan and Ansari (2018, Chapter 4) for a review of some of the criticisms from various perspectives.
25. A similar point was made by Motiram and Osberg (2010) in the context of drinking water supply in India.
26. Das and Sarkar (2011) similarly conclude that women's involvement in Joint Forest Management in West Bengal could enhance social capital for collective action in preserving forests.

References

Baland, J.M., S. Bowles, and P. Bardhan. 2006. *Inequality, Collective Action and Environment Sustainability*. Princeton: Princeton University Press.

Beitl, C.M. 2014. Adding Environment to the Collective Action Problem: Individuals, Civil Society, and the Mangrove-Fishery Commons in Ecuador. *World Development* 56 (4): 93–107.

Bising, E., et al. 2014. Social Capital, Collective Action and Access to Water in Rural Kenya. *Social Science and Medicine* 119 (October): 147–154.

Bourdieu, P. 1986. The Forms of Capital. In *Handbook of Theory of Research for the Sociology of Education*, ed. J.E. Richardson. New York: Greenwood Press.

Cleaver, F. 1999. Paradoxes of Participation: Questioning Participatory Approaches to Development. *Journal of International Development* 11 (4): 597–612.

Cleaver, F. 2001. Institutions, Agency and the Limitations of Participatory Development. In *Participation: The New Tyranny?*, ed. B. Cooke and U. Kothari. London: Zed Books.

Cleaver, F. 2005. The Inequality of Social Capital and the Reproduction of Chronic Poverty. *World Development* 33 (6): 893–906.

Cooke, B., and U. Kothari, eds. 2001. *Participation: The New Tyranny?* London: Zed Books.

Coppock, D.L., and S. Desta. 2013. Collective Action, Innovation, and Wealth Generation Among Settled Pastoral Women in Northern Kenya. *Rangeland Ecology & Management* 66 (1): 95–105.

Cornwall, A. 2003. Whose Voices? Whose Choices? Reflections on Gender and Participatory Development. *World Development* 31 (8): 1325–1342.

Cramb, R. 2005. Social Capital and Soil Conservation: Evidence from the Philippines. *The Australian Journal of Agricultural and Resource Economics* 49 (2): 211–226.

Dahal, G.R., and K.P. Adhikari. 2008. Bridging, Linking, and Bonding Social Capital in Collective Action: The Case of Kalahan Forest Reserve in the Philippines CAPRi (Collective Action and Property Rights). Working Paper No. 79, IFPRI (International Food Policy Research Institute), Washington, DC.

Das, N., and D. Sarkar. 2011. Network Externalities Under Social Capital: Lessons from Gender Sensitive Forest Management Programme in West Bengal. *Indian Economic Review* 46 (2): 243–274.

Davenport, M., and R.M. Hassan. 2019. Social Capital and Self-Organised Collective Action: Lessons and Insights from a South African Community Project. *Development Southern Africa*. https://www.tandfonline.com/doi/abs/10.1080/0376835X.2019.1628708?journalCode=cdsa20, consulted October 29, 2019.

de Hann, N. 2001. Of Goats and Groups: A Study of Social Capital in Development Projects. *Agriculture and Human Values* 18 (1): 71–84.

D'Silva, E., and S. Pai. 2003. Social Capital and Collective Action: Development Outcomes in Forest Protection and Watershed Development. *Economic and Political Weekly* 38 (14): 1404–1415.

Durlauf, S., and M. Fafchamps. 2004. Social Capital. National Bureau of Economic Research Working Papers No. 10485, Cambridge, MA.

Faraizi, A., T. Rahman, and J. McAllister. 2011. *Microcredit and Women's Empowerment: Case Study of Bangladesh*. London: Routledge.

Fine, B. 2001. The Social Capital of the World Bank. In *Development Policy in the Twenty-First Century: Beyond the Post-Washington Consensus*, ed. B. Fine, C. Lapavistsas, and J. Pincus. London: Routledge.

Freire, P. 2000. *Pedagogy of the Oppressed*. New York: Bloomsbury.

Funder, M. 2010. The Social Shaping of Participatory Spaces: Evidence from Community Development in Southern Thailand. *Journal of Development Studies* 46 (10): 1708–1728.

Gebremedhin, B., J. Pender, and G. Tesfay. 2004. Collective Action for Grazing Land Management in Crop-Livestock Mixed Systems in the Highlands of Northern Ethiopia. *Agricultural Systems* 82 (3): 273–290.

Healy, K. 2002. Building Networks of Social Capital for Grassroots Development Among Indigenous Communities in Bolivia and Mexico. In *Social Capital and Economic Development: Well-Being in Developing Countries*, ed. J. Isham, T. Kelly, and S. Ramaswamy, 197–214. Cheltenham, UK: Edward Elgar.

Hoogesteger, J. 2013. Social Capital in Water User Organizations of the Ecuadorian Highlands. *Human Organization* 72 (4): 37–357.

Ido, A. 2019. The Effect of Social Capital on Collective Action in Community Forest Management in Cambodia. *International Journal of the Commons* 13 (1): 777–803.

Isham, J. 2002. The Effect of Social Capital on Fertilizer Adoption: Evidence from Rural Tanzania. *Journal of African Economies* 11 (1): 39–60.

Karim, L. 2011. *Microfinance and Its Discontents: Women in Debt in Bangladesh*. Minneapolis: University of Minnesota Press.

Khan, S.R. 1999. *Government, Communities and NGOs in Social Sector Delivery*. Brookfield, VT: Ashgate.

Khan, S.R., and N. Ansari. 2018. *A Microcredit Alternative in South Asia: Akhuwat's Experiment*. London: Routledge.

Khan, S.R., S. Kazmi, and Z. Rifaqat. 2007. *Harnessing and Guiding Social Capital for Rural Development*. New York: Palgrave Macmillan.

Kihiu, E.N. 2016. Basic Capability Effect: Collective Management of Pastoral Resources in Southwestern Kenya. *Ecological Economics* 123 (March): 23–34.

Krishna, A. 2001. Moving from the Stock of Social Capital to the Flow of Benefits: The Role of Agency. *World Development* 29 (6): 925–943.

Krishna, A., and N. Uphoff, 2001. Assessing Social Factors in Sustainable Land-Use Management: Social Capital and Common Land Development in Rajasthan, India. In *Economic Policy and Sustainable Land Use: Recent Advances in Quantitative Analysis for Developing Countries*, ed. N. Heerink, H. van Keulen, and M. Kuiper, 335–350. Heidelberg and New York: Physica.

Krishna, A., and N. Uphoff. 2002. Mapping and Measuring Social Capital Through Assessment of Collective Action to Conserve and Develop Watersheds in Rajasthan, India. In *The Role of Social Capital in Development: An Empirical Assessment*, ed. C. Grootaert and T. van Bastelaer, 85–124. Cambridge: Cambridge University Press.

Kyamusugulwa, P.M., and D. Hilhorst. 2015. Power Holders and Social Dynamics of Participatory Development and Reconstruction: Cases from The Democratic Republic of the Congo. *World Development* 70: 249–259.

Li, H., and M. Li. 2011. Collective Water Management and Technical Efficiency in Rice Production: Evidence from China. *The Journal of Developing Areas* 44 (2): 391–406.

Lyon, F. 2000. Trust, Networks, and Norms: The Creation of Social Capital in Agricultural Economies in Ghana. *World Development* 28 (4): 663–681.

Mabuza, M.L., G.F. Ortmann and E.Z. Wale. 2012. Collective Action in Commercial Mushroom Production: The Role of Social Capital in the Management of Informal Farmer Groups in Swaziland. Paper presentated at the International Association of Agricultural Economists, (IAAE) Triennial Conference, Foz do Iquaçu, Brazil. https://www.researchgate.net/publication/254387572_Collective_action_in_commercial_mushroom_product

ion_the_role_of_social_capital_in_the_management_of_informal_farmer_groups_in_Swaziland, consulted October 30, 2019.
Mansuri, G., and V. Rao. 2013. *Localizing Development: Does Participation Work*? Washington, DC: World Bank.
Marín, A., S. Gelcich, J.C. Castilla, and F. Berkes. 2012. Exploring Social Capital in Chile's Coastal Benthic Comanagement System Using a Network Approach. *Ecology and Society* 17 (1): 1–16.
Mayoux, L. 1995. Beyond Naivety: Women, Gender Inequality and Participatory Development. *Development and Change* 26 (2): 235–258.
Michener, V.J. 1998. The Participatory Approach: Contradiction and Co-option in Burkina Faso. *World Development* 26 (12): 2105–2118.
Molinas, J.R. 1998. The Impact of Inequality, Gender, External Assistance, and Social Capital on Local Level Cooperation. *World Development* 26 (3): 13–31.
Mondal, A.H. 2000. Social Capital Formation: The Role of NGO Rural Development Programs in Bangladesh. *Policy Sciences* 33 (3 and 4): 459–475.
Mosse, D. 2001. 'Peoples Knowledge', Participation and Patronage: Operations and Representations in Rural Development. In *Participation: The New Tyranny?*, ed. B. Cooke and U. Kothari. London: Zed Books.
Mosse, D. 2006. Collective Action, Common Property, and Social Capital in South India: An Anthropological Commentary. *Economic Development and Cultural Change* 54 (3): 695–724.
Motiram, S., and L. Osberg. 2010. Social Capital and Basic Goods: The Cautionary Tale of Drinking Water in India. *Economic Development and Cultural Change* 59 (1): 63–94.
Mubangizi, B.C. 2003. Drawing on Social Capital for Community Economic Development: Insights from a South African Rural Community. *Community Development Journal* 38 (2): 140–150.
Nawaz, F. 2018. Social Capital, Collective Action and Women's Empowerment: An Empirical Study on Micro-finance Groups in Bangladesh. *South Asian Journal of Policy and Governance* 42 (1): 23–48.
Oakley, P., et al. 1995. *Projects with People: The Practice of Participation in Rural Development*. Geneva: ILO.
Olson, M. 1971. *The Logic of Collective Action*. Cambridge, MA: Harvard University Press.
O'Meally, S. 2014. The Contradictions of Pro-poor Participation and Empowerment: The World Bank in East Africa. *Development and Change* 45 (6): 1248–1283.

Ostrom, E. 1990. *Governing the Commons: The Evolution of Institutions for Collective Action.* Cambridge: Cambridge University Press.
Ostrom, E. 1993a. Constituting Social Capital and Collective Action. Working Paper 93-18, Department of Political Science, Indiana University, Bloomington, IN.
Ostrom, E. 1993b. Self-Governance, the Informal Economy, and the Tragedy of the Commons. In *Institutions of Democracy and Development: A Sequoia Seminar*, ed. P.L. Berger. San Francisco: Institute of Contemporary Studies.
Ostrom, E. 1996. Crossing the Great Divide: Coproduction, Synergy, and Development. *World Development.* 24 (6): 1073–1087.
Ostrom, E. 1997. Investing in Capital, Institutions, and Incentives. In *Institutions and Development: Growth and Governance in Less-Developed and Post-Socialist Countries*, ed. C. Clague. Baltimore: Johns Hopkins University Press.
Ostrom, E., and T.K. Ahn. 2007. The Meaning of Social Capital and Its Link to Collective Action. Working Paper 07-19, Department of Political Science, Indiana University, Bloomington, IN.
Platteau, J.-P., and A. Abraham. 2002. Participatory Development in the Presence of Endogenous Community Imperfections. *Journal of Development Studies* 39 (2): 109–136.
Pretty, J., and H. Ward. 2001. Social Capital and the Environment. *World Development* 29 (2): 209–227.
Reid, C., and L. Salmen. 2002. Qualitative Analysis of Social Capital: The Case of Agricultural Extension in Mali. In *Understanding and Measuring Social Capital: A Multidisciplinary Tool for Practitioners*, ed. C. Grootaert and T. van Bastelaer, 85–107. Washington, DC: World Bank.
Rodriguez, L.C., and U. Pascual. 2004. Land Clearance and Social Capital in Mountain Agro-Ecosystems: The Case of Opuntia Scrubland in Ayacucho, Peru. *Ecological Economics* 49 (2): 243–252.
Ruben, R., and J. Heras. 2012. Social Capital, Governance and Performance of Ethiopian Coffee Cooperatives. *Annals of Public and Cooperative Economics* 83 (4): 463–484.
Sandler, T. 2015. Collective Action: Fifty Years Later. *Public Choice* 164 (3 and 4): 195–216.
Sapkota, L.M., R.P. Shrestha, D. Jourdain, and G.P. Shivakoti. 2015. Factors Affecting Collective Action for Forest Fire Management: A Comparative Study of Community Forest User Groups in Central Siwalik, Nepal. *Environmental Management* 55 (1): 171–186.

Schroeder, C., and M. Zeller. 2013. Women, Social Capital and Collective Action—The Case of NERICA Rice Technology in Benin. *Quarterly Journal of International Agriculture* 52 (4): 329–356.

Smale, M., and V. Ruttan. 1997. Social Capital and Technical Change. In *Institutions and Development: Growth and Governance in Less-Developed and Post-socialist Countries*, ed. C. Clague, 182–200. Baltimore: Johns Hopkins University Press.

Uphoff, N. 2000. Understanding Social Capital: Learning from the Analysis and Experience of Participation. In *Social Capital: A Multifaceted Perspective*, ed. P. Dasgupta and I. Serageldin, 215–229. Washington, DC: World Bank

Van Bastelaer, T., and H. Leathers. 2006. Trust in Lending: Social Capital and Joint Liability Seed Loans in Southern Zambia. *World Development* 34 (10): 1788–1807.

Wade, R. 1988. *Village Republics: Economic Conditions for Collective Action in South India*. Cambridge: Cambridge University Press.

Westermann, O.J., J. Ashby, and J. Pretty. 2005. Gender and Social Capital: The Importance of Gender Differences for the Maturity and Effectiveness of Natural Resource Management Groups. *World Development* 33 (11): 1783–1799.

Willy, D.K., and K. Holm-Müller. 2013. Social Influence and Collective Action Effects on Farm Level Soil Conservation Effort in Rural Kenya. *Ecological Economics* 90 (June): 94–103.

Winters, P., B. Davis, and L. Corral. 2002. Assets, Activities and Income Generation in Rural Mexico: Factoring in Social and Public Capital. *Agricultural Economics* 27 (2): 139–156.

Woolcock, M. 2002. Social Capital in Theory and Practice: Where Do We Stand? In *Social Capital and Economic Development: Well-Being in Developing Countries*, ed. J. Isham, T. Kelly, and S. Ramaswamy, 18–39. Cheltenham, UK: Edward Elgar.

Part II

Constructed Social Capital and Induced Collective Action

3

Local Support Organizations: An Exit Strategy for Rural Development NGOs

Introduction

The government and donor-supported Rural Support Programs (RSPs) engage in participatory rural development in Pakistan.[1] Via social mobilization, they form community organizations (COs) at the grassroots level, which subsequently become partners in the development process.[2] The ten organizations of the Rural Support Programs Network (RSPN), established in 2000 by the RSPs, collectively operated in 149 of 154 districts of Pakistan (2018) and had a total outreach of 53.5 million people, about a fourth of Pakistan's population.[3]

In response to funding constraints, the Rural Support Programs (RSPs) began to steer their grassroots initiatives toward institutional sustainability with support from the RSPN. This entailed forming apex local support organizations (LSOs) at the Union Council (UC) level

This chapter draws on the authors' report "Local Support Organisations: Rural Support Programmes Letting Go, Citizens Taking Charge," written for the Rural Support Program Network, September 2010. We also drew on this report from "Local Support Organizations: An Exit Strategy for Rural Development NGOs," *Development Policy Review* 30 (3): 347–367, 2012.

S. R. Khan and S. R. Khan, *Social Capital and Collective Action in Pakistani Rural Development*, https://doi.org/10.1007/978-3-030-71450-5_3

building upon cognitive and structural forms of social capital.[4] The aim was two-fold. First, as apex organizations, the LSOs could replicate the work of the RSPs in mobilizing communities, creating COs and ensuring their participation in social, development, welfare, and credit activities. The vertical structure was designed to ensure that the apex organizations formed effective vertical ties (linking social capital) with the government, NGOs, donors, and the private sector.

Second, LSOs could go beyond merely substituting for the RSPs; they represented an indigenization of the social mobilization process reflecting their cognitive genesis, thus ensuring a permanent support system which was locally owned, self-reliant, and capable of formulating context-specific development programs (Azizi 2006; Mehr 2007; Khan 2008; RSPN 2009). In effect, the LSOs represent both a consolidation of participatory development and an exit strategy, enabling RSPs to focus on other communities more in need of their assistance. The objective, in short as framed by Azizi (2006), was to have organizations *of* the people rather than organizations *for* the people at the grassroots level.

This chapter explores whether LSOs did indeed strengthen the capabilities of COs to mobilize and harness social capital, generate diversified collective outcomes and induce process change (social, economic, and cultural), and if in this capacity LSOs could act as substantively independent entities. Since the LSOs had only been active for only a few years prior to our fieldwork, our findings may understate their potential.

In more detail, we first recount LSO history, structure, and governance and then frame LSOs in the context of the discussion of social capital and collective action in Chapter 2. We follow with a review of LSO-like apex or multitiered community organization federations regionally and beyond. Next, we present our research design and method and then explain our criteria for assessing LSO effectiveness. After that, we report our findings, which constitute the bulk of the chapter and then end with a summary of findings.

LSO History, Structure, and Governance[5]

The LSO model in Pakistan was first envisioned in the 1980s by the development practitioners of the Aga Khan Rural Support Program (AKRSP).[6] The model provided the template for wider replication, but it was not the first initiative of its kind, and, indeed, ran concurrently with, or was preceded by, similar initiatives in Ecuador, India, Sri Lanka, and Tajikistan.

The AKRSP advocated the formation of village organization (VO) clusters to sustain social mobilization efforts and implement larger infrastructure projects.[7] The LSO is an apex organization of COs and VO/VDOs of a particular union council. It is formed at the UC level and, at a minimum, requires 60% of the potential member households to be organized in men and women COs. By definition, an LSO is a formal and representative body of grassroots organizations to support participatory, equitable, and sustainable development of a defined geographical area. Its main objectives are to: (a) provide a localized permanent support system to foster and nurture grassroots organizations; (b) scale-up social mobilization through low-cost measures; (c) facilitate linkages with external agencies and provide a mechanism to address development challenges on a larger geographic scale.

Success would enable the transformation of AKRSP's role to one of capacity-building (Khan et. al. 1992). AKRSP records show that a number of apex organizations are still functional around the management of micro hydel projects that require continuous maintenance and management.

Since the establishment of the original apex organizations, the RSP institutional development approach has evolved through several iterations. In the late 1990s, RSPs started to shape COs into Local Development Organizations (LDOs). The LDO model, too, was conceived as a broad-based, two-tier, multi-purpose organization that could articulate and organize the common development concerns of a particular locality, mainly at the village level. However, over time, RSP staff noted that the LDOs were transforming into small professional NGOs and distancing themselves from the communities.

To counter this "professionalization phenomenon" the Rural Support Program Network (RSPN) developed in 2005/6 a graduated strategy to scale-up existing COs. In an effort to ensure that this form of institutional development would be sustainable, LSO development occurred in two stages: (i) the COs would form a Village Development Organization (VDO) at the level of a village or revenue village[8] and (ii) over time the VDOs would form an LSO. The decision was both time- and location-appropriate, in as much as COs were already in place and working informally. However, they were not registered and had virtually no administrative or financial systems, which prevented them from accessing additional donor funds or initiating large-scale development projects.[9]

The main objectives of the LSO, therefore, are to: provide a localized permanent support system to foster and nurture the grassroots organizations of COs and VDOs; scale-up social mobilization locally through low-cost measures (compared with RSP staff support); and provide an institutional facility to promote development linkages with service agencies in the government, donors, NGOs, and the private sector.[10]

The RSPs facilitate LSO formation at the UC level when the CO spans a significant proportion of households. The RSP's role is to provide both financial and technical support in the development of the LSO. The RSPN has developed operational guidelines and sample by-laws for the LSO, training modules for LSO activists, orientation and management training modules for RSP field staff actively involved in the program, and monitoring tools for the LSO program (Azizi 2006). Figure 3.1 illustrates the LSO structure.

As the figure shows, the LSOs are set up at the UC level. They form the apex of a triangular three-tier structure built up from household-level COs, which coalesce into VOs/VDOs. In turn, these merge into LSOs. The three tiers are linked through an electoral process aimed at ensuring transparency and grassroots representation.

The LSO structure combines representative and participatory aspects. The representative aspect is vertical linkage such that each tier elects representatives to the next higher tier. Participation is both lateral and vertical (bonding and linking aspects of social capital). Vertical integration is necessary for two reasons. First, village- and UC-level projects and

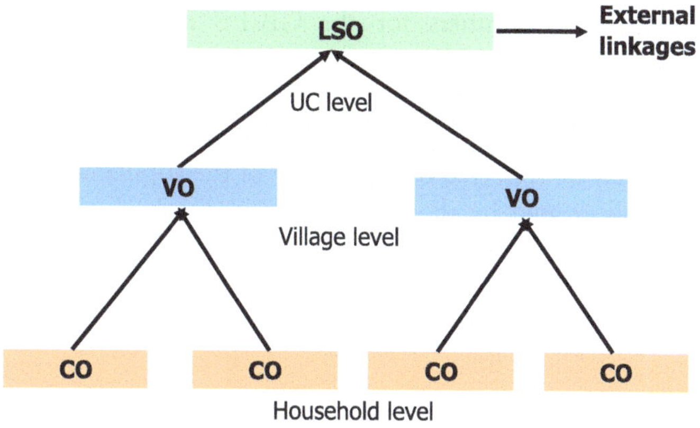

Fig. 3.1 LSO structure

activities need to be grounded in community needs. Second, a circular feedback loop ensures bottom-up and top-down communications. LSOs also aim to form financial and program linkages with external agencies such as donors, local government, and NGOs which is not possible at the CO level. LSOs can also bring about social and cultural change within the community, which is important in itself and also key to sustainable project outcomes.

The LSO governing structure is two-tiered, consisting of the general body (GB) and the executive body (EB). The GB comprises at least two nominees from each member organization (CO, VO). Its functions are to: approve and amend the by-laws of the LSO; approve the minutes of the previous GB meetings; approve the annual plan of operation prepared by the EB and; appoint the members of the EB.

An executive body (7–11 members) is elected by the GB from among itself. The EB functions are to: appoint its chairperson, vice-chairperson, and secretary; establish policies; create subcommittees on a needs basis; approve, amend and reject recommendations of subcommittees; raise funds for its own operations; prepare annual plans and budgets; provide strategic guidance and insights; keep financial records in a proper and easily retrievable manner and; ensure the audit of accounts on an annual basis.

The election of members for the GB/EB and subcommittees is required to be on merit. The process must be transparent and democratic. The GB is elected for a period of 3–5 years. On the expiry of its term, the entire GB is reelected. The EB is elected for a period of 2–3 years and may be reelected on the expiry of the stipulated period. The subcommittees created by the GB or EB are dissolved with the dissolution of the respective body. Similarly, the term of office of the office bearers of GB and EB automatically comes to an end with the dissolution of the respective body. The LSOs are registered under any government act deemed suitable by them.

Representation of women in the GB, EB, and Special Committees of the LSO is mandatory. In case the number of woman COs are negligible, there is provision for the nomination of more woman members from among the available women COs. A position has been reserved for a woman vice president in the EB of the LSO. The GB and EB are supported by paid staff for office functions such as accounting and book-keeping. The LSO assets and liabilities are owned and borne by its members, with the EB as the custodian.

LSOs continue to be a key aspect of RSP social capital construction for collective action (1,128 by 2019). There are numerous case studies (over fifty) on the RSPN website suggestive of LSO achievements in this regard. The LSOs have provided a platform for securing national identification cards for members and government assistance and support the members were entitled to via organization and activism. They have solicited and mediated disaster relief, charitable donations and agricultural inputs for the poorest, collectively donated to the poorest in case of crop failure, solicited and ensured education and health services, particularly for females and the poor.

Other examples of numerous initiatives included LSOs breathing life into traditional community institutions that became defunct and social infrastructure like school management committees that were set up by the government for monitoring and accountability but became dormant. Similarly, grassroots level accountability instituted by LSOs assured a proper functioning of government schools, basic health units, and drinking water supply facilities, at times by using the Right to Information Act which RSPs coached them on.

The LSOs have created employment opportunities by fund-raising to establish collective businesses like fruit dehydration, garment production, bee farms when self-employment was not possible or did not work due to over competition. They charged a modest commission from the profits to add to LSO savings. They have successfully negotiated with outside businesses to hire locally.

They have also become a political force to contend with during elections in which reputable office holders get elected to local, provincial, or national elections or they secure services that the area has been deprived of in exchange for political support.

LSOs engage in awareness raising on key issues like child rights, environmental degradation, and health hazards and organize activities for mitigation (anti-polio and malaria drives and disaster mitigation) and afforestation campaigns. They have ensured more female mobility and participation and run interference when male family members object or became obstreperous. Some of the notable induced collective action initiatives are summarized in Appendix 3.1.

LSOs as Constructed Social Capital for Collective Action

Following from the discussion in Chapter 2, LSOs represent and embody social capital in several ways. First, community organizations as the building blocks of LSOs embody cognitive/bonding and bridging/structural social capital. They represent an association based on mutual trust, norms, and reciprocal obligations. Second, community organizations can also be viewed as constructed social capital in the sense that the organizations formalize or give shape to indigenous social capital. Third, linking social capital is embodied in the association between the community organization and the development NGO (RSPs in this case). Fourth, the network of community organizations, or apex organizations (LSOs), created to address supra-village needs, represent social capital. Thus, we view the grassroots organizations at the various tiers, the relationships they embody within and across tiers and the foundations of these relationships as social capital. The expectation is that this stock of social capital will lead to a flow of collective action that enhances well-being.

In Chapter 2 we argue that, in the context of rural development, indigenous or autonomous social capital can be critical for mobilizing communities. Some of its typical manifestations are traditional village institutions, organizations, events, mutual aid traditions, the preeminence of customary law and traditions of social and development work. As indicated above, conceptually the LSOs represent the upper end of a process in which social capital takes the form of community organizations at different tiers that interact with each other and engage in institutionalized collective action. There are examples of the federation of community organizations from around the world and we review some of them below.

Other Examples of Community Organization Federations

The original AKRSP approach inspired the UNDP-funded South Asia Poverty Alleviation Program (SAPAP), launched in 1993 (UNDP 2004a, b; World Bank 2004). Six countries, Bangladesh, Nepal, India, Sri Lanka, Maldives, and Pakistan, participated in this regional program. The AKRSP methodology was common to them all, although the title differed in each country. The first organizational tier consisted of self-help groups (SHG), which coalesced into village organizations (VO) or, if the village was large, into community organizations (CO). In turn, the COs or VOs federated into sub-district (UC for Pakistan) or district-level bodies. They are known by several names, such as LSOs in Pakistan or Mandil Mahila Samkhyas (MMSs) in India. From the outset, SAPAP cultivated close relations with the host governments, whether at the central, state, or district levels. Anticipating bureaucratic resistance, it inducted senior retired government officials into its country management structure, thus ensuring familiarity with government methods and procedures and links with local government institutions.

The most rapid take-up of the SAPAP project, both spatially and over time, occurred in Andhra Pradesh, India. The project built upon existing women's SHGs, federating them into VOs and then into MMS. As project successes became visible, the World Bank agreed to finance an adapted version of the project. Under its District Poverty Initiatives Project (DPIP), the program, called VELUGU (light), gave greater emphasis to livelihood and income-generation activities. The program was built around the Community Investment Fund (a form of community-managed micro credit to poor rural women) but was extended to embrace excluded minorities, such as the untouchables.

A second project, the Andhra Pradesh Rural Poverty Reduction Project (APRPRP), established community-managed procurement centers for assessing, storing, and selling agricultural commodities.[11] The project benefited small and marginal farmers, traditionally exploited by moneylenders, traders, and middlemen. By 2007, 630,000 female SHGs were federated into 28,282 VOs, 910 sub-district organizations, and 26 district organizations. Farmers started having easy access to procurement centers, price and quantity information (accessible via mobile phones), and cash on delivery.

The project freed them from distress sales to middlemen and from credit on onerous terms. Trained female grassroots professionals (who grew to 100,000 by 2007) managed the supply chain. Their functions included handling logistics, quality control, weighing, book-keeping, and research and development. Committees of 3–5 members handled functions like purchase, quality control, social audits, and sales. The direct benefits to farmers and members and the indirect benefits via replication and job-creation were impressive.

A third project, which built upon and funded these projects was the state-sponsored Community Investment Fund (CIF) managed by the Society for Eradication of Rural Poverty (SERP), similar in nature and functions to the RSPs. The CIF supported the micro plans of SHGs, which embraced both farm and non-farm activities. These were agriculture, animal husbandry, business enterprises, commodity marketing, and food security. In addition, the CIF provided resources at the VO and MMS level for social development, infrastructure, and land purchase and development.

Another demonstration of the LSO approach was the Tajikistan Governance and Livelihoods Program (TGLP), implemented by the

Mountain Societies Development Support Program (MSDSP).[12] The TGLP was a project of the Aga Khan Foundation in a two-year partnership with VOs and the local government. The TGLP strove to institute democratic governance and generate sustainable livelihoods among the rural poor in selected pilot districts of Gorno-Badakhshan Autonomous Oblast (GBAO), geographically the largest province in Tajikistan.

One of the TLGP's key objectives was to build capacities within civil society and local government so that the two could collaborate effectively to promote development at the local and regional levels. Higher competencies on both sides were expected to contribute to building a civil society that held government more accountable, and a local government that helped civil society to better articulate and meet the needs of the people. The project aimed to provide insights for joint civil society-local government cooperation, which could be replicated in future across the country.

TGLP helped create a mechanism for collaboration and co-ordination between the existing sub-district level network of VOs called the Social Union for Development of Village Organizations (SUDVOs), and the sub-district governments. Positioning the VOs and SUDVOs as key players in the program design ensured that the government would accept the VOs as a credible institution that could represent village communities and identify and implement village development needs and priorities. Financing for micro-projects at the sub-district and district level was used as the entry point for discussion and formed a substantive basis around which the collaboration and engagement of civil society and local government was established.

The pilot was assessed to be a success in securing government involvement and financing; it addressed a major weakness of the MSDSP, i.e., excluding government. The subsequent and more inclusive approach also represented an exit strategy for the MSDSP in that the government could gradually be expected to assume its expected role of social sector delivery, but in a symbiotic partnership with the VO. The VO retained its autonomy, while the MSDSP focused upon facilitation and capacity-building (of SUDVOs and VOs). Building the capacity of the apex organizations was the key to their sustainability and the phased disengagement.

Sri Lanka had used this approach even prior to AKRSP's initiatives. Srivardana (2004) documented the case study of collective action by a federation of farmers' organizations in the Raana region of Sri Lanka.[13] The Participatory Institute of Development Alternatives initiated the process in 1983 via a series of social mobilizations, each more intense than the last, taking the collective action to a higher plane. Small neighborhood groups formed the village farmer organizations and these came together across 26 villages to form a district farmers' organization. The federation took control of the town market center to facilitate selling their products and proceeded to buy their own lorry, after negotiating a bank loan, to get better prices in the city. They also cut costs by sharing labor and buying agricultural machinery jointly.[14]

The villages had earlier been ignored by the state, but as the federation acquired more influence, the state interacted with it to deliver social and physical infrastructure including a reservoir, drinking water, lift-irrigation, network of gravel roads, electricity, and social services. The federation successfully fielded candidates for local government elections to influence local-level politics and took over the task of social mobilization. As the fame of the federation spread, farmers from other regions replicated the collective action via their own federations. By 1992, the federation had registered as a development NGO and was negotiating independently with donors and the government.

The "LSO approach" has also been tried beyond South Asia and Central Asia. Bebbington and Perreault (2003) described a process for multitiered rural development in the Guamote Canton in Ecuador. The lowest tier represented the creation and consolidation of community-level organizations, the second tier was the consolidation of these organizations into federations, and larger scale organizations drew on these federations to establish national outreach.

These organizations replaced the *hacienda* as the dominant mechanism for rural governance, and the church, as the proponent of liberation theology, was instrumental in the social mobilization which brought about this transformation via land reforms and land buy-outs. The state in turn required the formation of community organizations to mediate the delivery of services, and the church facilitated the process. Literacy programs built up the organizational and human capacity to link communities to the state. The establishment of canton-wide federations of community organizations followed this grassroots activity.[15] These federations negotiated successfully with the state, via national development NGOs, for resources and development investments.[16]

This attainment of independent status by NGOs is basically similar to the objective the RSPN is seeking for the LSOs, inasmuch as LSOs remain people-centered organizations and thus avoid the pitfalls of becoming detached from the communities they are meant to serve. This literature search establishes that there were precedents for what the RSPs are attempting in rural Pakistan. However, this strategic and deliberate use of apex organizations, built on grassroots effort and initiative, as an exit strategy is new. An investigation of this initiative should provide key lessons within and outside the country.

Research Design and Method

By the end of the first decade of the twenty-first century, 306 LSOs, the unit of analysis, had been formed, 23 of which were exclusively women's organizations. Appendix Table 3.1 lists the 49 LSOs which the RSPN was supporting at the time of the field survey. Of these, the RSPN identified 18, 3 exclusively female, for us to review, based on temporal, spatial, and performance criteria, as indicated on the map appended as Appendix Fig. 3.2. Appendix Table 3.2 shows the provincial distribution of these LSOs.[17]

We added a comparative dimension by introducing a control group for each LSO we evaluated. We twinned the nearest UC without an LSO with the LSO under investigation in order to determine whether the LSO had made a difference in terms of well-being and autonomous collective action. It is important to keep in mind that the control groups had an RSP presence but no LSO. While RSP refers to a whole program, for convenience we refer going forward to a LSO-RSP comparison as it pertains to a specific location.

The RSPs' mandate is to work with the poor across Pakistan; their development interventions, social and microfinance, specifically target the poor. As such, they constitute the population from which we drew our sample for the household survey. The RSPs use poverty scorecards to identify poor households.[18] They entail using poverty indicators based on expenditure patterns, starting with a large number (150) and paring down to less than a dozen. The process entails using correlation with observed and verified poverty so that it is possible to predict the likelihood of being in poverty with a high level of confidence. The paring down process eliminates indicators such as those not relying on direct observation or those that are overlapping. The ten indicators arrived at by the RSPs cover diet, durable goods in use, house facilities, and cooking fuel in use. The scores range from 0 to 100.

Originally, in selecting the samples for the target and control groups for the household survey, we opted for a combination of random and purposive sampling. The reason for the latter was two-fold. First, we planned to use the poverty scorecards of the UCs that the RSPs-LSOs had prepared. Many UCs were large, with dispersed villages which would have spatially extended us beyond our logistical and budget capabilities. Second, female-headed households were underrepresented in the poverty scorecards. We imposed a cut-off, reducing the sampling population to only those villages which exceeded a specified population. Second, in an effort to correct gender underrepresentation we stipulated that 15% of the sample should consist of women. After these deliberate adjustments, we opted for a 5% sample size in proportion to the village population to attain equal probability of selection.

Subsequently, we made changes based on field experience. First, several poverty scorecards contained flaws, in that they included children as household heads; household heads had migrated with their families; the scorecard included family heads who had passed away; and some names were in duplicate or triplicate. Thus, cleaning was needed in the field. Second, we discovered after about 100 interviews that there was little variation in responses. Thus, we settled for a fully purposive approach. First, we opted for a uniform sample size of 100 respondents each for the target and control groups across all LSOs, regardless of the union council population.

In addition, we stipulated that there be gender balance (50:50) in the sample, a focus on the poorer households (verified by poverty scorecards), ethnic and religious representation, and that at least 90% of the respondents be simple community organization members and not officeholders.

Based on these stipulated conditions, LSO management bodies identified the households from their records to facilitate the interviews. We selected the target group from the UC which included an LSO. The questionnaire consisted of 3 parts: Part I focused on identifying the stock of social capital that existed in the village before the RSPs and other NGO initiatives; Part II represented an institutional assessment focused on procedures, systems, and inputs; Part III was an outcome assessment focused on tangible (income, assets) and intangible (social empowerment) benefit perceptions.[19]

The questionnaires went through several iterations at RSPN and were pre-tested prior to implementation. The survey teams consisted of four to five enumerators headed by a field survey supervisor. Local teams were used for each region to cater to linguistic needs and to ensure local commitment. At the end of each day in the field, the principal investigator reviewed a sample of the questionnaires and conducted periodic brain-storming sessions to obtain feedback and to ensure that the enumerators remained on track. The principal investigator accompanied the teams for the substantive part of the survey, which lasted 5.5 months, from August 2009 to mid-January 2010, and conducted intensive training sessions in each region to familiarize the enumerators with the study scope, objectives, and methodology.

The premise underlying the RSP institutional maturity index (IMI) is that in UCs where the RSPs have had a sustained presence, COs have internalized the concept of collective action and are capable of launching their own initiatives and moving in new directions. It is also reasonable to assume that they would be receptive to the opportunities offered by vertical linkages. However, premises always need to be tested and we added two sets of questions to the control group questionnaires aimed at determining the following: were the COs active in those UCs where the RSPs were reducing their presence, for instance, due to reduced funding? Did the CO know what an LSO was and were they receptive to the idea of establishing one in their own UC?

Checklists were developed for the focus group discussions, one each respectively for males and females in the target group, and identically for the control group. Each focus group discussion was restricted to 10–15 participants; at a minimum, three community organizations were represented; we ensured that the participants had not been interviewed previously and they were not community organization officeholders.

Key informant interviews were conducted with a cross-section of community members and representatives (local elders, school teachers, and social activists), RSP field staff members, both active and retired, government line department officials and representatives of microfinance banks. We also conducted discussions with the LSO board, executive body and general body members, and with RSP management staff. While we recognized that staff responses could contain biases, it was necessary to gain perspectives on policy, programmatic, and operational issues with which households might not be familiar.

The final survey instrument we utilized was LSO profiles. These are normally constructed by LSO officials and management staff but given the conflict of interest, overstatement is to be expected. In order to obtain an independent assessment, we asked 10 CO members in each LSO to complete profiles.

Based on the description of the research instruments, it is evident that methodologically we used a triangulation approach (Olsen 2004) for the LSO evaluation and collected data through project observation, questionnaires soliciting agent/beneficiary perceptions, interviews, Focus Group Discussions (FGD), case studies and secondary sources/documents and LSO profiles. Since there were no benchmarks we could draw on, a "before/after" study was not possible. While we are confident that we collected valuable social information, given our sampling, the findings are suggestive given the sampling. The details of the survey implementation for the target and control groups are provided in Appendix Table 3.3.

Criteria for Assessing LSO Effectiveness

We assessed LSO effectiveness on the basis of three related sets of indicators. The first set, social capital stock, constituted the foundation of the assessment. The second set was framed around institutional indicators. The third set focused on benefit perceptions. Alternatively, we can also present these indicators as process and outcome indicators. In other words, past traditions of collective action contribute to present institutional sustainability which, in turn, generates outcomes. The indicators were derived from the research instruments used including the household survey questionnaire, checklist for the focus group discussions (FGD), and key informant interviews.

The key research questions embedded in the questionnaires to ascertain the social capital stock pertained to institutions of authority, the role of social institutions, social cohesion, mutual aid traditions, household participation in collective action, and customary laws and their impact.

The institutional assessment of procedures/systems focused on the election of office holders, frequency and quality of meetings, record keeping and auditing of accounts, The institutional assessment of inputs focused on the pace of social mobilization (CO and VO formation), quality of social mobilization, multi-ethnic and gender representation in the COs, participation by the village poorest, gender representation, discussion of women's issues, stakeholder linkages, activities at different tiers, the extent of community participation, credit disbursed and savings, women's access to credit and internal CO lending.

The potential benefits at the CO/household level included assets, income, credit, social empowerment, women's empowerment, education, health, and nutrition. At the VO/VDO/Village level they included community productive infrastructure (CPI), education, health, water, and sanitation. At the LSO/Union Council level they included cross-cutting infrastructure projects, credit disbursed, social and cultural change, and policy change through local government interface.

Findings

Before turning to the stated assessment criteria above, we provide an overview based on the ten LSO profiles we constructed and then bring to attention some details of LSO community development work to provide a broader perspective.

Based on the LSO profiles, the median number of households per UC was 3,000 and the median number of organized households was 1,500.

The median number of VOs/VDOs per UC was 10. Compared to 50 for the men's COs, the median number for women's COs, at 25, was half that of men. The LSO profiles confirmed the imbalance between male and female members of the general and executive bodies. While the median for male EB members was between one and ten, it was less than one for females.

The profile respondents endorsed the household survey perceptions that LSOs were being well managed on all counts as indicated below. The respondents' perception was that the LSOs were involved in a range of self-help activities, with an emphasis on training. The median beneficiary number was about 300 households. The LSOs had undertaken activities with external support, quite similar in nature to its self-help initiatives, with drinking water and irrigation schemes ranking highest.

The LSOs we reviewed had launched diverse initiatives. These were being implemented at the UC, village, and household levels. Some of the larger projects were innovative and ambitious in scope in that they involved the whole community. They were the result of linkages established with donors, NGOs, the government, and the private sector. While for space considerations we report on the successful LSOs, which were impressive in terms of their outreach and innovation, by the same token, there were also examples of weak governance and implementation flaws. Details of selected survey LSO activities are reported in Appendix 3.2 a–c.

Social Capital Stock

Traditional systems of governance, law, and collective action have a bearing on the new constructions of social capital, namely, the COs, VOs, and LSOs. As envisaged, the LSO architecture aims to combine participatory interventions with democratic governance. Traditional authority structures are autocratic. Our primary concern, therefore, was whether traditional systems, with patriarchy as one of its components, could coexist with representative norms? Also, was it reasonable to assume that LSOs would be able to deliver services in a consultative, participatory mode in such traditional societies? However, while seemingly incompatible, we noted a convergence which was partly driven by expediency and partly by the manner in which local governance systems had evolved over time.

Such systems have their roots in two diverging traditions. Autocratic rule represents one extreme. This existed to a greater or lesser degree in, successively, the hereditary, precolonial, and postcolonial periods. The *raja*, *nawab*, *malik*, *khan*, or *maiter* were the hereditary overlords, extracting taxes (*qalang*) and free labor (*begar*) from the communities. A retinue of advisers (*viziers*) and intermediaries (*zaitoon*, *zaildars*) provided administrative back-up. With few exceptions, their rule was harsh and autocratic.

Colonial governance imposed a new fiscal burden in the shape of *abiana* (water) and other taxes, which were administered by an appointed *numberdar*.[20] The British rulers also created new indigenous landed gentry, to serve as intermediaries. These were the feudal *jagirdars* and *waderas* who proved no less autocratic than the hereditary rulers.

Post-independence, hereditary rule waned and in our Northern survey areas mini-states merged into Pakistan. However, feudal oppression remained overtly present during military regimes and, in more covert forms, during periods of elected government when governance lapses created space for it. The extent and intensity of feudal oppression vary across the country, with the greatest intensity being in parts of Sindh and Southern Punjab. However, the historical autocratic and hierarchical system of local governance is mirrored across the whole country in different forms.

A parallel facet of governance was people-oriented. First, absolute rule was not watertight, partly through default, and partly because the traditional ruler did not wish to intervene in small disputes. The latter became the remit of village elders adjudicating through *panchayats* and *jirgas*. Over time, as traditional and colonial rule faded, these village institutions became more prominent. They provided alternative recourse for weak and inept state governance.

Second, strong traditions of mutual aid and collective action have always existed, the latter in the domain of natural resource management (NRM). Rural communities were and continue to be dependent on local resources for sustenance. The NRM systems that have evolved over time are technically and socially sustainable. In fact, communities have skillfully adapted them to present conditions (see below).

The survey responses on the presence of indigenous social capital were encouraging. The village leadership (titles location-specific) has become more egalitarian and accountable. The incumbents occupy these positions through their hereditary status. While the *numberdar* acquired hereditary status over time, he can also be an elected representative. The leaders' primary responsibility is to preside over *panchayats/jirgas*, entrusted with settling intra-family, intra-village, and inter-village disputes. However, they also engage actively in social and development activities. To a much lesser extent, they oversee the maintenance of law and order and tax collection.

A little over 65% of the respondents indicated that local leaders continue to retain their influence. The remaining 35% attribute their declining influence to evolving political changes. Community perceptions regarding leadership functions suggest governing through traditional institutions is dominant (over 40%) followed by social welfare activities conducted by the leadership (over 30%).

Village events (festivals, weddings, funerals, religious celebrations) maintain cohesion and harmony within the community. Over 90% of the respondents stated that they meet and discuss family and village problems on various social occasions, religious and otherwise.

Maternal and paternal relatives, friends, and neighbors constituted the main source of assistance, indicating the strength of bonding social capital. The responses about assistance are about 25% for patrilineal relative or neighbor, 18% friend, 16% matrilineal relative, and 8% for CO member.

Over 35% of the respondents stated that they participated in collective activities as members of various local *tanzeems* (organizations). Of these, a roughly similar percentage observed that women from their households were also members of local *tanzeems*. The bulk of these *tanzeems* were local community-based organizations (CBOs), women's organizations, and religious welfare committees. The collective activities were diverse in nature and included lending, support for the poor, NRM, and local infrastructure development.

Close to 60% of the respondents noted that customary law (*rivaj*) was the prevalent law in the villages. They also ranked it higher than formal legal recourse. By and large, this was the trend across LSOs. A quarter of the respondents observed that both *rivaj* and statutory law (*qanoon*) worked in tandem. The villagers explained that they preferred to have their disputes settled quickly and fairly by the village leaders, and only elected to go to the courts as a last resort. As a check on their understanding, we asked them to correlate the law with the institution and they were clear about the difference. Over 60% of the respondents stated that the informal institutions (*panchayats*, *jirgas*) also performed development and social functions.

The most striking demonstration of indigenous social capital was demonstrated by traditional natural resource management (NRM) practices. In our survey area, the snowcapped mountains, sparkling springs, and gushing rivers are the true treasures of Gilgit-Baltistan. They provide water to the vast plains of Pakistan and the coastal delta. Natural resources and communities are interwoven in Gilgit-Baltistan. These resources have been used under simple and elegant management techniques that have valley-specific terminologies but are, essentially, similar.

Water management embraces drinking and irrigation water. Water storage tanks, referred to as *ghulk*, are constructed in each *muhallah* (neighborhood). This tank is underground and fully covered, with a small door for filling water pots. The space is also used as a cold room in summers to store meat, milk, and butter. The water is constantly replenished via channel through-flows. It is strictly prohibited to pollute the channel and violators are fined Rs.50/- on the spot.[21]

Arable lands face scarcity of water in spring and autumn when reduced snowmelt depletes *nalas* (streams). The response is two-fold. First, communities construct channels (*khul*) from the river or perennial streams to strategically placed outlets. The free labor that they contribute is referred to as *rajaki* in *Shina* and *Burushaski*, and *aashar* in *Wakhi* (local languages and dialects). Second, and to use water efficiently, a water management committee develops a schedule to ration the water and ensure compliance. Communities are also responsible for planting trees along the channel as soil binders and for periodically cleaning the channels.

Wild trees and shrubs are the primary source of fuel and need to be used sustainably to ensure their availability for future generations. The communities establish a limit of 20 maunds (about 82 pounds) of fuelwood and shrubs per year per household, which the *nambardar* monitors. To ensure propagation, cutting is restricted to the period from September to December. The local terms for this practice are *golos* in *Khawar*, *gahin* in *Shina*, and *ghuz-kutak* in *Wakhi*.

Another traditional practice is not to plant trees in close proximity to arable land. There are also spacing requirements: 20 steps between apricot and walnut trees; six steps between almond trees and; eight steps for cherry and other fruit trees. Young trees are protected from cattle by coating the trunks with a paste of animal waste and mud. Tree leaf ash provides warmth during the extreme winter months. Since the leaves are in scarce supply their collection and distribution according to household needs is determined communally.

Livestock, a major food, livelihood, and work source for communities, are taken to the upland and alpine pastures (*nullahs*) during the spring and summer months. The process of collecting livestock, delegating responsibility for accompanying them, and negotiating rates is referred to as *kuch* in *Wakhi*, *hiamas* in Shina, and *biganik* in *Khawar*. The livestock graze a particular area of the pasture for two weeks and then move on, allowing the grass to regenerate. During this period, households retain a cow and a few goats for milk and stall-feed them, as livestock are not allowed to graze freely during the crop season. The person contracted to look after the livestock in pastures is called *payalo* in *Shina*, *huyeltarch* in *Burushaski*, and *shupun* in *Wakhi*. The caretaker, generally from the Gujjar (traditionally nomadic) community, charges the livestock owners a grazing tax (*qalang*), in cash or in kind at the rate of one sheep per 40 sheep, or Rs.30/- per sheep and Rs.400/- per horse. The livestock are brought back from pasture in November and this activity is called *dumankiy*a in *Shina* and *khorikhomi*c in *Khawar*. Wild animal hunting is prohibited but trophy hunting is allowed to ensure the existence of wildlife as well as to benefit local communities.

Traditional village institutions, organizations, events, mutual aid traditions, the pre-eminence of customary law and traditions of social and development work and natural resource management traditions in particular are evidence of vibrant local social capital. Such social capital also has transformative potential in that, all else remaining unchanged, it can be shaped into new organizational forms such as the COs, VOs, and LSOs. Further, it also underscores the sustainability of these constructed forms. While we recognize that traditional institutions retain regressive tendencies,[22] the manner in which they have evolved will determine the rate and resilience of the transformation.

Institutional Assessment

This assessment is in two parts. First, we examine LSO governance as embodied in management systems and procedures. The envisaged LSO governance structure blends democratic and participatory elements. The structure is three-tiered with inbuilt checks and balances, designed to prevent it from becoming top-heavy. These checks and balances take the form of stringent accountability and transparency requirements and open channels of communication. The LSO guidelines emphasize merit and service to the community. The aim is to ensure that as they become entrenched, the risk of *biradari* (clan) capture, or politicization is minimized.

However, management systems and procedures are preconditions for institutional sustainability. In and of themselves they only constitute a framework or, in mathematical terminology, necessary but not sufficient conditions. Institutional vigor and outreach are premised on more active elements. We have defined these as "inputs" and analyze them in detail below.

The election process for the governing bodies was democratic and transparent. Elections (secret ballot, open show of hands) and community selection were the two primary modes for inducting members to these bodies. The perception of influence peddling in the selection process was highest in the Khaplu LSO but even that did not exceed 37% of the responses. Thus, merit was the determining factor in selecting members of the governing bodies. Further, even the subset of respondents who conceded influence was a factor chose, based on the perception of effectiveness. Ultimately, the majority of the respondents chose freely and this has a three-fold attribution: first, relational transformations within the communities over time demonstrate a tilt toward egalitarianism; second, the RSPs have played a role in weaning communities away from traditionally subservient mindsets and; third, RSPN policy and planning staff have built accountability into the LSO system and procedures.

We assessed the community's post-election engagement with the LSOs, using several awareness indicators, such as frequency and record of meetings, and the implementation and nature of audits. A high proportion (over 70%) of the respondents were aware of the executive and general body meetings, the majority noting that these meetings were held monthly. Over 95 of the respondents indicated that minutes of meetings were noted. Similarly, over 80% were aware the LSO/VO accounts were audited and of the auditing mode adopted (internal, external).

The FGD feedback confirmed that the LSO executive committee and general body meetings were held regularly, and that the frequency with which they were held was appropriate. Close to three-fourths responded in the affirmative to adequate regularity in the survey.

There was a high level of satisfaction with RSP and LSO/VO staff in terms of their ability to inspire confidence and for their accessibility. For the most part, satisfaction varied between 80 and 100% with regards to both RSP and LSO/VDO/VO staff. The FGD additionally indicated that the LSOs had imparted training in a diversity of skills.

A high percentage (over 80%) of the respondents stated that the pace of social mobilization had picked up once the LSOs were formed, as evident in the formation of new male and female COs and the reactivation of dormant COs. An equal proportion of respondents also concurred that the LSOs had become more active, with a focus on credit, development projects, and training.

Almost three-fourths of the respondents concurred that the LSO had established links with various external agencies compared to under three-fifths for the control group. This suggests that the LSOs were under greater pressure to establish these linkages as they did not have the benefit of endowments or government support, or the comfort of ongoing RSP funding. Both the LSOs and control group UCs found donor agencies and NGOs were more receptive than government agencies. This was a measure of relative responsiveness to the LSOs, and does not denote lack of effort on their part. In fact, the LSOs, facilitated by the RSPs, repeatedly attempted to establish links with government line departments but with moderate success. Gilgit-Baltistan and AJ&K LSOs fared comparatively better, which is not surprising, as the governments in these regions were known to be people-friendly.

A key reason for LSO formation was to ensure multi-tier interventions. We found the LSOs to be active at all levels (household, village, and UC) in the aggregate. Across LSOs, household-level activities were comparatively the highest, followed by UC-level activities. The latter was an encouraging development and correlated directly with external linkages established. The comparison across LSOs and the control groups showed a dearth of infrastructure projects for the former and this was not surprising considering that LSOs were funding-constrained. However, the flip side is that they were relatively more active in establishing linkages in an effort to secure funding. Over 70% of the respondents stated they contributed to LSO projects/activities with a response variation ranging from 60 to 100% across LSOs. The contributions were in labor, cash, and in kind—in that order.

Over 75% of the respondents noted that the LSOs had secured external funding to on-lend to CO members. While the RSPs and RSPN contributed substantial funding, donors, and banks provided an equally large chunk, which indicated that the LSOs were diversifying their loan sources. Nearly 85% of the respondents stated they had access to these loans and a higher 92% indicated that women could access them. Livestock, small enterprises, and agriculture constituted the three primary activities for which loans were extended. Consistent with socially collateralized credit, both target and control group FGD indicated that a social boycott was the primary deterrent for default.

A roughly equal proportion of the LSO and control group COs had extant saving schemes. Overall, the savings profile was less than satisfactory as more than 50% of the COs had accumulated savings of less than Rs.5,000/- while the control group situation was even worse at 60%. The LSOs and the control group had a similar savings profile with the LSOs marginally outperforming the control group on a number of counts. About 43% of the respondents indicated savings ranging from Rs.5,000 to Rs.50,000/-, compared to only 30% in the control group. The weighted average savings for the LSO-managed COs were Rs.17.6 thousand, while the control group COs averaged Rs.16.6 thousand. Further, over 50% of savings were kept in a bank; it was even higher for the control group COs at 72%.

It was encouraging to note that LSO-managed COs recycled 30% of their savings as internal lending compared to 24% for the control group, a fact confirmed qualitatively by the FGD. Over 80% of the FGD respondents indicated that the savings were being used for internal lending. Nonetheless, insofar as savings are an index of CO performance the emerging picture revealed LSOs to be underperforming in this regard.

While overall the findings were positive, we observed some negative factors in some cases. Evolving management systems in some LSOs exhibited a tendency toward centralized decision-making. Communities either held their hereditary rulers in respect or a cult of leadership had emerged. So, while the LSO precepts were egalitarian, the mode of governance at times tended to exhibit an autocratic bent, with a marked gender bias.

Also, two management modes appeared to have evolved while retaining the common overarching structure specified in the LSO guidelines. In Gilgit-Baltistan-Chitral, over twenty-five years of AKRSP efforts had resulted in well-entrenched VOs and women's organizations (WOs). The LSO had divided its responsibilities. Policy decisions resided with the board of directors/executive body, and their implementation was the remit of the professional management staff (referred to as the management committee). While the separation had a priori merit, the practice revealed defects. Weak communications between the board, the general body, and the VO/WO members were an identified problem in some cases. Communities expressed dissatisfaction with the manner in which board/executive body members were elected. The perception was that the process was not entirely transparent. Furthermore, communities observed that they neither knew the constituent members nor were decisions taken at the meetings of the general body conveyed to them, even though they had elected representatives to this body.

Weak communications led at times to defective projects and activities in terms of their quality and distributional focus. While member communities identified these at the outset, their involvement tapered off during the course of the project cycle, especially at the implementation and monitoring stages. Instead, the LSO engaged contractors, which meant added expense, shoddy work, and a general lack of ownership. LSO projects and activities were made possible through efforts to establish external linkages with various agencies, each of which had its own particular way of doing business. Government agencies work through their own designated contractors, with an entrenched culture of corruption and kick-backs. Unfortunately, LSOs did not enjoy the luxury of picking and choosing. Their own internal governance structures therefore needed to be watertight to counteract the lack of transparency in government agencies.

While critical of the board/executive body members, the VO/WO members appreciated the efforts of the managers or social organizers who interacted with them regularly. The AKRSP provided one-off funding for infrastructure and financed management salaries (Rs.25,000–30,000 per month) with the stipulation that they be phased out over three years. On the one hand, its concern was that paid professional staff detracted from the spirit of volunteerism which, ideally, should drive the LSOs. On the other hand, the paid staff complained that the salaries were too low in relation to their strenuous job requirements. Indeed, the younger and better managers tended to leave for better-paid jobs. In view of the fact that relations with communities were built laboriously over time, their departure left a vacuum and led to a visible slackening of activities.

In the other provinces and Azad Jammu and Kashmir (AJ&K), the locus of mobilization was the CO, with relatively few VOs being formed at the village level. In this case, policy, planning, and management responsibilities were combined in the LSO Executive Body. On the upside, the LSO leadership was strong, effective, and community-oriented. This last attribute appears to reflect an election process which was democratic, accountable, and immune to influence peddling and *biradari* (clan) dominance. Only a secretary counted as paid staff, which was consistent with the spirit of volunteerism. On the downside, we noted a tendency toward centralization in four of the five LSOs surveyed in AJ&K (Kotli and Bagh) and the Khyber Pakhtunkhwa (Haripur). In group discussions with the LSO officeholders, the LSO chairman tended to dominate. Both tendencies pointed to a traditional "cult of leadership."

The target group FGD provided valuable information on leadership roles. Almost half the LSOs had experienced leadership changes. A little over 27% of the respondent groups indicated that the leaders had completed their tenures; while slightly higher than 30% revealed that the leaders had to be removed because they did not measure up. The respondent groups felt that the process for changing leadership was transparent with an established mechanism in place. In a departure from the more ambivalent responses in the household survey the perception was that leaders were from the community at large rather than from influential families. By the same token, LSOs were viewed as reasonably capable of resolving community disputes.

Community Assessment of Benefits and Outcomes

Almost three-quarters of the target-group respondents reported that the LSOs had contributed to an increase in their household incomes, while the corresponding number for the control group was 62%. Credit, training, and livestock grants were noted as the main source of income growth. Only about 30% of respondents indicated an increase in asset growth, about 60% of which constituted housing improvements and livestock purchases. Both target and control groups reported a similar rate and pattern of asset growth.

LSOs and RSPs implemented a similar range of projects/activities, the only difference being the comparatively larger disbursement of credit and drinking water supply schemes by the LSOs and, not surprisingly, more training by the RSPs. Also as expected, LSO funding sources were more diversified than those of the RSPs.

We asked the respondents to rank the LSOs (1–3 with 1 as the highest) according to their management of projects and activities. Close to three-fifths of the respondents gave the LSOs a ranking of "1," the best possible. Disaggregated by LSO, ten LSOs received more than a 50%

positive endorsement on this scale. Based on our effectiveness index, women LSOs secured the top two positions (see Chapter 4).

We also ranked perceptions of LSO effectiveness, measured by several indicators, such as gender equality, savings generation, credit disbursement, reduced dependence on RSPs and ability to secure internal and external funding. Close to four-fifths of respondents consistently ranked the LSOs high. Comparing effectiveness and management across LSOs, the trend lines were similar but the management measure exhibited far more variability. The attribute contributing most to LSO credibility was the trust in which it was held by the community. This trust created a virtuous circle since LSOs held in high trust were subsequently viewed as being more effective which added to the trust.

We asked respondents to comment on key decisions made by the LSOs and the decision-making process, namely, whether they considered it open and consultative. Respondents across LSOs observed that decision-making was a participatory process, with almost 90% concurring on the four criteria of openness and consultations. When asked about what would improve LSO effectiveness, not surprisingly respondents felt that increased funding was the primary requirement of the LSOs and a precursor to all other activities.

Are the LSOs a Viable Exit Strategy for the RSPs?

The state of LSO dependence at the time of the survey establishes a benchmark for taking the exit strategy forward. Close to 55% of respondents thought that LSOs continued to remain dependent on the RSPs. Dependent LSOs indicated a need for continued RSP funding, training, and technical support.

In general, there was a poor correlation between reduced dependence, on the one hand, and good management of projects/activities and overall LSO effectiveness, on the other. However, such a correlation was evident in six of the LSOs (a third of the total), and we argue that these LSOs became institutionally and financially sustainable. This level of independence, inferred from community perceptions, is an impressive achievement in view of the relatively short time that these LSOs had been in existence. The respondents attributed the self-reliance to social mobilization, external links established with other organizations, financial independence, and a sense of pride in doing their work themselves.

The manner in which the RSPs engaged with the LSOs had a bearing on their performance. Some RSPs, notably AKRSP in Gilgit-Baltistan-Chitral, had substantively terminated their engagement after providing one-off funding for LSO office infrastructure, because of their own financial constraints.[23] While they continued to provide limited salary support, the links, otherwise, were tenuous. This had left the LSOs floundering and unsure of themselves.

There was an ongoing internal RSP debate revolving around whether the LSOs and RSPs roles were interchangeable or complementary. Some argued that it was unrealistic to expect the LSOs to replace the RSPs, rich as the latter were in technical, financial, and human resources. Others countered that the LSOs could rely on activists and volunteers and that being an integral part of the community would ensure that projects and activities were implemented cost-effectively.

Institutional resistance could delay the transition. It was not uncommon to hear RSP staff referring to LSOs as mini-RSPs. Also, we noted some dissent within the RSPs, where some were of the opinion that the LSOs should be the product of a felt need. However, such reservations deferred to policy, which was to form LSOs proactively. Nevertheless, the lack of complete buy-in by middle-level RSP staff may have slowed down the transition in some areas.

External constraints, too, were present. First, donor funding had become scarce, especially in Gilgit-Baltistan-Chitral, with the result that the RSPs had disengaged prematurely. The nature of the RSP–LSO relations has a regional context. In Gilgit-Baltistan-Chitral, the AKRSP was coming to grips with declining donor support. As such, the LSOs were being accorded relatively low priority. This took the shape of a one-off contribution for salary support and office infrastructure, occasional training and some linkage development—somewhat of a cookie-cutter approach. On the whole the LSOs felt they have been abandoned prematurely, when there was a need for continued capacity-building and help in promoting linkages.

Many of the organizations had become inactive in those UCs where the AKRSP had reduced its presence. There were several complaints that the president or manager had defaulted on loans or absconded with the savings. This made it all the more difficult for the LSOs to reorganize. In other cases, we noted strong donor dependence, in the sense that funding infusions were the main lifeline for these organizations. Indeed, in many UCs the LSOs had taken on the added burden of reactivating dormant COs, which appear to have mobilized around projects rather than the indigenous community social capital. A repeated complaint was that the RSPs had formed COs, but there had been no substantive follow-up. The AKRSP could have anticipated and averted this dependence mindset.

In contrast, the NRSP's interface in the Punjab was more nurturing and sustained. However, even here, in some cases, RSP–LSO relations were strained because they were implementing similar programs. The microcredit and development programs of the RSPs were well-entrenched and tended to swamp LSO efforts. In an ideal complementary relationship, both these activities would be channeled through the LSOs, concurrent with focused efforts to building their capacity—especially when the LSO credit record was exemplary.

In yet other cases, the original organizations in the Punjab transformed themselves into savings societies and cooperatives and limited themselves to internal lending. The bulk of the COs became credit organizations partly through intent and partly by default. In other words, they were organized around credit at the outset, or were reduced to it because of the RSPs' inability to deliver broader development benefits.

Dependence was not the only factor in the COs' inability to self-motivate. A key change was altered cognitive perceptions, especially in Gilgit-Baltistan-Chitral, the AJ&K, and Haripur. A combination of high unemployment and down-country opportunities had made male communities more outward-looking. In turn, this had inhibited the spirit of volunteerism. In contrast, women not only continued to remain area-confined, they were also stepping into typically male domains—forced to do so by economic necessity. This is not to depreciate the increased employment opportunities for men down-country. Livelihoods would always take priority over volunteerism. Indeed, the relocation was temporary—during the winter months, when men cannot plant or harvest crops and they can get paid employment via outmigration. However, such labor movements detract from the continuous efforts required to nurture and sustain male COs. Women were, therefore, able to step into the spaces vacated by men (Chapter 4). The RSPs have no stated position on this; in fact, they were actively involved in promoting women's economic and social participation.

A priori, an established need formed a good foundation on which to build an LSO. In some UCs the CO members had expressed this need. In one UC in particular, members had even offered to pay higher fees if the RSP approved its request for an LSO. Among other things, the respondents envisaged the LSO's role as one of forming linkages, mobilizing and monitoring community activities and organizing training. The expressed need for LSOs was strongest in those areas where the RSPs were easing out, leaving the communities feeling vulnerable.

Decentralized services, infrastructure, and financing were effectively provided to local communities by the RSPs. They also established linkages with provincial governments and government line departments, specifically in the shape of one-off block grants and collaborative projects. However, their primary source of funding and technical support continued to be multilateral/bilateral donors and NGOs. As we have indicated, the LSOs reflect RSP efforts both to indigenize development and, equally important, to address their capacity constraints. LSO links with provincial and local government bodies were tenuous at the time of the survey. Unless the local government process is institutionalized, both the RSPs and LSOs will continue to remain dependent on donor resources as well as their own ability to generate these resources.[24]

In survey responses LSOs consistently out-performed the RSPs in the public perception. The institutional comparisons show the LSOs in a favorable light. They had been relatively more successful than the RSPs in obtaining grants and scholarships for the poor and in securing government services. RSPs were not underperforming as they scored high with the communities as well; it is just that the LSOs were doing even better. Ultimately, this should be a source of satisfaction for the RSPs as the LSOs are eventually meant to replace them. Both institutions achieved comparable success in raising social awareness among CO members and in increasing their visibility and confidence. Aspects of increased social awareness were increased social cohesion; focus on health, hygiene, and sanitation and; greater attention to women's rights and contributions.

Ultimately, our take on the question was that, yes, the LSOs are a viable exit strategy for the RSPs, but the processes necessary to affect this transition needed strengthening. In our view, the RSP–LSO interface needed to become more proactive. At the outset, the LSOs were a creation of the RSPs, giving them an induced rather than an autonomous flavor. The transition from the former to the latter would require strong process interventions, such as technical, human, and financial empowerment. We note the key difference, namely, that the LSOs represented embodied social capital while the RSPs were facilitators. But it is the RSPs which occupied center-stage in community perceptions and these perceptions change only if the required process interventions are carried out. Most critical in this regard is setting LSOs on the track to financial sustainability.

Achieving financial sustainability can be viewed as a two-part strategy. Part one was the RSPN facilitating LSOs via a community investment fund (CIF). This entailed giving the LSOs a grant in the form of a revolving fund of either one or two million rupees. The CIF generated interest when disbursed as credit and part of this was used for LSO operational expenses and part ploughed back into the revolving fund. The accrued returns at the time of the survey ranged from Rs. 100,000 to 400,000 and had the potential for becoming small LSO endowments.

The second part of the strategy followed the adage, "necessity is the mother of invention." The LSOs devised various innovative ways to generate additional resources. These include voluntary community contributions, donor-funding set-asides, room and implement rentals, among other initiatives.[25] LSOs had been more successful than the control group in raising an endowment fund, not surprising as their need was more pressing. Thus, close to 70% LSOs had an endowment fund compared to about 50% for the control group. However, the main source of this LSO endowment was the RSPN, whereas the RSPs had more diverse funding sources.

Summary

Partly because of financial constraints but also as a sustainability exercise, the RSPs, with the assistance of the RSPN, explored an exit strategy from some of the extensive social mobilization, grassroots organization construction, and participatory development activities RSPs were engaged in. The issue at hand was whether LSOs as apex organizations could be used as a mechanism to consolidate the work that RSPs had done so that the latter could move on to capacity-building activities and mobilizing other marginalized communities not yet reached.

While our review of the literature indicated the existence of other multitier apex organizations as an institutional entity in grassroots participatory development, we are not aware of any systematic attempt to create and strengthen such organizations as a mechanism to consolidate, strengthen, and indigenize the process so that the organizations are *of* the people and not only *for* the people and to use such organizations for a development NGO exit strategy.

Exploring whether this is a viable exit strategy for the RSPs was our key research question. Our working hypothesis was that the ability to tap indigenous social capital in communities and build on that to construct new forms of institutional social capital, which included the various tiers of the LSO, would be central to the success of such a strategy. Success is measured as the ability of the LSO to deliver sustained benefits to the households and communities via collective action.

The findings based on observation of the outstanding projects and processes reflect the ability of LSOs to mobilize successfully for ambitious collective action for community betterment. The projects tackled were much needed, ambitious in scale, and demonstrated a surprising level of innovation in finding solutions to difficult problems. Observation of processes demonstrated the LSOs' ability to bring about cultural change that empowered communities, women, and the poorest of the poor and enabled them to engage in collective action.

The LSOs were active and over four-fifths of respondents expressed satisfaction with the pace of the work. About three-quarters observed that linkages with donors, the private sector, and other development NGOs were picking up. Since linkages were a key part of the strategy for diversifying the resource and activity base, this is encouraging. Other successes included the greater ability of LSOs rather than RSPs in raising endowment funds, though their sources were less diversified. LSO-run COs showed a greater recovery rate in micro lending than control groups; LSO projects were more likely to be perceived as pro-women and pro-poor; LSOs were perceived as more successful than RSPs in securing government services and scholarships for the poor and; LSOs were perceived as more successful than RSPs in increasing income and social well-being.

The communities for the most part appeared to be aware and engaged with regard to process which they viewed as participatory. There was an awareness that meetings were being held, minutes taken, and accounts audited. Communities had started saving, and these savings were being recycled as internal lending, where 85% had access to loans. Four-fifths rated the LSOs high on effectiveness.

The RSPN and the RSPs have developed a sound exit strategy. In our assessment, a third of the LSOs have become institutionally and financially sustainable, an impressive achievement given the short time they had been in existence. There appeared to be two prevailing strategies on how to proceed. One view can be characterized by a "sink or swim" approach. At times, such as in Gilgit-Baltistan-Chitral, this seemed to be motivated by necessity, as financial constraints impelled the RSPs to move on. An alternative was a more nurturing strategy, and this is the one we endorse to ensure a higher success rate.

Notes

1. For details on RSPs see Khan et al. (2007, Chapter 2) and Khan (2009). The general RSP social mobilization method, as adopted by the National Rural Support Program (NRSP), is explained in Chapter 5. While the last elected government of the Pakistan Muslim League supported RSPs financially and administratively, the current Pakistan Tehreek-e-Insaf government has been hostile and hounding development NGOs. Thus, while the RSP-government complementary relations were in evidence

during the PML-N era there is no evident interest shown by the PTI government towards the RSPs.

2. These COs comprise anywhere from 5 to 10 households and the number of COs in a village varies depending on its population. In peri-urban areas, the COs are essentially lane committees, comprising households in the neighborhood.
3. https://www.rspn.org/, consulted November 2, 2019.
4. Union Councils are the lowest administrative tier; above them are *tehsils*, districts and provinces.
5. This section is a synthesis of Azizi (2006).
6. Shoaib Sultan Khan, the first General Manager of the AKRSP, conceptualized these multitiered federations of community organizations in the early 1980s.
7. Other RSPs, especially the National Rural Support Program and the Sarhad Rural Support Program, also supported apex bodies of COs at the village, union council and *tehsil* levels in relatively mature communities.
8. Revenue villages are defined for tax purposes and are much larger entities than a regular village. The latter represents more cohesive communities on which social mobilization is centered.
9. In 2002, mature community organizations also began to register themselves as Citizen Community Boards (CCBs) as envisioned in the Local Government Ordinance (Government of Pakistan 2000); but even these organizations relied heavily on the technical support of the local RSP.
10. In several areas LSOs have federated into LSO Networks at the district level (e.g., Chitral, Ghizer, and Dargai Networks) to benefit from scale advantages; a total of 15 LSO Networks had been established by 2019, https://www.rspn.org/, consulted November 18, 2019. For an account of Chital's network, refer to https://www.rspn.org/wp-content/uploads/2016/05/The-Network-of-LSOs-in-Chitral-A-Case-Study-of-Chitral-Community-Development-Network.pdf, consulted November 18, 2019.
11. Close to 100 centers were established by 2007, Rao et. al. (2007).
12. The MSDSP was funded by the Aga Khan Foundation following the success of the Aga Khan Rural Support Program in Gilgit Pakistan and its successful replication in the rest of Pakistan.
13. See also Van Mele and Samsuzzaman (2005) for farmer federations in Bangladesh.
14. This process is likely to have marginalized the poorest engaged in day labor.
15. The authors point out that the federations waxed and waned but survived, and, as is generally true, individuals played a key role in the process.

16. Bebbington (1997) mentioned the critical role of market demand in enabling such organizations to market their produce and role of the state in this context.
17. Of these, subsequently, two in the Khyber Pakhtunkhwa and one in Baluchistan were replaced for security reasons. Ideally we should have studied only LSOs which had been in operation for at least three and preferably five years. While 21 LSOs qualified for selection on this criterion, their distribution across the RSPs was skewed, the bulk being concentrated in the AKRSP—and NRSP—(National Rural Support Program) managed areas.
18. The scorecard was developed by Mark Schreiner as a tool that is straightforward and easy to implement in the field, www.uniteforsight.org/global-health-university/poverty-scorecards, consulted November 4, 2019.
19. The questionnaires will be made available by the authors on request.
20. The *numberdar* has acquired hereditary status and remains a figure of respect, consulted on diverse village affairs and a permanently inducted member of village institutions. He also continues to collect *abiana* (water tax).
21. The 2010 exchange rate was Rs.85 to one $.
22. Culturally embedded regressive practices include *karo kari* (honor killings), *watta satta* (bride exchanges between families) and *vani*, *swara* (forced child marriage). On the one hand, the harsher *panchayat* and *jirga* rulings evoke the most brutal punishments of past hereditary rulers. On the other hand, such institutions also offer hope for quick remediation in civic and property disputes.
23. This may be due to in part to funding constraints but it was also policy driven, the premise being that early disengagement with the LSOs will force them to become sustainable.
24. Local bodies in Pakistan have been constituted to serve the interests of authoritarian rulers (Generals Ayub Khan, Zia ul Haq and Musharraf) and bypass provincial governments that posed a threat to them. Their tenure has never lasted longer than their sponsors. Consequently, they were inept bodies at best, constitutionally out on a limb and financially disempowered. While devolution now has constitutional protection, much of the power devolved to the provincial level with no fiscal powers at the local level.
25. Some examples include contributions from the sale of wheat, rice and fruit (Alimpur and Nabipur), sub-letting rooms in the office complex for daily occupancy (PHKN), savings from donor-funded projects (PHKN),

community (CO, general body) contributions (Goth Mehrab, PHKN), rental from agricultural implements (Goth Mehrab—planned), earnings from the sale of greenhouse vegetables (Goth Mehrab—planned), savings from matching government grants (RCSO) and water charges from irrigation schemes (Khaplu—planned).

26. Maternity centers were a critical need as expecting village women often expired en-route to hospitals.

Appendix 3.1: Selected Notable Examples of LSO Induced Collective Action

See Tables 3.1 and 3.2.

LSO Surhan, Union Council Bhakuo, District Tharparker, Sindh
A Karachi businessman leased salt-mines near LSO villages. Twenty-two wheeled trucks utilized the road that served the LSO villages. Since the trucks were way too large and heavy for the road, they damaged the roads and culverts causing dangerous driving conditions and accidents. In addition, the trucks delayed traffic and killed livestock (without accountability when travelling fast during odd hours). When an accident resulted in 10 deaths, about 300 of the 3,500 LSO members took direct action and blocked the road. LSO activists were

Table 3.1 RSPN-supported LSOs (as of 30 June 2009)

RSPs	Total	Formed before 30 June 2006	Formed before 30 June 2007
AKRSP	12	10	1
BRSP	2	0	0
SRSP	7	3	2
NRSP	14	5	3
TDRP	8	3	2
PRSP	2	0	0
Women's LSOs	4	1	3
Total	49	21	8

Source RSPN (2009)

Table 3.2 Households interviewed by province/area

Province/area	LSOs	Control group
AJ&K (3 LSOs, 3 control groups)	324	323
Khyber Pakhtunkhwa (2 LSOs, 1 control group)	173	82
Chitral (1 LSO, 1 control group)	113	114
Gilgit–Baltistan (3 LSOs, 3 control groups)	283	273
Punjab (4 LSOs, 4 control groups)	401	383
Sindh (3 LSOs, 3 control groups	242	278
Balochistan (2 LSOs)	155	0
Total	1691	1453

Source Author survey

able to convert the spontaneous collective action into a negotiated settlement that resulted in the improvement of the roads, culverts, and social investments by the business in LSO villages.

Another remarkable success was the LSO legally fighting the diversion of funds by the Department of Education initially sanctioned for a high school in an LSO village. The LSO got wind of the diversion on political grounds and formed a committee to block the diversion. The LSO filed a petition with a Sessions Judge and won their case.

LSO Society Development Foundation, Union Council Rawali, District Bagh, Azad Jamnu and Kashmir

Apart from several other initiatives, the recycling program was particularly notable. Villages would clean and return glass bottles to a pharmacy for a small sum. Plastic bags were being eschewed for cloth bags that several LSO members were producing and marketing for Rs. 20–25. School books were collected at the end of the year and donated to less advantaged students.

LSO Rural Community Development Organization, Union Council Topi, District Bagh, Azad Jamnu and Kashmir

The LSOs environmental collective action initiatives included tree planting, forest protection, and rainwater harvesting. It formed a conflict resolution committee consisting of eight executive body members and 25 general body members to provide speedy local justice on issues including murder, land disputes, kidnapping, robbery, and fights. The courts were only used as a backup when resolution was not possible by the committee. Committee decisions were enforced by a social boycott if not heeded.

LSO Mamta, Union Council Mithrio Bhatti, District Tharparker, Sindh
Only eight of the 47 LSO villages had electricity and the district had the highest number of nocturnal snake bites in the country, several fatal. Solar lighting had come to a nearby region and members approached the LSO for credit. The LSO formed a three-person committee, delegated one LSO member for training in installation and maintenance and subsequently provided credit, initially to 30 applicants after an appraisal. Snakebite incidents dramatically declined, schooling outcomes improved as children had longer study hours, and women were able to engage in more home-based activities for income.

LSO Saleem Khan, Union Council Saleem Khan, District Swabi, Khyber Pakhtunkhwa
The Union Council LSO members had rights over a large tract of fertile commons. However, the plots were small and distributed, access difficult, and conflicts arose over boundaries so farming was difficult. The LSO successfully undertook the complex task of consolidating and distributing the land and subsequently raised the funds to build eight access roads.

LSO Abasind Rural Support Organization, Union Council Komila, District Kohistan, Khyber Pakhtunkhwa
Kohistan is one of the poorest districts in the country because it is so remote. It is where the Himalayas, Karakorum, and Hindukush systems meet. Despite gushing mountain streams, many of the villages were not electrified. Micro hydel projects had been funded by donors but expensive to install and maintain. The LSO innovated by replacing iron with a wooden turbine and reduced the cost ten-fold. Other advantages included longer life (no rusting), lower maintenance cost, higher efficiency (rotates faster since it is lighter and needs less water

pressure—great advantage in winter when water level declines), better health (since kerosene lamps could be dispensed with) and also less outdoor environmental pollution. After successfully piloting in one village in which all electricity recipients regularly paid dues deposited into a CO account, the LSO decided to diffuse the technology to other LSO villages.

LSO Rhod Mullazai, Union Council Rhod Mullazai, District Pishin, Baluchistan
A *kareze* is an ingenious underground water channel that uses a network of wells and gravity to move water in water-scarce areas while avoiding loss through evaporation. These were traditionally collectively maintained but the LSO found a loss of flow due to a lack of collective annual cleaning. The LSO organized joint maintenance and dues collection and success in some villages resulted in their plans to extend this to all the *karezes* in the union council. Other activities included liaising with a development NGO to provide wind-driven drinking water supply, a ban on cutting and marketing Juniper trees (threatened with extinction), replanting, and establishing rules for extraction and local use of fallen trees and banning pheasant hunting until successful conservation was attained.

Appendix 3.2: Selected Illustration of Survey LSO Community Development Work

See Fig. 3.2 and Table 3.3.

a. *Mehrab Goth LSO, Bahawalpur, Sindh*

The Goth Mehrab LSO was instrumental in extending local irrigation systems from a seasonal to an annual basis. The process also represented a non-intrusive and complementary public to private sector transition. In particular, the private sector operation drew upon embedded social capital to forestall a zero-sum game or "the tragedy of the commons."

The public sector (provincial irrigation departments) primarily managed Pakistan's canal irrigation systems. In Mehrab Goth,

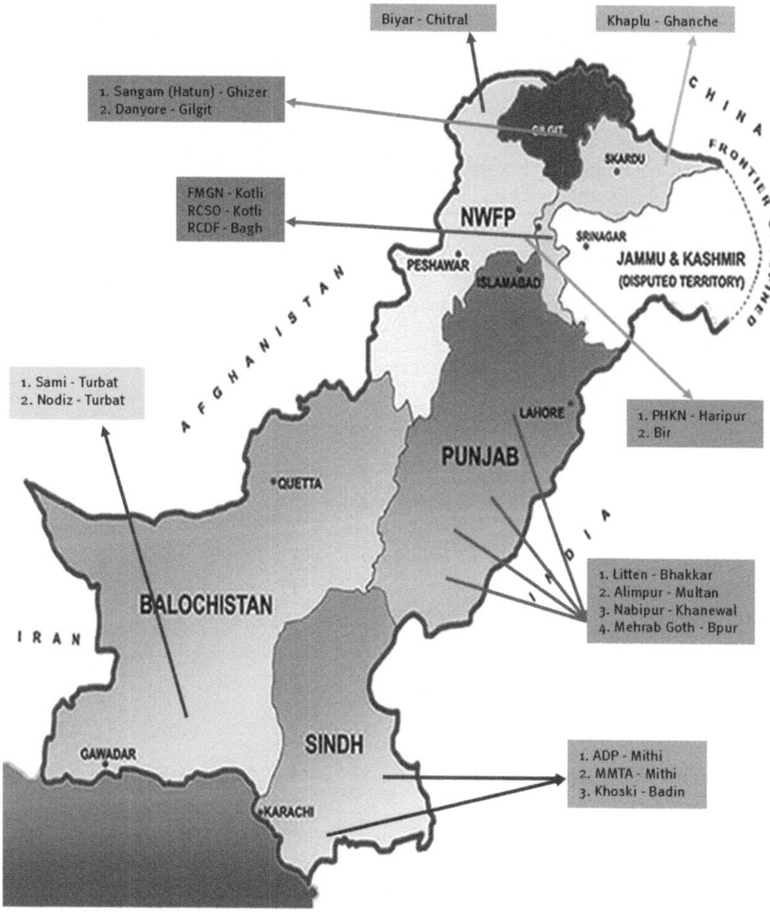

Fig. 3.2 LSO national survey sites (*Source* Authors)

Bahawalpur, irrigation water was seasonally available during the *kharif* (summer) season. Various factors, including competing demands for this water and, possibly, climate change, further constricted water availability.

The project involved installing 300 feet deep turbines along the minor, which tapped aquifers replenished by seepage from the minor. The water was then conveyed via underground GI pipes into arid zones which lay beyond outlying farmers' fields. Although fertile, cultivation was not

Table 3.3 Survey implementation details for target and control groups

	Target group					
LSO	Union Council	Household Questionnaire	FGD check list	Group discussion (LSO office holders)	LSO profile	Informant interviews
AJ&K						
RCDF, Kotli	Tarala	128	2		1	4
FMGN, Kotli	Goi	118	2		1	4
RCSO, Bagh	Degwar	78	2	1	1	4
Sub-total		*324*	*6*	*1*	*3*	*12*
Khyber Pakhtunkhwa						
PHKN, Haripur	Pind Hashim Khan	72	2	1	6	2
Bir, Haripur	Bir	101	2	1	0	0
Sub-total		*173*	*4*	*2*	*6*	*2*
Chitral						
Biyar,Chitral	Charun	113	2	1	10	2
Sub-total		*113*	*2*	*1*	*10*	*2*
Gilgit–Baltistan						
Khaplu, Baltistan	Khaplu	92	2	1	7	3
Sangam (Hatun), Gilgit)	Hatun	94	2	1	9	2
Danyore, Gilgit	Danyore	97	2	1	10	2
Sub-total		*283*	*6*	*3*	*26*	*7*
Punjab						
Litten, Punjab	Litten	100	2	1	10	0
Alimpur, Punjab	Alimpur	105	2	1	10	0
Nabipur, Punjab	Nabipur	96	2	1	10	0
Goth Mehrab, Punjab	Goth Mehrab	100	2	1	10	3
Sub-total		*401*	*8*	*4*	*40*	*3*
Tharparkar						

(continued)

Table 3.3 (continued)

LSO	*Target group* Union Council	Household Questionnaire	FGD check list	Group discussion (LSO office holders)	LSO profile	Informant interviews
Aurat Development Program (ADP), Mithi	Mithi	96	2	1	10	4
Megh Malhar Tariqiati Idara (MMTA)	Mithrio Bhatti	77	2	1	9	2
Sub-total		*173*	*4*	*2*	*19*	*6*
Sind						
Khoski, Badin	Khoski	69	2	1	10	3
Sub-total		*69*	*2*	*1*	*10*	*3*
Balochistan						
Nodiz, Turbat	Nodiz	75	2	1	10	
Sami, Turbat	Sami	80	2		10	
Sub-total		*155*	*4*	*1*	*20*	
Total		**1691**	**36**	**15**	**134**	**35**

Control group

Union Councils (with RSP, no LSO)	Related LSO	Household Questionnaire	FGD check list	Group discussion (RSP office holders)
AJ&K				
Atkora, Kotli	RCDF	90		
Qamrotie, Kotli	FMGN	149		
Kalali, Bagh	RCSO	84	1	1
Sub-total		*323*	*1*	*1*
Khyber Pakhtunkhwa				
Mankara, Haripur	PHKN	82	3	1
Sub-total		*82*	*3*	*1*
Chitral				

(continued)

Table 3.3 (continued)

Control group				
Union Councils (with RSP, no LSO)	Related LSO	Household Questionnaire	FGD check list	Group discussion (RSP office holders)
Owir, Upper Chitral	Biyar	114	2	1
Sub-total		*114*	*2*	*1*
Gilgit–Baltistan				
Sailing	Khaplu	89	2	1
Bubur	Sangam (Hatun)	94	2	1
Jalalabad	Danyore	90	2	1
Sub-total		*273*	*6*	*3*
Punjab				
Goharwala	Litten	100	2	0
Matti Tal	Alimpur	101	2	1
Kot Bahadur	Nabipur	100	2	0
Jundido Misson Mari Sheikh	Goth Mehrab	82	2	0
Sub-total		*383*	*8*	*1*
Sindh				
Mithi	ADP	101	2	1
Joruo	MAMTA	90	2	1
			4	*2*
Khalifo Qasim, Dehi Jarkas	Khoski	87	2	1
Sub-total		*278*	*2*	*1*
Total		**1453**	**26**	**10**

Source Author survey

possible in these arid areas because the underlying groundwater aquifers were brackish. The deep turbine-GI pipe extension made it possible to reclaim and cultivate large swathes of arid land. Farmers claimed that the soil's productivity was twice as high as the fields they cultivated traditionally.

The LSO forwarded turbines, which were provided by NRSP free of cost, to several community organizations (COs). These COs managed the turbines and sold the water. Two modes of water sales became prevalent. One was a not-for-profit sale for land reclamation. The other was sale-for-profit to farmers who drew water from the minor during the *kharif* season and were water-deprived during the *rabi* (wheat) season, when the irrigation department shut off canal water. Water from the turbines was pumped into the minors and its distribution precisely synchronized. The downstream farmers bought this water at hourly rates (Rs.200 per hour), extracting the water through pipes which matched the diameter of pipes discharging water from the turbines.

The synchronization of discharge and withdrawal—sometimes several kilometers downstream—was affected through cell phone communications. The system was so finely tuned that often several turbines and outlets operated simultaneously. No Irrigation Department officials were involved in the process; the minor merely served as a vehicle for conveying water. The system was trust-based.

While we are tempted to attribute this to embedded social capital, there was also an inbuilt check avoiding a zero-sum game. Any deviation from the rules of the game would result in a collapse of trust, system breakdown, and a loss to all, including the culpable farmer. These are the same farmers who were not above *mogah* (outlet) tampering when the irrigation department released water from the canals, but who operated their own system with no cheating.

The LSO also established linkages with other organizations. It signed a memorandum of understanding with the World Wildlife Fund (WWF) to establish a resource center adjacent to the LSO office. The project was worth Rs.1.8 million, with the LSO contributing 20% from its own sources and member contributions. The resource center was to be a repository for agricultural implements (land levelers, ploughs, drills), to be rented out below market rates to small farmers. The implements, provided under the WWF grant were to remain the property of the LSO. The LSO planned to build in a small profit margin for its endowment fund.

Another example of a linkage was the establishment of demonstration plots in collaboration with the Fauji Fertiliser Corporation (FFC). The LSO regularly facilitated farmers meetings where trained FFC staff advised farmers on good agronomy. Also, WWF funding was used for the upgradation of a primary school to middle level in a remote area.

b. *Litten LSO, District Bhakkar, Punjab*

The Litten LSO is located on rain-dependent desert terrain. With NRSP support, the LSO initiated an ambitious project with the communities, which generated both environmental and economic benefits. The technology was simple and elegant. It involved extensive plantation of the tamarisk tree (*khagal*) on private lands, where the tree was intercropped with peanuts. The *khagal* is hardy, regenerates easily, and needs little water in the initial stage. It has multiple uses (fuelwood, timber for construction, and simple furniture). The average sale price of a five-year-old tree is Rs. 800/- which is a valuable source of income for the household. The LSO prepared a plan which envisaged the plantation of 100 trees by every member of each CO. The environmental windfall generated by a project of this magnitude is self-evident.

A road clearing initiative was another illustration of close community collaboration. The key roads—communication and market lifelines for the communities—were often covered with layers of sand thanks to recurring sandstorms. In this particular case, a two-kilometer stretch of one of the trunk roads had accumulated enough sand to become unserviceable. The LSO mobilized the communities which contributed Rs.70,000 and free labor and cleared the road.

The LSO also managed adult education (functional literacy), training (stitching, embroidery) prior to credit to women (the LSO provided the credit via its community investment fund (CIF)), assistance to the marginalized (livestock/poultry to the poorest of the poor), water pumps for vegetable growing for farmers who owned a maximum one-half acre of land and facilitated ID card procurement for communities.

c. *Nabipur LSO, District Khanewal, Punjab*

The mere existence of the Nabipur LSO in a feudal environment raised the hopes of an oppressed and impoverished community where the *wadera* (landlord) presence was strong. Feudal oppression was manifested in the blocking of gainful employment opportunities to perpetuate the captive labor market of landless and homeless tenants, the absence of schools that changed serf attitudes and therefore represented a threat to feudal dominance, the absence of health centers, forced labor, especially of young girls in feudal households, and the oppressive use of police and local thugs to quell resistance.

The LSO framed an agenda which, although ostensibly developmental, indirectly aimed to counter *wadera* excesses. Among the existing and planned initiatives were the establishment of a girl's college, the conversion of an abandoned government building into a school, maternity and health centers,[26] and technical training and vocational centers to prepare unemployed youth for the job market. The most ambitious initiative was providing low-cost housing for homeless tenants, thus reducing their dependence on the landlords.

Another initiative aimed to minimize the influence of the *mullahs* (local religious leader). It involved donating the skins of sacrificial animals to the LSO rather than the mosque. These were then sold and the money was used to purchase essential items which were distributed among the indigent and needy.

The absence of contractual stipulations and penalties in the LSO credit program was a measure of collective trust, also evident in a 100% recovery rate. While not strictly kosher to a micro credit practitioner, deviation from the norm of this nature spoke volumes for inter-community trust.

References

Azizi, M.A. 2006. Guidelines for LSO Program. RSPN, Islamabad, Pakistan.

Bebbington, A. 1997. Social Capital and Rural Intensification: Local Organizations and Islands of Sustainability in Rural Andes. *The Geographical Journal* 163 (2): 189–197.

Bebbington, A.J., and T. Perreault. 2003. Social Capital, Development, and Access to Resources in Highland Ecuador. *Economic Geography* 75 (4): 395–418.

Government of Pakistan. 2000. Devolution of Power and Responsibility: Establishing the Foundation of Genuine Democracy—Local Government Proposed Plan. National Reconstruction Bureau, Islamabad, Pakistan.

Khan, N. 2008. Extending the Frontiers of Social Capital for Local-Level Development: A Case Study of Local Support Organizations Fostering Linkages with State and Non-State Agencies. Rural Support Program Network (RSPN), Social Mobilization Section, Islamabad, Pakistan.

Khan, M.H. 2009. *Participatory Rural Development in Pakistan: Experience of Rural Support Programs*. Karachi: Oxford University Press.

Khan, M.H., et al. 1992. *Rural Change in the Third World: Pakistan and the Aga Khan Rural Support Program*. New York: Greenwood Press.

Khan, S.R., S. Kazmi, and Z. Rifaqat. 2007. *Harnessing and Guiding Social Capital for Rural Development*. New York: Palgrave/Macmillan.

Mehr, L. 2007. Scaling Up Community Organizations A Case Study of Social Mobilization Best Practices. Rural Support Program Network (RSPN), Islamabad, Pakistan.

Olsen, W. 2004. Triangulation in Social Research: Qualitative and Quantitative Methods Can Really Be Mixed. In *Developments in Sociology*, ed. M.H. Olmskirk. Edinburgh: Causeway Press.

Rao, K.P., et al. 2007. "Making Markets Work for the Poor: Community-Managed Procurement Centers for Small and Marginal Farmers in Andhra Pradesh, India." *South Asia* 1 (December): Note No. 2.

RSPN. 2009. Note on Importance of VDOs in the Three Tier Model. Rural Support Program Network, Islamabad, Pakistan.

Srivardana, S. 2004. Innovative Practice Amidst Positive Potential for Paradigm Shift: The Case of Sri Lanka. In *Pro-poor Growth and Governance in South Asia: Decentralization and Participatory Development*, ed. P. Wignaraja and S. Sirivardana, 241–259. New Delhi, Thousand Oaks and, London: Sage.

UNDP. 2004a. Scaling Up Poverty Reduction: South Asia Poverty Alleviation Programme. Regional Bureau for Asia & the Pacific, Islamabad.

UNDP. 2004b, South Asia Poverty Alleviation Programme—A Case Study. Regional Bureau for Asia & the Pacific, Islamabad, Pakistan.

Van Mele, P., and S. Samsuzzaman. 2005. Innovating with Federations: Community Institutions Take the Lead in Seed Marketing. In *Innovations in Rural Extension: Case Studies from Bangladesh*, ed. P. Van Mele, A. Salahuddin, and N. Magor. Wallingford: CABI Publishing.

World Bank. 2004. The World Bank and People's Republic of China, Reducing Poverty, Sustaining Growth: Pakistan Case—Scaling Up RSPs. World Bank, Islamabad.

4

Gender and Livelihood Support Organizations

Introduction

This chapter relies on the same data bases we relied on for Chapter 3. We start this chapter with an overview of the gender balance attained by LSOs. As indicated in Chapter 3, some of the LSOs were run exclusively by women. After the overview, we narrate how women rose to the challenge of filling spaces vacated by men in LSO management. This becomes more evident when comparing the performance of female run LSOs with those run by men. The conceptual framework for social capital and collective action has been covered in Chapters 2 and 3 and the research design and method in Chapter 3. Thus, we proceed straight to the findings.

This chapter draws on the authors' report "Local Support Organisations: Rural Support Programmes Letting Go, Citizens Taking Charge," written for the Rural Support Program Network, September 2010. We also drew on this report for "A Rural Support Programme Exit Strategy: Women Filling Vacated Spaces and Excelling in Community Development," *Development in Practice* 22 (2): 154–163, 2012.

S. R. Khan and S. R. Khan, *Social Capital and Collective Action in Pakistani Rural Development*, https://doi.org/10.1007/978-3-030-71450-5_4

Findings

Overview of Gender Balance in LSOs

The majority of the women respondents, from 60 to 75%, noted a predominantly male representation in the LSO/VO governing bodies. However, empowering women was viewed as an LSO priority and women found the decision-making process to be open and consultative.

Women responded to questions regarding the degree to which the LSOs were sensitive to their concerns. The gender disparity in governance did not prevent discussions on a wide range of women's issues at the general and executive body meetings, with over 80% of the respondents indicating as much.

The key issues and concerns raised at these meetings affecting women included health, education, livelihoods, and vocational training. The majority of female respondents also confirmed that they were consulted on activities affecting them at the LSO general body meetings and that the decisions taken subsequently were consensus-based (by show of hands).

A large proportion (between 70 and 85%) of the women respondents observed that LSO-managed projects/activities were pro-poor and pro-women. The benign training–credit nexus formed the dominant part of both LSO and RSP activities. However, RSP projects/activities were more diverse, and understandably so as they had the edge in terms of time and experience. More than 90% of female respondents noted that women were able to access the credit the LSOs were on-lending. An almost equal proportion indicated that women could use community organization savings, both for their own use and in the form of internal lending.

More than four-fifths of the female respondents observed that women's income had increased. Building their capacity through training and providing credit to utilize this capacity were the two key contributing factors. A nearly equal proportion of women indicated they resultantly enjoyed higher social benefits in the form of improved nutrition, health, and education for children. The LSOs performed better than the RSPs in terms of improvements in both income and social well-being.

One reason could be the socialization process, whereby the RSPs initially and LSOs subsequently sensitized women to their important role in the family. In fact, over 60% of the female respondents in the target group observed women's decision-making powers had increased, compared with slightly over 50% for the control group. The perception was uniform across LSOs, with only six LSOs not concurring. These powers were fairly wide-ranging. Women's rights and contributions formed a key component of the LSOs' awareness-creation efforts. Reprising global findings, this study affirms that women are beneficiaries of microcredit; in this case through the instrumentality of the LSOs. Women exhibited a strong need for the organizational and financial support extended by the RSPs and the LSOs. Both represented avenues for economic, social, and cultural empowerment and for easing their cultural shackles.

While the focus of this book is on collective action, induced collective action also enables individual enterprise. Appendix 4.2 documents case studies where women said they had become economically and socially empowered via microcredit. While we are aware from other studies (Khan and Ansari 2018, Chapter 4) that men appropriate either the credit or the income accruing from it, we did not come across such admissions from the women in our study.

Women LSOs: Filling Vacated Spaces

This section demonstrates that women were more rooted in their local environment than men and, therefore, more receptive to RSP and LSO initiatives. The primary reason was that men, driven by economic necessity, out-migrated to supplement family income and women filled the spaces vacated by them. Where women were assigned such a central role, they rose to the challenge. We present survey evidence which shows them outperforming their male counterparts in the next section.

As indicated above, men's livelihood opportunities extended beyond the village, which may explain why their community organizations and village organizations tended to become dormant once the RSPs disengaged. In contrast, women's spaces continue to be centered on the household. They were more receptive to initiatives that allowed them to be home-based, such as skills-development, credit, education, health, water, and sanitation. They were also process- rather than outcome-oriented and hence adapted to changes in the external environment. Indeed, in some cases we noted that the withdrawal of funding had induced internal transformations, where the women's organizations had become self-sustaining entities—both credit and project-driven. Many of these organizations had internalized the participatory principles that the RSPs had instilled in them and had launched independent initiatives, mostly income-oriented but some focused on education. Women were also more responsive to training and income-generation opportunities offered by the LSOs.

LSOs were an important instrument for empowering women. Where women had successfully overcome male-defined cultural barriers, they were confident and protective about their hard-won spaces and rights, and set about asserting them quietly and effectively rather than in an overtly confrontational manner. Further, they represented a cohesive force, which transcended ethnic and religious differences.

However, the organizational complexion of the LSOs did not reflect their needs in as much as gender representation in the constituted bodies (executive body, general body) still had a distinctly male slant. We turn next to how female managerial performance showed up in the LSO rankings compared with that of males.

Comparative Performance

Of the 18 LSOs we reviewed, 3 (namely Sami, Pakistan Hoslamand Khwateen Network [PHKN] and Aurat Development Program [ADP]) were exclusively female-run LSOs (for details refer to Appendix 4.1). We ranked the 18 LSOs on various criteria (Chapter 3) to illustrate how effectively and efficiently the LSOs responded to the needs of their members. The women's LSOs ranked highly on most criteria.

LSO effectiveness was measured by several indicators including: gender equality; savings generation; credit disbursement; reduced dependence on RSPs; and ability to secure internal and external funding. Sami and PHKN ranked first and second, while ADP ranked thirteenth.

PHKN and Sami also ranked first and second respectively in terms of their success in raising endowment funds, hence ensuring their financial sustainability.

The women's LSOs also scored highly on project management. PHKN ranked second and Sami seventh on these criteria. One way of assessing the success of the exit strategy was to ask respondents about how dependent the LSO remained on the RSP. In the ranking of reduced dependence, Sami and PHKN ranked first and fourth. There is a very close correlation between reduced dependence and high scores on project management and overall LSO effectiveness.

Summary

Overall, we found that women fared well in LSO management and performance. Even though the representation in the governance bodies of LSOs/VOs was disproportionately male, attitudes for gender inclusion were surprisingly positive across the board (90% favorable). There was also a high degree of gender sensitivity in terms of the importance of separate discussion of women's issues, and women found the decision-making process to be open and consultative. Over four-fifths of the women responded that they had access to community organization savings and a similar number responded that their incomes had increased as a result of LSO activity. As has been found to be more broadly the case, this was viewed to have had a positive impact on the education, nutrition, and health of their children. Two-thirds felt their decision-making powers had improved and in this regard were more empowered.

The women organizations were more active and also more adaptable, and hence capable of doing without RSP support. While the men in general were more outward-looking as a livelihood strategy, women were willing and able to fill the spaces vacated. Perhaps this also explains why women LSOs took the top two spots in the ranking of LSO's effectiveness.

Appendix 4.1

Pakistan Hoslamand Khwateen Network (PHKN), Haripur

PHKN was the oldest LSO among the 18 surveyed. It was initially constituted as a network of local COs in 1998 and subsequently registered as a women's LSO. Among the LSOs we surveyed, the PHKN is the clearest illustration of process change leading to sustainable outcomes.

By process change here we mean women's empowerment. Our observations showed that women crossed cultural barriers by contributing actively to the household economy and by making a political impact. They had become confident, articulate, self-sufficient and protective about their hard-won spaces and rights that took many years of struggle to achieve. As a cohesive force, which transcended ethnic and religious barriers, they began to enjoy equal status with men, but in a mutually reinforcing rather than a confrontational relationship.

Process change also catalyzed sustainable outcomes. PHKN achieved a level of local outreach which could be the envy of any local government department/agency. Some of its achievements include social mobilization and training and enterprise development. They implemented projects in collaboration with the Rural Water Supply and Sanitation Programme [RWSSP] and the Barani Rural Development Programme [BARD].

They arranged for financial sustainability by developing an endowment fund (Rs.9.5 million) based on projects funded by the ILO, UNDP and, Inter-cooperation-Pakistan), enterprise earnings (AHAN), income generated from a guest house, profits from micro credit disbursements, consultancies and resource services and CO contributions.

During our survey, it was evident that by engaging in a division of responsibilities they were creating a second-tier leadership. Meanwhile, the leadership in place focused on social mobilization, linkages and resource generation, project implementation, district-level outreach, acting as resource persons for government and donor projects at the district level and providing services including a credit program with special provisions for the marginalized. As a result of their efforts and achievements, they acquired political clout in local elections.

Appendix 4.2: Successful Microcredit Case Studies

a. *Lehri Bai of Mithi, Tharparkar (LSO ADP)*

Lehri Bai made *khatiya paapar* (savory snack) in her house. She took a loan of Rs.10,000/- from LSO ADP to start this business. Previously she purchased her ingredients from Mithi, but as her sales increased, she decided to go to Hyderabad, which was cheaper and offered more variety. She started supplying *paapar* to Hyderabad and Mithi and made *paapar* *w*orth Rs. 500/- daily. She is a widow but with the income she earned she raised three children, got her daughters married, and gave them a reasonable trousseau including four *tolas* (47 grams) of gold. She proudly stated she was financially independent and her self-confidence was visible.

b. *Warya of Mithi, Tharparkar*

Warya is a resident of Mithi, Tharparkar. She has four daughters and one son. Her husband was holding down a low paying job. His meager income was insufficient to manage their household expenditure and educate their children. Warya was a house-bound woman, without qualifications and the confidence to go out and get a job. At the same time, she was desperate to augment the family income so that her family could enjoy a decent standard of living and she could provide her children with quality education.

She took a loan of Rs.10,000/- and started stitching clothes. Not only did she repay the loan but began to add to the family income. Encouraged, she took another loan and this time bought a sewing machine. Now she was generating an income of nearly Rs.300/- daily. As the income increased so did the family standard of living—including the health of the children and their education. Her elder daughters completed their matric, two younger ones were enrolled in school and the son was studying in the regional city, Hyderabad. The elder daughters joined Warya in her tailoring business. She took a third loan and added her own money to buy two more machines and added to the family income. Warya also conducted stitching lessons for young girls in the neighborhood.

Diligence, perseverance, and hard work enabled Warya to pay back all her loans and become the proud owner of sewing machines valued at a couple of hundred thousand rupees. She was able to save money by going to Karachi to purchase thread. With her savings she added another room to their house which was used exclusively as the sewing room where she worked and stored her threads and materials.

From a shy, lonely recluse, Warya became a confident woman with a high self-esteem. In appreciation and recognition of her hard work, the Pakistan Poverty Alleviation Fund (PPAF) gave Warya a cash award of Rs.70,000/-. It all began with Rs.10,000/- loan.

c. *Kasturi of Mithi, Tharparkar*

Winding through narrow lanes with open drains clogged with plastic bags, we arrived at Kasturi's house. Outside the door sat three plump black buffaloes, languidly swishing their tails to ward off the flies swarming all over them. On the *charpai* (bed) sat a cheerful woman clad in a colorful *ghagra* (skirt) wearing traditional *Thari* anklets, bangles, and jewelry.

Coming from a very poor family but blessed with drive and resilience Kasturi took a Rs.10,000/- loan. She purchased a buffalo, the LSO trained her, and she started selling milk. She paid off the loan within a year, took another loan, and bought a second buffalo. After that there was no looking back for this resourceful and dynamic woman. At the time of the survey, she owned 5 buffaloes, sold 60 kilos of milk at Rs.40 per kilo, and involved her entire family in the dairy business.

During the interview there was a commotion outside. A three-year-old calf was suffering severe convulsions; with its back arched and a heaving chest it fell to the ground. Then its limbs became rigid. Kasturi sprang up, took a syringe, snapped an ampule, filled it and deftly plunged it into the neck of the calf. She administered two doses while her husband held the calf down. It was a pleasure to witness her cool efficiency and the warm, friendly, and jovial relationship between the married couple.

d. *Momal Mallhi of Mithi, Tharparkar*

Momal Mallhi was a 45 woman at the time of the survey. She supported seven family members, including a 60-year old husband—formerly a taxi driver and then unemployed. Momal had *biri* (local cigarette) making skills but did not have money to purchase tobacco from the local market. She borrowed Rs.10,000/- from the LSO, purchased tobacco, and started making *biris* at home. Neighborhood women and children, who could not venture out to the market, were now able to purchase *biris* from her house (in which she had opened a small shop) for their menfolk.

She paid off her first loan and took a second one. Momal's business was growing and it changed her and her family's life. Once a shy woman, she developed enough confidence to travel from Mithi to the wholesale market in Hyderabad to purchase supplies. With the increased income, the family ate better, wore good clothes, and bore the children's education expenses. Momal became the family decision maker, her self-image and status in the neighborhood improved and she also became her LSO's chairperson.

Reference

Khan, S.R., and N. Ansari. 2018. *A Microcredit Alternative in South Asia: Akhuwat's Experiment*. London: Routledge.

5

Rural Water Supply Scheme Sustainability: A Comparative Institutional Analysis

Introduction

This chapter is based on a report that was a follow-up to an earlier study conducted for the Government of Punjab,[1] in which we investigated the sustainability of rural water supply schemes (RWSS) that had been managed by a government agency, Public Health Engineering Department (PHED), and returned to rural communities to manage.[2] Our investigation showed that the transfer process was hasty and not accompanied by adequate social capital construction and training. Nonetheless, several communities were successfully managing their RWSS and we investigated the factors responsible.

Need, due to the lack of viable alternatives, played an important role in galvanizing communities to engage in collective action for water supply. Water committees (WCOM), with representation duly given to each *biraderi* (clan), contributed significantly to scheme sustainability. In

This chapter has been drawn from Sustainable Development Policy Institute Monograph Series No. 3, 1998, Islamabad. The report was subsequently published as Khan (1999, Chapter 2).

S. R. Khan and S. R. Khan, *Social Capital and Collective Action in Pakistani Rural Development*, https://doi.org/10.1007/978-3-030-71450-5_5

fact, our main finding was that there was considerable raw potential for collective action that could be tapped into and formalized.

None of the fifty communities whose RWSS schemes were in our sample for that study had undergone any social capital construction or systematic training. We conjectured, but were not able to establish, that this may play an important role in scheme sustainability and highlighted this as an important area for further study. Fortunately, another World Bank research study was awarded to the Sustainable Development Policy Institute that enabled us to explore this issue.

Thus, this chapter explores how the construction of social capital impacted rural water supply scheme (RWSS) sustainability via induced collective action. This chapter is based on research that was part of a larger UNDP-World Bank Water and Sanitation multi-country study which included Bolivia, Honduras, Indonesia, Pakistan, Benin, and Uganda.[3] The focus of the multi-country study was on the impact of project institutional rules on rural water supply scheme sustainability.

A "project" represented a funding/implementing agency with a particular set of rules for funding community RWSS. The focus was on demand responsive rules that conform to mainstream economics demand theory with regard to allowing communities to choose a level of service and requiring communities to at least partially pay for the service. The logic is that demand responsive project rules would result in self-selection on the part of communities and those communities would opt for the service they could pay for and, given this, would own the scheme and participate in its maintenance. The public policy logic was that since not all communities could be served, there should be selection criteria for social investment. We view potable water as a basic human right and were mainly interested in researching the impact of social capital construction on collective action and scheme sustainability.

Those whose needs are not met may be fairly homogeneous economically.[4] They are generally poor and their capacity to pay may barely be enough to cover the operating cost.[5] In fact, in many cases, need would not get translated into demand because of the limited capacity to pay. Thus, we consider water supply to be in the domain of public sector provision as a subsidized or as a public good.

In each of the six countries, two projects were selected and data was collected for 15 schemes of each project (delivering agency). In Pakistan, given our interest in social capital construction, we argued for the inclusion of the National Rural Support Program (NRSP) in the study. NRSP is an autonomously run partly government funded organization that has adopted the social capital construction approach of RSPs as described in Chapter 3.

The second project in our sample was the IDA (International Development Association) funded Local Government and Rural Development Department (LGRDD) schemes. We also included five IDA funded Public Health Engineering Department (PHED) schemes in the sample. The government line departments were naturally of interest due to their much wider coverage for social sector delivery. The project selection enabled us to frame the study as a comparative institutional analysis.

In the rest of this chapter we first present the conceptual framework for the research. We follow by outlining the sampling procedure and study design and then a description of the three projects and project rules and implementation procedures. Findings are presented next based on an analysis of field reports. These reports were written by the field team after completing a two-day survey of each scheme. We add to these findings in the subsequent section by analyzing the data collected via structured questionnaires. We end with a summary of findings.

Conceptual Framework

This conceptual framework for this chapter is contextualized within the broader discussion of this issue on social capital and collective action in Chapter 2. "Participation" has been and still is a catchword in the development studies.[6] It is associated with concepts of decentralization and collective action. Briefly, the idea is if communities, on their own or via social capital construction and training (outside interventions), take full or partial responsibility for providing for their needs via collective action, the results will be sustainable. The reasoning is that such participation gives communities a sense of ownership and involvement and therefore the construction and O&M (operation and maintenance) of a scheme are sound. In terms of the broader conceptual framework introduced in Chapter 2, participation here represents the collective action based on autonomous or constructed social capital.

Collective action in the context of rural water supply schemes refers to the community selecting or electing a water committee (WCOM) and entrusting its O&M to the committee, participating in community meetings for collective decisions, collectively agreeing upon and paying the tariff in a timely manner. One key collective decision involves resolving uneven benefits resulting from the scheme design. For example, in gravity schemes profligate practices at higher elevations can lead to lower water pressure and delivery at lower elevations and such problems need to be collectively resolved by mandating and enforcing responsible usage.

A collective sense of ownership would result in using peer group pressure when others default on fees, reporting leaks, and mal-practices—such as deliberate breakage (for cattle ponds), illegal connections and the use of suction pumps on the mainline—to the WCOM. Thus, collective action is the broader framework that includes individual responsibility and effort harnessed for the provision of an individual and collective need.

Several possible motivations for collective action could be identified in the context of a rural water supply scheme. There could be a social motivation that includes altruism and a sense of well-being that comes from the social affirmation of performing a community role. This would be the case, for example, if an individual activist makes a social contribution to a scheme that exceeds the individual benefit from such an effort. There could be an individual motivation, to be part of a collective effort, driven by personal and household needs.

In the case of rural water supply, spontaneous collective action may or may not occur in response to community need and constructed social capital could act as a catalyst in engendering it. In addition, even if communities are adequately motivated for collective action, they may lack the necessary skills and this could be an additional intervention by development NGOs. One could conceive of social capital construction and skills training as reducing the transaction costs of collection action.

The social capital construction needs to be viewed in a dynamic perspective. There may be community resistance to social capital construction based on an innate suspicion of outsiders and because of scams that rural communities may have been subjected to in the past, like a cooperative banking scandal in rural Pakistan. However, once an organization is formed and the benefits of collective action demonstrated, the skeptical may join in as was the case with COs/VOs and LSOs discussed in Chapters 3 and 4.

Sustainability is inferred to exist by the physical condition of the scheme, the quality of service provided and the consumer satisfaction with it, the willingness and ability to operate and maintain the scheme and the organizational (which includes enforcement mechanisms) and financial skills of the WCOM. If observations based on the above indicators suggest that there is a high probability of the maintenance of an acceptable level of water supply service throughout the design life of the scheme, it is viewed as being sustainable.[7]

Sampling and Study Design

Given the nature of the investigation, we viewed two-stage PPS (probability proportionate to size) sampling as appropriate (Appendix 5.1). In the first stage, the village/scheme was selected based on population size and in the next stage 15 households were randomly selected.[8] This procedure enabled us to maintain an equal probability of selection of each household (EPSEM) in the targeted populations. While EPSEM was maintained at the second stage, in almost all cases, we had to deviate from PPS at the first stage such that some schemes were included with a probability of one. This was because age of the scheme, as one of the specified inclusion parameters that we needed to conform to (Appendix 5.1), impinged on the original design.

In order to investigate sustainability, it was preferable to include older schemes in the sample. In AJK, the phase I LGRDD schemes were completed in 1994 or 1995. Out of the 30 relevant schemes, we included all twelve of the relevant 1994 schemes with a probability of one. Three 1995 schemes were then selected based on the PPS criteria out of the 18 relevant 1995 schemes. Out of the 32 NRSP/AJK schemes in the population, we did not consider the 14 1996 schemes. Of the remaining 18, we selected four of the five 1994 schemes with a probability of one and excluded one because of the small size of the community. One, out of the ten relevant 1995 schemes, was selected on a PPS basis. We selected all four of the 1995 schemes out of the 15 relevant NRSP schemes in Rawalpindi and the oldest 1996 scheme. In Sindh, we selected all four of the 1995 NRSP schemes and the oldest of the three relevant 1996 schemes. Similarly, we selected all four of the 1995 schemes and the oldest of the 6 relevant 1996 schemes.

Appendix Table 5.6 shows that there was no significant systematic difference between the selected and remaining schemes. It turned out that the average number of beneficiaries in sample schemes was lower and that the cost per beneficiary therefore higher. If anything, this should make collective action more difficult. The analysis was structured to enable a multi-layered comparative institutional comparison as indicated by the schema below.

LGRDD

} AJK

NRSP

NRSP Punjab

NRSP

} Sindh

PHED

The study design enabled us to compare NRSP's performance with the two government projects, its performance across the three provinces and the two government projects with each other.

Information was drawn from several sources. The main source of information was field reports of two three member trained field teams including an engineer, and a male and female social scientist.[9] The fieldwork included observations, a Focus Group Discussion (FGD) with the community, 15 household surveys per village, one technical survey, a one page survey to review the scheme implementation process and a one page survey to solicit information from the field workers.

Apart from observations of the field team, we had three data sets generated from structured community, household and technical questionnaires. Multiple sources of information are welcome when the information is all consistent but contradictory information can also result from multiple sources. In making a final assessment, we gave the most weight to the field reports and technical evaluations. Also, we viewed data generated from one-on-one household interviews to be more reliable than those based on the FGD.

While FGDs can bring hidden information to light and contradictions in the group can bring the researcher closer to social reality, we felt that responses designed to please project personnel or those following the views of the local notables were equally likely. At the end of the data analysis section, we conducted a robustness test to indicate how consistent field reports were with the technical evaluations and household and community responses.

Project Descriptions, Rules, and Implementation Procedures

NRSP drew its inspiration from the Agha Khan Rural Support Programme (AKRSP) which is an internationally and nationally renowned development NGO in Northern Pakistan. NRSP was formed to replicate the AKRSP development approach across the country. The first NRSP management team realized that rapid expansion would dissipate quality. Also, they realized that anticipated targets were, in any case, literally not achievable in the time envisaged. They therefore converted the first government grant for operations into an endowment that subsequently partially financed its operations.[10]

The AKRSP approach relies on social capital construction by a trained professional social mobilizer.[11] The goal is to form a community organization (CO) which can then serve as a platform for multi-sectoral initiatives. The first initiative is referred to as a PPI (productive physical infrastructure), which is partially funded by the project, and this also serves as an incentive for communities to organize. The PPI is expected to be identified and implemented via a series of interactive dialogues between the communities and the project management groups. If a RWSS emerges from this process as a high priority of the community, one can infer community demand for it exists, since the community has to make a substantial contribution.[12] A mechanism for holding the CO together, after the completion of the PPI, is regular meetings at which mandatory savings are deposited. Community savings can then be used as collateral for loans mediated by the project for other community initiatives. In addition, the project provides training for various income generating and income defending activities. NRSP quite successfully adapted and adopted this approach.

NRSPs interactive engagement of communities was referred to as a diagnostic survey which comprised three dialogues. In the first dialogue, the NRSP introduced itself, explained its participatory approach and interactively developed a detailed village profile based on a "needs analysis." The result of the first dialogue was the identification of a small productive scheme required by the community. The second series of dialogues with the community, in which the project senior engineer and the social organization unit were involved, resulted in blueprints and cost estimates prepared by the field unit which were sent to the management group for approval. In the third series of dialogues between the community and the management group the terms of partnership between the two parties were explored and the CO, consisting of all scheme beneficiaries, was formed.

The execution, maintenance, and monitoring of the scheme was entirely the responsibility of the CO. During scheme construction, the general body of the CO met weekly to manage all aspects of the scheme and collectively assign responsibilities. The project social organization unit provided technical and financial assistance, supervised progress of scheme construction and CO functioning and made recommendations about payments of project installments and provision of support services. Management responsibility became vested in the CO after the scheme was completed.

In the LGRDD schemes, the needs were again identified by the villagers who lobbied their elected representatives. While in practice, political considerations were paramount, in theory prioritization was also based on need as defined by the distance and quality of the present water source, the field assessment of the per beneficiary cost, the technical feasibility of the scheme and evidence of previous community work. Once the scheme was approved, the District Office of the LGRDD conducted a feasibility study. The District Council (DC) or Union Council (UC), which are the tiers of local government, then decided if funding was available. In this case, the funding was made available by the IDA.

For implementation, a scheme committee was set up consisting of three to five members. Usually a UC member or supporter invariably became the scheme leader and the others played supportive roles such as keeping accounts and supervising purchases. Unlike the NRSP, where the terms of partnership were between the community and the project, the contract was between the scheme leader and the LGRDD. The scheme leader was responsible for the utilization of the funds and materials provided by the project.

The LGRDD's responsibilities included the scheme survey and design in consultation with the community, planning and arranging the work, arranging the government contribution, paying for the materials including pipes, fittings, and other stand post materials to be transported to the nearest metaled road from the village, assisting the community in procurements including design specifications, quality control, and bill and contract preparation, imparting training to plumbers and technicians chosen by the community and overseeing the implementation of the civil work construction.

The responsibilities of the community included the following: forming a committee; co-operating with LGRDD for surveying; planning and designing the scheme; providing the local materials like sand, stone, clay, and gravel; opening a bank account and depositing the government contribution; collecting local donations and the water rate fee; acquiring the land and water rights; placing the order for the GI (galvanized iron) pipes and certifying the quality and quantity; arranging transportation of the project supplied material from the nearest metaled road to the site; installing the pipes according to the design; arranging the funding and construction of community civil works such as spring intakes; constructing spring protection works, pump houses, reservoirs of less than 5,000 gallons (approved reservoirs of greater than 5,000 gallons are paid for by the project); returning unused material to the project and providing skilled and unskilled labor free as required.

Once the scheme was complete, the scheme committee was expected to be dissolved and a WCOM established which was entirely responsible for operating and maintaining the scheme. The WCOM was required to collect the water tariff established by the community and emergency dues when needed, facilitate the training of suitable persons from the community for scheme O&M, settle local disputes by reconciliation, prevent or disconnect unauthorized (not authorized by the project) connections, maintain accounts as advised by the project and educate water users in hygiene and sanitation. The project was expected to continue to monitor and supervise the scheme after its completion and provide assistance (up to 25% of rehabilitation cost) to the WCOM to rehabilitate the scheme if damaged by natural calamities.

The PHED project also responded to community requests for schemes. The request was forwarded to the project implementation team (PIT) which conducted a needs assessment based on the cohesiveness and willingness of the community to make land available for the scheme and assume O&M responsibilities. PIT and PHED community mobilizers visited selected villages for social and technical feasibility and to discuss and decide upon affordable technology and form a CO (with a PHED sub-engineer as a technical member). The technical design was prepared jointly by PIT, PHED, and the CO and submitted for approval.

A CO bank account was opened and CO members trained for O&M and other sustainability issues. The next stage was the formal signing of a Memorandum of Understanding (MOU) between the CO and a high ranking official of the PHED (the executive engineer). The PIT signed as a witness and a senior district administrative official (the deputy commissioner) verified the MOU.

After the signing of the MOU, PHED called for bids, selected the contractor, and awarded the bid. The CO signed as a witness and identified community members for training in O&M and account keeping. PHED supervised the construction while the CO provided labor for assisting in the laying of distribution pipes and collected the water tariff for the first month. The contractor test ran the scheme for two weeks prior to handing it over to the community. This handing over process was formally documented.[13]

The PHED committed to paying energy charges (for four hours of daily operation) for four years, to clearing the schemes financial liabilities and to operating the scheme for the first three months. It also undertook to provide community assistance for major repairs and rehabilitation, including extension, at no financial cost to the community. The community undertook to pay for the trained operator and the power connection fee.

On paper, the project rules and procedures (Appendix Tables 5.7 and 5.8) were very similar so the real issue was implementation. The "ideal" implementation procedures for the two government projects, as outlined above, deviated considerably from practice for the two government projects as described in the next section.

Findings

Field Report Analysis

Some of the main village characteristics drawn from the technical data set are reported in the summary Table 5.1. These provide a context for

Table 5.1 Comparative village background characteristics (percentages)

	LGRDD	NRSP	PHED
At or below poverty line	40	60	60
Village electrified	93	80	100
Mean travel time from the nearest city (mins.)	154 (95)	100 (45)	10 (22)

Note Parentheses contain standard deviations
Source Technical evaluation data set

the field report evaluation that follows. In these and subsequent comparisons, the reader needs to keep in mind that there were only 5 PHED schemes but 15 LGRDD and NRSP schemes in the sample.

LGRDD villages were in general more remote and also more of them gave the impression of being at or below the poverty line. The extent of village electrification, as a proxy for village infrastructure, was quite high across the board.

LGRDD/AJK

The AJK terrain in which the RWSSs were constructed is very hilly with a scattered population in clusters of households.[14] While spring water is available, this is often seasonal and a good distance away over hilly terrain. The average total cost of the LGRDD gravity schemes was Rs.463,000.[15] The total cost of the schemes was high because IDA requires schemes to cover the whole population of the village. The use of GI pipes was another cause of the high cost. Water was generally collected in a big storage tank with a storage capacity ranging from 2,000 to 5,000 gallons. Small storage tanks connected with the distribution network were provided for the scattered population clusters. The level of service in all the LGRDD schemes was public stand posts, although local notables managed illegal house connections.

Given the seasonal nature of spring water availability, the gravity schemes generally resulted from an expressed need. In most cases, a local notable managed to deliver the scheme to the village and such local notables were also the entry point of the project into the community. The decision-making was therefore usually confined to the local notables who had the major say in critical decisions such as the location of the stand posts.[16]

All but two of the 15 LGRDD schemes we investigated were completed either in March or April 1994. The remaining two were completed in August and October 1995. Two-thirds of these 15 schemes were judged to be non-sustainable by the field team according to the criteria defined above. Many of them were in poor physical condition despite the recent completion dates. Of the remaining five, one was a borderline case and four were judged to be clearly sustainable. In three of these four schemes, success was attributed to an important individual contribution. In one case, a plumber, as a permanent employee of the scheme (which was exceptional) and, in the other two cases, an interested activist and a selfless activist made the difference. The activist was described as selfless since he derived no personal benefit from the scheme. He managed to galvanize the community which met to deal collectively with crisis situations. The community also paid a regular monthly tariff of Rs.10 and later agreed to raise this to Rs.50.

In all cases, the males of the community generally participated quite wholeheartedly in the scheme construction which included transporting the project pipes over long distances, laying them underground in difficult terrain, and constructing the tanks.[17] However, in most cases, this was the extent of the participation. This was as could be expected, since there was no sustained social mobilization. In most cases, the community felt little sense of ownership and the scheme was perceived as belonging to the project, the World Bank or the chairman of the WCOM and there was little collective action, beyond the initial effort, to maintain the scheme. Local notables personally benefitted the most from the schemes mediated through them.

NRSP/AJK

The gravity-based NRSP schemes operated essentially on the same principle as the LGRDD schemes. The average per beneficiary cost of NRSP schemes in AJK was about 60% of the comparable LGRDD cost.[18] In fact, the scheme was delivered by the project for even a lesser amount, since about a third of total cost was contributed by the community. The use of HDP (high-density polyethylene) pipes by NRSP, which were very cheap in comparison with GI pipes,[19] was an important factor in reducing per beneficiary cost. The level of service depended on demand and took the form of either public stand posts or house connections.

While the LGRDD and NRSP schemes were physically comparable, there was a qualitative difference between the community management of the schemes. The NRSP communities in general were well mobilized, chose their level of service, were familiar with project rules and had a sense of ownership. One problem was that NRSP focused on the interests of the community organization whose members, rather than the community at large, represented the project beneficiaries. Since the NRSP mandate is to focus on the "poorest of the poor," this is not necessarily a problem if they realize their objective.

Four of the five schemes were judged to be sustainable by the field team. In the sustainable schemes, the communities worked well together. The physical condition of the schemes was good, the pipes were laid underground as required and leaks were not evident, the community was willing to repair the scheme in case of damage via collections and had regular meetings and a saving scheme. In all cases, consumer satisfaction was high and the community demonstrated a sense of ownership of the schemes.

The project mobilized the communities effectively, relied on them to identify their own needs, involved them in all phases of the project and imparted training to a plumber. Given this standard format, it was instructive to find out what went wrong in the one NRSP scheme not found to be sustainable. Interestingly, participation appears to have been impeded by the project's reliance on a local notable. This local notable/activist was the sole decision maker and it seemed that consequently there were no regular meetings, tariff collections, or a sense of ownership of the scheme by the community. The local notable was also the only person with a direct connection to the mainline.

NRSP/Punjab

The analysis of the five NRSP schemes in the Punjab reinforces the main conclusion drawn from the AJK schemes. The mean cost of the scheme was Rs.125,000 and on average just over two-fifths of the total cost was contributed by the community. The average beneficiary cost was somewhat higher than the cost of the AJK/NRSP schemes because of the pumping and the more elaborate distribution network. Four of the five schemes were completed in 1995 and one was completed in 1996.

The source of almost all the Punjab NRSP schemes was ground water pumped with the help of an electric motor and stored in an elevated tank. A distribution network then delivered the water stored in the tank to the community.[20] The level of service was public stand posts shared, in principle, by not more than seven families, although, in practice, more than seven families sometimes utilized a public stand post.

Two of the five schemes were found to be clearly non-sustainable, two clearly sustainable, and one fits into the "may be" category. The two non-sustainable schemes and the one with a non-determined status all had the problem of the scheme being captured by a local notable and consequently of a non-participating community. In one case, the secretary was entirely influential in decision-making and he and his family were the sole beneficiaries. Even the president of the CO was excluded from the scheme benefits. In the second non-sustainable case, the community relied entirely on the activist who enjoyed the bulk of the benefits from the scheme. In the third scheme, with the undetermined status, the president and CO manager were once again the most influential in decision-making and the remaining community members showed little awareness of the project rules.

The unsustainable schemes were in poor physical condition and provided limited service. The communities were not satisfied with the service, did not own the schemes, did not pay a tariff and had little awareness of O&M responsibilities. The project failed by working via local notables, the absence of community mobilization and the lack of maintenance or hygiene training.

NRSP clearly demonstrated the capacity to do much better judging by the performance of the well-functioning schemes in AJK, from the performance of the two Punjab schemes that were found to be sustainable and the four sustainable schemes in Sindh (described in the next sub-section). In the case of the sustainable Punjab schemes, the NRSP field officers performed well in implementing the project software and hardware.[21] They provided all the necessary information and training and ensured broad-based participation of the community in all phases of the project. As a result, the schemes were in good physical condition, the record keeping was good, tariffs were paid regularly and the community was willing and able to maintain the scheme. For non-routine maintenance, there were emergency meetings for collective decision-making and implementation. There were no mal-practices and the community revealed a sense of ownership of the schemes.

NRSP/Sindh

Four of the five surface water NRSP schemes, built in the Sindh plains, were completed in 1995 and the fifth in 1996. The average beneficiary cost was 15 times less than that of the more elaborate PHED schemes in Sindh discussed in the next sub-section. On average, 37% of the total cost of the scheme was contributed by the community. The NRSP schemes were very basic and used canal water as a source since ground water was very saline and generally not potable. This water was stored in well built but open storage reservoirs. These were low-cost schemes with no full-time employees required. The level of service was a shared delivery chamber or house connections.

Four of the five schemes were found to be sustainable. The one problematic scheme in Sindh had similar problems of an exclusive reliance by the community on the activist and hence a lack of broad-based participation. Moreover, the poor and the minorities (Hindu and Qadiani) were excluded. The project social activist was clearly not up to the task, since he himself was unaware of the project rules.[22] By helping cement the floor of a community-built reservoir, contaminated by the upward push of saline water, the scheme had improved the quality of water and hence created a sense of satisfaction among community members, particularly women. However, the water quality continued to be poor and the lack of community mobilization or collective action was evident from individual households engaging in their own water purification by crude techniques.

The other four schemes were found by the field team to be sustainable. The project was very successful in delivering on its part of the contract. The community was involved in all stages of the project and all the relevant information was provided. Training was provided in leadership and management skills, water purification, hygiene, and scheme maintenance. As a result, in general, the physical condition of the tank was good and the sense of ownership, willingness to maintain the scheme, and consumer satisfaction were high.

Thus, across the three regions, 10 of the fifteen NRSP schemes were found to be sustainable. In the three non-sustainable schemes and the two not completely satisfactory schemes, the big failing was the project reliance on a local notable and hence the lack of broad-based community participation and ownership of the scheme. In this regard, the non-satisfactory NRSP schemes resembled the bulk of the LGRDD schemes which were non-sustainable and, interestingly, the few successful LGRDD schemes managed to replicate the broad-based participation of the NRSP schemes. This same lesson once again comes through from the review of the PHED schemes.[23]

PHED/Sindh

The dates of completion of the five PHED schemes varied from August 1995 to January 1996. The average cost of the PHED schemes was Rs.5.9 million but they were more elaborate than the NRSP schemes. As indicated earlier, the average beneficiary cost was 15 times more than the average for NRSP Sindh schemes.

Once again, canal water was generally the source.[24] The scheme design included two reservoirs surrounded by a boundary wall. Water was required to be stored in these reservoirs and sufficient time was provided for sedimentation. After this, it was to be filtered through a chlorine tank and pumped directly into the distribution network. Since electricity load shedding was a serious problem in rural Pakistan, a diesel engine was to be provided. An operator-cum-plumber was to be provided to look after the scheme, although the salary of the employee was expected to be paid by the community. The level of service was house connections.

Of the five schemes, two were found to be unsustainable, one sustainable, and two were of indeterminate status. In all cases, the community expressed a strong need for the schemes. In most cases, even when the scheme was sustainable, the project software and hardware was not well executed. There were technical errors in the design or construction, not enough information or training was provided for O&M, community members were not clear on the project rules and hygiene education was either not provided or only informally provided.

The physical condition of the two unsustainable schemes was poor. Equipment such as the chlorinator and sluice gate valves were not in working order, spider webs were found in the manhole, direct pumping endangered pipes due to high static pressure and resulted in leaky pipes, valves, electric pumps, and chlorinator. Further, the sedimentation tanks were dirty and not being utilized and there were acute drainage problems. However, the communities chose the level of service and in one case made a cash contribution and, in another case contributed the land. Even so, in the former case, they refused to contribute for an overhead tank to avoid direct pumping from a slow sand filter.

Social capital construction was weak as evident from the lack of implementation of a tariff regime, no formal training, and there was a lack of community ownership or community awareness of its responsibility. There was little community participation in decision-making and the CO and project officials or local notables were viewed as responsible for the scheme. Not surprisingly, there was inequality in the distribution of benefits. In some cases, households had more than one connection and in other cases they had none. There was little likelihood that the communities would be able to pay the electric bill once the PHED subsidy phased out.

The two schemes of indeterminate status had a more mixed record. Drainage and static pressure due to direct pumping was still a problem. However, the physical structure was good in both cases and consumer satisfaction was high. The scheme was perceived to be a World Bank scheme in one case and so there was no sense of community ownership.

In both cases, there was no formal training, and, in one case, no record of tariff collection. In the other case, the tariff collection was regular and, since the names of defaulters were announced in the Friday sermon, collection was not a problem. However, the tariff rate was too low to pay the electricity bill once the PHED subsidy phased out.

The communities chose the level of service but were not involved in planning or decision-making. Once again, this was viewed to be the prerogative of the local notables represented in the CO. There were no regular CO meetings. In one case, the poor were excluded entirely from the scheme because they could not afford the pipes for the house connections. While default was low in one case, even in that community, people did not bother to report leaks and were not aware of the project rules.

Once again, the one sustainable scheme had much to do with the community being mobilized prior to contact with PHED. A CBO (community-based organization) was present in the village since 1971. They established links with some of the most prominent national capacity-building organizations such as the Trust for Voluntary Organizations and Strengthening Participatory Organizations. Thus, they had a long-established history of collective action on a self-help basis which included building school rooms for the high school and community drains. They solicited the PHED project to upgrade from stand posts to yard connections.

The scheme worked like a blue print of successful community action. The physical condition of the project was excellent, it was well maintained, no leaks were evident, a proper tariff structure was in place, payments were prompt and there was virtually no default. The level of community satisfaction with the scheme and ownership of it was high. The community indicated a capability and willingness to operate and maintain the scheme in every way.

Appendix 5.2 presents two case studies that highlight two of our main points from this section. Case study 5.2.1 is probably the worst LGRDD scheme with regard to the rudimentary implementation of project rules and the lack of social mobilization. We chose it to highlight the danger of using local notables as an entry into village communities. The likely consequence is a capture of scheme benefits by local notables and the alienation of the rest of the village community. Such an approach is unlikely to lead to successful social sector service delivery, even if the community has the capacity to pay for the service.

Case study 5.2.2 does not represent the best example of NRSP's social capital construction, which can produce sustainable social sector service delivery. However, we selected it because it is geographically a very similar community to Patthi (Appendix 5.2.1) and also subject to the same kinds of social tensions. As the case study will indicate, the social capital construction and community organization provided enough of a glue to enable the villagers to collectively address problems pertaining to RWS.

Data Analysis

Technical Evaluation Data Set

The results in the last section are more optimistic than those evident from the technical evaluation. The most striking finding resulting from the technical evaluation was that, in a fundamental sense, only one and perhaps none of the 35 schemes in the sample were financially sustainable. Only 2 LGRDD schemes and 3 NRSP schemes had instituted regular tariff collection. While tariff collection was in place in all PHED schemes, in only one case was it high enough to cover O&M, repair, and expansion. Four schemes (three PHED and one NRSP scheme) had adequate reserves available at the time of the survey for O&M. These results need to be qualified for NRSP since the COs had a regular saving scheme which could be drawn on by the community by consensus for any one of their schemes across different sectors. Also, the NRSP schemes in Sindh had no recurring costs and hence no need of a tariff. Twenty of the remaining schemes were gravity based and as such were low and irregular maintenance schemes.

Table 5.2 provides a technical overview of how well the schemes were performing in a comparative context.

Table 5.2 did not show NRSP to be as overwhelmingly superior in all respects as one might have expected given the field report analysis above. However, in critical categories such as the quality of construction, lack of defects in masonry work, lack of defects in water catchments,

Table 5.2 Comparative technical evaluation of WSS (percentages)

	LGRDD	NRSP	PHED
Possibility of source contamination	47	67	60
Efforts taken for protecting source	57	27	20
Good quality construction	27	67	60
Defects in water catchments	27	7	0
Defects in masonry	20	0	0
Pipes exposed and leaking	60	6	60
Many stand posts leaking	27	0	na
Highly capable operators	27	13	20
Most of the scheme working	73	73	20

Note na = not available
Source Technical evaluation data

and exposed and leaking pipes they clearly dominated. The category that NRSP did poorly in is the possibility of source contamination. This resulted mainly from low cost exposed open tanks of the five NRSP schemes in Sindh. PHED also rated well in construction but rated poorly in terms of leaking pipes and the fact that only one of the five schemes rated as mostly functional.

Just as we were able to explore physical sustainability conclusions arrived at in the field report analysis in greater depth using the technical evaluation data set, we were able to explore other issues such as need and demand assessment, social capital construction, participation and community satisfaction in greater depth using the household and community data sets.

Community and Household Data Sets

Since many of the same questions were asked of communities and households, it was possible to juxtapose the responses to indicate the consistency in the responses from the two different sources. As earlier mentioned, we attached more weight to household responses than community responses because there was a possibility of project coached responses or local notables influencing opinion even when FGDs were skillfully conducted.

In Table 5.3, we focused on the key variables and sorted them into the following three categories: social mobilization; need/demand, perceptions of performance, and sustainability. Since we attached the most weight to field reports followed by technical evaluation, our main interest in drawing on the community and household data sets was to investigate the additional insights that may be forthcoming to explain the relative institutional strength of NRSP. We indicated when there was a lack of concordance between the findings of the field report on the one hand and the community and household responses on the other hand.

Need could play an important role in galvanizing communities to work together. This can be identified both by subjective responses and by ascertaining the time the community spent in procuring water prior to the scheme. As expected, Table 5.3 shows need, as proxied by time spent to collect water prior to the scheme, was the highest in the AJK hilly terrain communities which had LGRDD schemes. However, expressed need was equally high in the LGRDD and PHED communities and

Table 5.3 Comparative community need and demand for WSS (percentage)

Project	LGRDD		NRSP		PHED	
Data set	COMM	HH	COMM	HH	COMM	HH
HHs spending more than 15 mins. to collect water before WSS	na	88	na	62	na	70
Water identified as main need	67	96	53	82	80	95
Project provided information on cost of alternative options	0	9	40	50	20	27
Aware of scheme cost	20	02	80	41	100	32
Community made the final decision about type of RWSS	7	31	93	63	100	64
Mean cash contribution	1,225 (14)	1,341 (150)	1,269 (14)	1,643 (116)	700 (1)	683 (9)
Paying tariff	27	19	27	20	100	89
Willing to pay for improvements	na	36	na	46	na	23

Note Parentheses contain the number of communities and households respectively who reported a cash contribution
Source Community and household data sets

higher than the NRSP communities visited. This is likely since NRSP has multi-sectoral interventions and alternative needs can be expressed. In any case, since the expressed need for rural drinking water supply was higher in the two government schemes, communities could in principle have been more easily galvanized for collective action holding other things constant.

Table 5.4 presents responses that were indicative of project efforts and success in social capital construction and training.

Awareness of project rules at the household level was much higher for NRSP than the other projects, although at 39% this awareness was low in absolute terms. At the community level, the awareness was matched by PHED. Participation was also greatest in NRSP schemes. Awareness of O&M responsibilities was recorded as greatest for PHED at the household level (88%) and greatest for NRSP schemes (87%) at the community level.

NRSP schemes were more participatory in that all of them were built by the communities. This was also true for most of the LGRDD schemes but for none of the PHED schemes. However, at the individual

Table 5.4 Comparative social capital construction: awareness, decision making and training (percentage)

Project	LGRDD		NRSP		PHED	
Data set	COMM	HH	COMM	HH	COMM	HH
Awareness of project rules	7	17	40	39	40	16
Aware of O&M responsibilities	53	67	87	84	80	88
Built WSS/Felt participation in WSS adequate	87	74	100	83	0	78
Felt community owned scheme	67	30	80	71	100	77
Trained (nos.)	6	13	10	22	25	18
Considered training sufficient/Considered training useful	13	69	53	59	20	61

Note Front slashes separate questions asked of communities and household when there was a difference in questions asked
Source Community and household data sets

level, 74% and 78% respectively of the LGRDD and PHED household respondents felt their participation in the RWSS was adequate. This perception of participation was again higher at 83% for NRSP schemes.

One way to infer if meaningful participation and collective action was actually underway is to gauge the sense of ownership of the scheme present at the community and household level. At both the household and community level, this was highest for PHED (77 and 100% respectively) followed by NRSP (71% and 80% respectively) with LGRDD a distant third at the household level (30%) and a closer third (67%) at the community level.

The investment in training was greatest by PHED since, in relative terms, they had the largest numbers of individuals trained on various aspects pertaining to water supply and sanitation.[25] However, the training delivered by LGRDD was considered useful by a larger percentage of households (69%) than was the case for PHED (61%) and NRSP (59%). At the community level a much higher proportion of schemes considered the training provided by NRSP as sufficient.

While the field report and technical evaluation sub-sections address issues of sustainability in an "objective" sense, it is nonetheless interesting to address this issue from the perspective of household and community responses as summarized in Table 5.5.

A great deal of confidence was placed in the schemes by communities and households. Thus, 97 and 95% of households for PHED and NRSP schemes respectively were satisfied with the scheme management (69% for LGRDD). Over four-fifths of all households and communities across the board rated the performance of the scheme as good. We were able to cross check this since information had also been solicited about the unreliability of the system. Only 1% of the households viewed the PHED schemes as unreliable and 9 and 11% respectively viewed the LGRDD and NRSP schemes as unreliable. A very similar response was also evident on the existence of mal-practices in the community.

Overall, the spirit of self-reliance evident from community and household responses was once again the highest for NRSP. Eighty-four percent of the NRSP households, 76% of the LGRDD households, and 61% of the PHED households viewed the community as a source of funds for major repair. The corresponding community data set percentages were

Table 5.5 Comparative perceptions of performance and sustainability (percentages)

Project	LGRDD		NRSP		PHED	
Data set	COMM	HH	COMM	HH	COMM	HH
Satisfied with WSS management	na	69	na	95	na	97
Rating the RWSS as good	80	84	80	83	80	88
Viewing the RWSS as unreliable	na	9	na	11	na	1
Cited existence of mal-practices	7	16	13	9	0	0
Viewing community as a source of funds for major repair	40	76	67	84	60	61
Felt community had financial capacity to keep scheme operational for 10 years	100	86	100	93	100	96
Felt community would have the funds to replace scheme when necessary	7	10	27	28	0	20

Source Community and household data sets

67, 40, and 60% respectively. All the communities across the board felt that the community had the financial capacity to keep schemes operational for 10 years although at the household level the expressed level of confidence was lower at 86, 93, and 96% for LGRDD, NRSP, and PHED respectively. However, only 7, 27, and 0% responses at the community level and 10, 28, and 20% responses at the household level for LGRDD, NRSP and PHED respectively suggested confidence in being able to replace the schemes when the current one became obsolete.

Overall, the household and community responses are broadly consistent. Also, the household and community data re-enforce the findings of the field reports and technical evaluations that NRSP was in general performing best in terms of social capital construction. This result is broadly consistent with the assessment of the field reports. However, PHED's performance evident from the community and household responses was much better than evident from the field reports or technical evaluation.

The field team also interviewed the field staff. On average the eight NRSP field staff interviewed (staff often were responsible for more than one project) were able to recall over 90% of the documented project rules (if we exclude one social organizer who virtually knew none or refused to cooperate) while the nine LGRDD staff and the two PHED field staff recalled 52 and 35% respectively. Better trained field staff was another reason for better performance of the NRSP schemes.

Exploring Data Robustness and Hypotheses Testing

To test the robustness of the findings from the different sources, we created a sustainability variable based on the findings of the field report. Schemes were classified as either non-sustainable or as sustainable based on the assessment of the field reports.[26] Using the non-sustainability variable, we re-computed Tables 5.2, 5.3, 5.4, and 5.5 The hypothesis is that non-sustainable schemes would consistently do worse than the other schemes on all criteria.[27] Response in the affirmative would mean consistency between field reports and the data sets based on the structured questionnaires. Such consistency was quite clearly evident in the technical, community, and household responses for NRSP and PHED. However, the results were mixed for LGRDD.

Notwithstanding this discrepancy, we went ahead and attempted to more rigorously identify the relative importance of social capital construction as a determinant of sustainability. For this purpose, we computed indices of sustainability and social capital construction and other variables based on the methodology for this developed for the multi-country study (reported as Appendix 5.3). Appendix Table 5.9 presents the results of the estimation.

Social capital construction and need are the only two variables that are significant and they are consistently so under alternative specifications. Overall, the results reported in Appendix Table 5.9 are consistent with the findings on scheme sustainability based on cross-tabulations. However, we view these findings as only suggestive for several reasons. First, we did not have enough observations to estimate separate estimation by project. Separate estimation would be useful in and of themselves but also represent a robustness test of the statistical model.

Summary

The performance of two Pakistani line agencies in delivering 15 and 5 rural water supply schemes (RWSS) respectively and one development NGO which delivered 15 such schemes are reviewed in this chapter. The delivering agencies are referred to as projects and the two government projects are the Public Health Engineering Department (PHED) and the Local Government and Rural Development Department (LGRDD). The development NGO is the National Rural Support Program (NRSP) which followed a tried and tested approach to rural social sector delivery in Pakistan (Chapter 3). The results reported are based on field reports written by trained field teams and on analyses of data generated from focus group meetings, household interviews, interviews with the project field staff, and technical evaluations.

The focus of the research was on how central social capital construction was to the success and sustainability of RWSS in particular and social sector delivery in general. It was important to include government projects in the study because of their scale of operations and the NGO project was included on our insistence into a multi-country study because of its focus on social capital construction.

Our findings based on the field reports showed that the NRSP schemes had a much higher success rate in sustainable delivery and that their schemes were also more cost-effective. NRSP staff managed to mobilize communities to construct social capital in three different provinces under very different social, economic, and technological conditions. The accomplishment was particularly noteworthy in Sindh where the communities were highly differentiated by ethnicity and income.

NRSP social mobilizers were much less inclined to use village local notables as their entry point into the village and as the individuals through whom subsequent scheme related work was mediated. In fact, the NRSP schemes where this did happen were judged to be among those performing poorly on the specified criteria for sustainability. The reason for this failure was the lack of broad participation in decision-making and hence the lack of ownership of the scheme by the community or any collective action to make the scheme a success. Typically, in such schemes, the local notables who made the key decisions also disproportionately captured the scheme benefits. Such NRSP schemes operated like the typical government scheme. Interestingly, government schemes where decision-making was much more broad based showed a success similar to the successful NRSP schemes.

In fact, the performance of LGRDD field workers showed that they managed to get a good participatory response from the communities in the scheme construction process but that they didn't attempt to carry the community participation process any further. This clearly indicates their more limited expectations. If they were trained, expected, and remunerated to take the process further, their performance suggests they could have. Similarly, if PHED could have success in forming water committees and having them implement regular tariff collection, they could have taken the process further.

The results of technical, community, and household data analysis for the most part confirmed the evaluations of the field teams contained in the field reports. There were two major differences. First, the field reports were much more sanguine about the overall financial sustainability of the schemes than was evident from the technical evaluations. For example, only five out of the thirty-five schemes had instituted a regular system of tariff collection and strictly speaking only one of the schemes could be viewed as financially sustainable. This result sounds more alarming than it was.

NRSP COs have savings they can draw upon if the community so decides. Also, the NRSP schemes in Sindh had no recurring costs and hence no need of a tariff. Twenty of the remaining schemes were gravity based and as such were low and irregular maintenance schemes. Second, and this is more difficult to explain, the field reports and the technical evaluations rated the PHED scheme performance to be much worse than indicated by the community and household responses. We placed more confidence in the field reports since structured questionnaire responses can be coached.

Exploring the data to understand why NRSP schemes were viewed as better managed, we discovered that the quality of construction, masonry, catchment, and better placing and condition of the pipes stood out. With regard to social capital construction, NRSP communities were better informed, better aware of project rules, and demonstrated more participation and self-reliance. Also, communities actually built the scheme, made greater cash contributions, and indicated a greater willingness-to-pay for improvements. The results of our econometric estimation supported the hypotheses that social capital construction and need are critical determinants of scheme sustainability.

Notes

1. Pakistan's four main provinces listed by population size are Punjab, Sindh, Khyber Pakhtunkhwa and Baluchistan. In addition, there are federally or provincially administered areas and Azad Jammu and Kashmir (AJK) is an autonomously run province.
2. See Khan (1999, Chapter 1). This study was funded by the Multi-Sectoral Support Unit which played a key role in Pakistan's Social Action Program in the early 1990s. It was directed at providing access to basic education, health, family welfare services and water supply and sanitation to rural communities.
3. Jennifer Sara was the task manager for the study and Travis Katz the global coordinator.
4. One reason why a collective market solution may not exist is that the more prosperous often cater for their demand by sinking their own tube wells (Khan 1999, Chapter 1).
5. Our earlier research showed that in poor rural communities the tariff rate would need to be sensitive to the capacity to pay. Khan (1999, p. 61) found the willingness-to-pay, even for improved service, gravitated to what communities were actually paying and it ranged from Rs.16 to Rs.30 per month. It would be preferable to identify willingness-to-pay (WTP) based on a survey of communities without a rural water supply scheme. In any case, to get some perspective on the WTP, it is interesting that Rs.20 represented, during the survey period, the cost of an ice-cream cone which many urban middle class parents routinely bought for their children. One dollar exchanged for Rs.41.38 in September 1997.
6. Narayan (1995) and Khan et. al. (1998, Chapter 1) empirically test this concept in the context of rural water supply and also provide other references to the associated literature.

7. Sustainability in this narrow sense can be viewed as a pre-condition for sustainability in the broader sense of concern with the well being of future generations.
8. Village household lists as sampling frames were made available by NRSP and PHED. For LGRDD, the household sampling frame was constructed at site by the field team.
9. To save on time in the field, two teams were trained. The training included in house sessions, a pre-test survey, follow-up in house sessions, another pre-test survey and further follow-up in-house sessions. The engineers had a BA degree while the rest of the field team had MA degrees from various social science disciplines. The fieldwork period was March 25, 1997 to May 15, 1997.
10. Public private partnership (bidding for government service delivery) and donor project funding subsequently became sources of ongoing funding.
11. Also referred to as social organizer or social activist.
12. Between a third and two fifths of the total cost for the 15 NRSP schemes we investigated was contributed by the community (Appendix Table 5.6).
13. This is in sharp contrast to the NRSP approach in which there was no handing over of the scheme, since the project believed the scheme belonged to the community to begin with.
14. For various problems confronted by hilly area schemes see Khan (1999, Chapter 1).
15. Appendix Table 5.6 presents comparative data across the projects.
16. The project decision not to give a choice with regard to the level of service to the community seemed to have been driven by project convenience rather than a scarcity of water since the source often had an abundant yield.
17. Donations of cash, in kind contributions and provision of land appeared by consensus to substitute for each other. Thus, those offering a portion of their land for the scheme or offering more cash, contributed less labor. In some cases, those whose land the pipe passed through did not pay a tariff. Thus, there was a developed sense of equitable contribution which revealed the ability to devise norms that enabled collective action.
18. Implicit in these numbers is a statement about NRSP being more cost-effective, i.e., at a lower cost it delivered a more satisfying service. Critics often claim that this ignores the large NGO overheads that are needed for the social mobilization. This is an important issue for investigation. However, two points are noteworthy in this context. First, the community

organizations that result from the social capital construction become a platform for multi-sectoral interventions. Second, the recurrent expenditure of each provincial ministry and district and lower tier offices represent part of government overheads. Thus, for a parallel treatment, these government administrative costs need also be taken into account in cost-effectiveness analysis.

19. Obviously, the HDP pipe is not as durable as the GI pipe. This is particularly important in hilly areas such as AJK where landslides can easily damage pipes, including GI pipes. However, the NRSP pipes were well laid underground.
20. One of the five schemes located in hilly Murree was gravity based as in the AJK.
21. It is also notable that in the two sustainable Punjab schemes, the communities were homogeneous in that they belonged to the same caste. This finding is consistent with the evidence reported in Khan (1999, Chapter 1).
22. Also, a Sindhi social activist trying to mobilize a Punjabi community settled in Sindh probably did not help much either.
23. We shared the first draft of our study with the projects and received a response from NRSP with supporting documentation. This indicated that the quality of the water in one of the schemes found to be non-sustainable in Sindh was poor because the water channel from the canal to the reservoir was unlined. One of the non-sustainable schemes in the Punjab was partly functional due to a delay in securing a three-phase electric connection. These explanations were useful but we need to reiterate that criteria used by the field team in assessing sustainability were multi-faceted as earlier indicated in the conceptual section.
24. There was one exception for which the source was ground water.
25. Training subjects included O&M, administration and finance, sanitation and hygiene education, organization and leadership and design and construction.
26. There was a loss of information in merging the intermediate category with the sustainable schemes to enable a sharper test to be conducted.
27. Of course, one could expect little difference when the percentage scores were already very high such as is the case with over 90% of household respondents satisfied with PHED and NRSP schemes.
28. See Kish (1965, pp. 217–218) for other such justifications and also for arguments concerning the statistical efficiency derived from such a sample design.

29. This is clearly a very incomplete characterization of the complex social mobilization process that facilitates social capital construction.

Appendix 5.1: Sampling

See Tables 5.6, 5.7, 5.8, and 5.9.

The sample design involved a random two-stage cluster sampling. In the first stage, 15 villages, in which the RWSSs were situated, were selected for the NRSP, and IDA/LGRDD projects and 5 for the PHED/IDA project. To ensure comparability, scheme/village selection was done on the basis of the following eligibility criteria:

1. Include communities with >15 HHs but <2500 HHs;
2. Include only rural communities in the sample;
3. Include, if possible, new (not rehabilitated) schemes that were initiated in 1995 or earlier;

Table 5.6 Comparative beneficiary and cost data for government and NGO schemes

Project	Avg. no. of beneficiaries		Scheme avg. total cost		Per beneficiary cost		Avg. project cost as % to total cost	
	S	NS	S	NS	S	NS	S	NS
LGRDD	578	388	462,604.5	336,164.7	800.0	866.4	*100	*100
NRSP								
Sind	239	438	83,821.6	129,909.0	360.7	296.9	69.4	68.1
Punjab	134	554	110,326.8	69,128.4	543.5	145.1	55.7	79.2
AJK	259	277	125,045.6	101,581.8	458.0	366.8	62.7	66.5
PHED	1,113	909	5,886,600.0	4,106,000.0	5,288.8	4517.1	*100	*100

Note
S—Data regarding the schemes included in the sample
NS—Data regarding the non-sample schemes
*—There was some community contribution but these two projects did not quantify it and only the project contribution was taken into consideration
Source Projects

Table 5.7 Project rules pertaining to communities

Project rules	PHED	NRSP	LGRDD
Forming of water committee	X	X	X
Participation of community at all levels of Implementations	X	X	X
Handing over of the scheme to the community	X	X	X
O&M—responsibility of the community	X (Partial)	X	X
Labor be provided by the community	X	X	X
Cash contribution by the community		X	
Land provided by the community	X	X	X
No more project financial responsibility after the completion of the scheme		X	
Committee will open a bank account	X	X	
Maintenance of accounts by the committee	X	X	X
Promotion of drainage and sanitation facilities by the community	X		
Civil works done by the community		X	
Periodic meetings of the community			X

Source Projects

To ensure regional representation, NRSP scheme/villages were selected from Sindh (5/7), Punjab (5/15), and AJK (5/17). The numerator in the parentheses represents the number of villages selected and the denominator represents villages that met the above eligibility criteria. Five out of ten PHED/IDA schemes were selected in Sindh. All the LGRDD/IDA villages (15/30) were situated in AJK. The sampling frames for the selection were procured from the projects with the assistance of the Water and Sanitation Programme housed in the Resident World Bank Mission in Pakistan.

In principle, the clusters/villages in the first stage of the two-stage sampling process were to be selected with probability proportionate to size (PPS). This would allow a fixed sample of 15 households in the second stage and still maintain equal probability of selection (EPSEM) for all the households (hhs) in the populations (project villages that met the eligibility criteria) we were sampling from, as explained below.

There are various rationales for this sample design. The total sample of hhs in a village can be subject to large variations following purely

Table 5.8 Project responsibilities

Project Rules	NRSP	PHED	LGRDD
Project will form a CO/VDA/WSC	X	X	X
- will socially mobilize the Community	X	X	X
- will sign TOP/MOX with the Community	X	X	X
- will seek labor contribution from the Community	X		X
- will seek in kind contribution from the Community	X	X	X
- will conduct a feasibility study	X	X	X
- will design the scheme	X	X	X
- will provide technical and organizational assistance on fiscal and other planning and management issues	X	X	X
- will construct the scheme		X	
- will supervise construction	X	X	X
- will impart hygiene education	X	X	X
- will impart LMST* training to activists	X		
- will impart training in plumbing to the nominated Community member(s)	X	X	X
- will rehabilitate the scheme by sharing up to 25% of the cost afterward		X	
- will transfer the scheme in proper working condition and free of all liabilities		X	X
- will provide assistance for repairs including extension free of cost		X	
- will monitor the scheme after completion	X	X	X
- will run the operation and clear all financial and other responsibilities of the scheme		X	
- will pay energy charges up to 4 hour of daily pumping for 3 months after scheme hand over		X	

* —Leadership and management skills training
Source Projects

random selection if the villages vary a great deal in size as they do in Pakistan. One reason to want to control the sub-sample size of hhs in the villages was that it became easier to make work-plans and administer the survey knowing roughly how much time the field teams needed for each village. This was necessary because project personnel needed to be informed in advance about the arrival of the field teams. Another reason for wanting a fixed sample of village hhs was to attain uniformity in the sample size of hhs across country for the cross-country comparisons.[28]

The above reasoning can be presented more formally. In the first stage, the probability of selecting a village with N hhs is N/F_b (where F_b

Table 5.9 OLS regression results (dependent variable: index of sustainability [SS])

	(1)	(2)	(3)	(4)	(5)
Constant	4.77*	1.32	0.50	0.73	0.11
	(3.67)	(0.73)	(0.25)	(0.32)	(0.05)
SCC	0.61**	0.75*	0.82*	0.83*	0.95*
	(2.17)	(2.84)	(3.00)	(2.96)	(3.26)
DR	−0.13	−0.17	−0.17	−0.17	−0.19
	(−0.91)	(−1.31)	(−1.27)	(−1.27)	(−1.40)
NEED	–	3.45**	3.17**	3.16**	3.53**
		(2.59)	(2.33)	(2.28)	(2.53)
WCOM	–	–	0.67	0.73	0.42
			(0.98)	(0.99)	(0.54)
EDU	–	–	–	−0.03	−0.01
				(−0.22)	(−0.06)
TRAINING	–	–	–	–	−2.90
					(−1.31)
n	35	35	35	35	35
Adj. R^2	0.12	0.25	0.32	0.30	0.34
F-Stat	3.24**	4.77*	4.95*	3.85*	3.89*

Note Figures in parenthesis are t-statistics
SCC—Index of social capital construction. Descriptions of all indices are contained in Appendix 5.3
DR—Index of demand responsiveness (see Appendix VIII)
NEED—1 If water supply scheme is the pressing need, 0 otherwise
WCOM—1 If water committee exists in the village, 0 otherwise
EDU—Mean level of education in the community across household (see Appendix VIII)
TRAINING—Mean household perception on the value of training (see Appendix VIII)
*—Significant at the 1 % level
**—Significant at the 5 % level
***—Significant at the 10 % level
Source Community data set
We tried interaction terms (NEEDSM, TRAINSM, and WCOMSM) but none of them were statistically significant

represents the zone size [explained below] for the relevant project household population, P). At the second stage, we select a fixed sample, b, of hhs from the N hhs in the village, i.e., b/N. Thus, this two-stage sampling design ensures EPSEM as earlier stated:

$$N/F_b * b/N = b/F_b = f$$

Systematic selection with a random start was utilized for the first stage selection of villages. Given the desired number of schemes for a project, a, in a region, the zone size F_b is computed as P/a. For example, for the NRSP project in AJK 20 villages met the eligibility criteria and 5 villages ($a = 5$) were to be selected. Thus, the zone size was $759/5 =$ 152, where 759 represents the total population, P, of the eligible villages for a project. The village household populations were stacked in a cumulative frequency distribution extending from 1 to 759. A random number (R_n) was selected between 1 and 152 to identify the first scheme with the probability of N/F_b (the larger villages had a higher probability of selection). The other four schemes were selected with the same probability as $R_n + F_b$, $R_n + 2F_b$, $R_n + 3F_b$ and $R_n + 4F_b$.

Household populations were again provided for the selected villages by the projects. We again used systematic selection to choose 15 villages with probability b/N. Note that in this second stage the probability of selection of the hhs from the larger villages was lower, exactly offsetting the higher probability of selection of the larger villages.

Appendix 5.2

Appendix 5.2.1: Scheme Patthi Wala, Muzaffarabad, AJK, LGRD

Village Profile

Patthi Wala was a small village with 61 widely dispersed households. However, only 8 households were not connected to the scheme. It is located at a distance of 40 km (ninety minutes by bus) from the district headquarters which is also the nearest city. Most of the households were engaged in labor and could be categorized as poor. The village contained a primary school for boys and girls and had electricity.

Scheme Delivery

This scheme was not delivered to the community based on an expressed need or demand. One version was that the delivery was based on bureaucratic bungling. Another version was that the chairman of town committee had good relations with the then Prime Minister, AJK and that the scheme was delivered as political patronage. A few notables did however make cash contributions.

The village already had an LGRDD scheme which was functioning and few people even had house connections. Also, there were several private springs in the village. The community did not have prior knowledge about the scheme and were not given a choice about the level of service.

Social Mobilization

One respondent mentioned that the community did not know that a scheme had been sanctioned for the village. The day the pipes reached the village, the chairman WCOM informed the community that a scheme had been sanctioned for the village and if they helped in carrying pipes, the village would get water supply.

Since the community was not taken into confidence, nobody knew much about the scheme before its implementation. The chairman of the WCOM and other village notables were influential in the decision-making. All the village notables had house connections while the rest of the population got water from the public stand posts.

The community neither had the ability nor the willingness to operate and maintain the system. The community had no managerial, financial, or technical knowledge and, in fact, the majority of the respondents were unaware of the presence of a WCOM in their village.

Sustainability

The physical condition of the scheme was very bad. There were a number of storage tanks which were built by LGRD in the earlier scheme.

For this scheme, the community constructed two storage tanks which every community was supposed to construct as a scheme requirement. However, the condition of these two tanks was very poor. One tank was destroyed by landslides and the other tank had big cracks. The main tank, damaged by landslide some months prior to the field team visit, had not been repaired. The community had resorted to direct supply from the source. There were a large number of leaks in the distribution network. The quality of service was not satisfactory and only the small segment of the community with house connections was satisfied.

Appendix 5.2.2: Androate, Rawalakot, AJK, NRSP

Village Profile

Androat is a hilly area in district Rawalakot. It is located at a distance of 30 km from Rawalakot toward Mang along the metalled road leading to Rawalpindi, and a 3.5 km un-metalled road led to the village. The village population was scattered over the hills. Small hamlets of about two to five houses clustered together. The residents generally worked abroad and so remittances were an important source of income for the poor village population. Other than that, small terraced agricultural land was a source of livelihood. The village had access to electricity.

Scheme Delivery

Due to the dispersed nature of the settlements, the scheme did not respond to the requirements of the whole community. The community actively contributed to the project in terms of cash and labor. Its cash contribution of Rs.24,870 amounted to 37% of total project cost. Consumers were given a choice regarding the level of service and they opted for house connections.

Social Mobilization

The community was provided the relevant information concerning the scheme by the project. A community organization was formed and made responsible for decision-making. The community was involved in the identification, planning, and implementation of the scheme. The community revealed a sense of ownership and was well aware of its responsibilities for O&M.

Sustainability

The main CO formed a water committee comprising of three persons and made them responsible for the O&M of the system. They had been appointed at each of three lines to monitor the system. The physical condition of the system was good.

The field team found that not all consumers were fully satisfied. Women especially complained about the abrupt stoppage of water due to the opening of the taps at the houses located at the upper level. There was no valve system to control the supply.

There was a feeling that the source selection was influenced by the interests of some influential CO members. Community members felt that another source should be tapped by the existing scheme in order to extend supply to current non-users who are members of the CO. The community was willing to contribute for such an extension. There was no tariff structure but the community undertook collective action when any kind of repair was required.

Appendix 5.3: Construction of Variables for Multivariate Analysis

The three main indices utilized and the variables used to construct the indices are as follows:
Index of scheme sustainability (SS)

1. Physical condition
2. Consumer satisfaction
3. Operations and maintenance
4. Overall ranking of sustainability

Index of demand responsiveness (DR)

1. Project initiation
2. Contribution—cash
3. Willingness to maintain the system

Index of social capital construction (SCC)[29]

1. Informed choice
2. Consumer satisfaction
3. Financial management

Scoring Method

There are four types of questions in the survey:

Yes/no questions: Score is +2 if the answer contributes positively toward the indicator and 0 otherwise.
Ordinal ranking questions: If the answer indicated positive performance in that indicator category, it was given a score of +2. If the answer indicated neither positive nor negative performance, it was assigned a score of +1 and if it did not contribute, it was given a score of 0.
Multiple choice questions: In some cases, multiple choice questions were used. Scoring of these can be explained with help of an example:
Whose idea was it to build the project?

The answer was scored as follows:

+2 water committee, neighbor, or community leaders
+1 local government
0 project

In the regression analysis, we used mean values for education (EDU) and training respectively.

EDU was defined as the mean level of education in the community across the household. They were given scores as follows:

0 if the person did not go to school
3 if the person attended primary school
5 if the person completed primary school
7 if the person attended secondary school
8 if the person completed secondary school
12 if the person attended college
14 if the person completed college
16 if the person studied beyond college

Training was defined as the mean household perception concerning the value of training and it has been given scores as follows:

2 if the person felt that training was useful
1 if the person felt that training was fair
0 if the person felt that training was useless/incomprehensible

References

Khan, S.R. 1999. *Government, Communities and NGOs in Social Sector Delivery*. Brookfield, VT: Ashgate.

Khan, S.R., F. Aslam, R. Bashir, A. Fatah, S. Kazmi, A. Mahmood, K. Pervez, and N. Saher. 1998. Rural Water Supply Scheme Sustainability in Pakistan: A Comparative Institutional Analysis. *Sustainable Development Policy Institute*, Monograph Series #3, Islamabad.

Kish, L. 1965. *Survey Sampling*. New York: Wiley.

Narayan, D. 1995. The Contribution of People's Participation: Evidence from 121 Rural Water Supply Projects. Environmentally Sustainable Development Occasional Paper Series No. 1, World Bank, Washington, DC.

Part III

Indigenous Social Capital and Spontaneous and Mixed Forms of Collective Action

6

Forest Depredations in Pakistan: Spontaneous and Mixed Forms of Collective Action

Introduction

The Sarhad Awami Forestry Ittehad (SAFI) represents a credible attempt by civil society to engage in forestry reform advocacy and activism in Khyber Pakhtunkhwa (KPK) Province, Pakistan (until 2010 known as the North Western Frontier Province, NWFP). SAFI aims to make headway against the existing top-down, predatory, forest management regime.[1] This regime, both by intent and default, is a major contributor to the large-scale degradation of Pakistan's primary forests; the devastation wrought by the 1995 earthquake and the 2010 floods are two tragic consequences of such degradation.[2] Therefore, it is important to document and analyze initiatives which attempt regime change with a focus on local participation, rights-based approaches, and accountability. An evaluation of SAFI's impact on the forestry reform process aimed at sustainable forest management could be of value to other budding collective action movements in the forestry sector.

This chapter drew on Khan et al. (2006, 2009) among other research works.

S. R. Khan and S. R. Khan, *Social Capital and Collective Action in Pakistani Rural Development*, https://doi.org/10.1007/978-3-030-71450-5_6

The evident deforestation in the KPK province tracks a chronology of management failure. Originally, customary law, with its genesis in collective action established community resource rights, and give them a stake in managing the forests sustainably. However, the steady attrition of such rights, followed by the transition to a statutory law regime, triggered the conditions for deforestation. Specifically, statutory law alienated communities from their resource rights; concurrently, weak enforcement of the law allowed encroachments in the shape of timber extraction and land-use changes. Collective action aims to arrest the deforestation–management nexus by reinstating customary law-based resource rights within a statutory law framework. This has taken the shape of forestry reform efforts and, on occasion, outright confrontation of communities with the establishment.

SAFI has managed to successfully channel anger over social injustice into sustained collective action. However, prior to SAFI's collective action, there was spontaneous collective action in Dir when the anger boiled over and resulted in violent conflict. The anger was dissipated by some state remediation but then festered again when promises were broken and it became evident that justice was denied. This chapter explores SAFI's success in the context of breaking the vicious cycle of social injustice, social anger, via spontaneous collective action.

In this chapter we first briefly describe the nature of the fieldwork we engaged in to cover the spontaneous form of collective action in Dir and the mixed form of collective action engaged in by SAFI (Chapter 2). We next present evidence of deforestation nationally and in the KPK province. After that, we describe the trajectory of forest management in Khyber Pakhtunkhwa (KPK), from its origins in customary law through its transition to statutory law. We narrate how the conflict between customary and statutory law and the denial of local rights led to spontaneous and violent collective action in Dir. Next, we present the mixed form of collective action undertaken by SAFI as an alternative. SAFI's origin, structure, focus, sources of finance, and collective action are described followed by a review of its advocacy initiatives and we end with a summary.

Field Work

Fieldwork that covered the Dir collective action was carried out over a 20-month period, from May 2003 to December 2004. Preparatory research combined site visits with information obtained from secondary sources. Observational data were supplemented by information gathered from community Focus Group Discussions (FGD), and interviews with policy makers, journalists, representatives of non-governmental organizations, and staff of the Environmental Rehabilitation in North-West Frontier Province and Punjab (ERNP) project working in Dir-Kohistan.

Stakeholder interviews were conducted in person, while FGD were held separately with members of different ethnic communities, to minimize inter-ethnic discord. Participants were selected to represent a cross-section of that community. The Pathan-Gujjar mix did not present problems as the interests of both groups were identical, as indicated below.

For the SAFI study, the data collection was done by SUNGI (a development NGO based in KPK) and the Sustainable Development Policy Institute (SDPI) Islamabad (a think tank). Qualitative data were collected through FGD and key informant interviews of the stakeholders. Stakeholders included Forest Department (FD) senior and mid-level officials, elected members of SAFI, civil society and NGO representatives, a provincial member of the national assembly, SUNGI staff, local leaders and national press members. The interviews and group discussions were conducted in the Malakand Division and Hazara Divisions; in both SAFI has a significant presence. The conversations were recorded in the local vernacular and translated into English during report writing. Secondary source information, books, articles, reports, office documents, and press clippings provided by SUNGI were also consulted. The area covered by our study consists of three northern districts of KPK province (Kohistan, Shangla, and Batgaram).

Evidence of Deforestation

The State of Pakistan's Forests

Pakistan's total forest area, estimated at 5.2% of its land area in 1998,[3] is well under an ideal 25% ratio.[4] Linear projections had showed that the rate of deforestation prevailing at the turn of the century would reduce forest area to 2.78 million hectares, or 2% of Pakistan's land area within two decades (Jafrey 2001). The Food and Agriculture Organization (FAO 2015) showed comparative national forest data over a 25-year period—from 1990 to 2015. The physical indicators suggest an almost uniform declining trend as evident in Table 6.1.

The bulk of Pakistan's primary forest resources and watersheds is situated in the KPK province and the Federally Administered Tribal Areas (FATA), constituting 7.8% of its total land area.[5] Over half of these forests are located in the Malakand and Hazara Divisions.[6] Malakand Division covers 29% of KPK's land area; its 0.36 million hectares of forests comprise 8% of this area. The smaller Hazara division constitutes 17% of the province's area with 0.32 million forest hectares covering about 5% of its land area. The difference reflects varying densities of forest stands (forest productivity). Not only have the forests in the KPK depleted significantly over time but they have also suffered declining productivity.

Data from a survey (Government of NWFP 1997) covering the forest rich areas in KPK indicated that 11% of the then existing timber volume was concentrated on standing forests (21% of the surveyed area). Another 42% of the forests comprised only 16% of the standing stock. This reflected an alarming decline in forest productivity. The condition of lowland forests was also precarious. Nearly 50% of these were open forest stratum accounting for a mere 5% of overall timber volume. The only forests with relatively high forest stands were situated in the high-hill regions where accessibility was restricted.[7] The maps in Fig. 6.1 highlight the continuing state of deforestation in the KPK province.

The latest, and in principle laudable, attempt to arrest and reverse deforestation trends is the PTI government's "Billion Trees Tsunami Program" in KPK which, at a cost of Rs.12 billion, undertook to plant

Table 6.1 Comparative forest data for Pakistan

	1990	**2015**	**Annual change rate (%)**
Forest area ('000 hectares)			
Extent of Forest	2527	1472	−2.1
Other wooded land	1191	1521	1.0
Forest Area—by characteristic ('000 hectares)			
Primary forests	0	0	0
Other naturally regenerated forest	2293	1110	−2.9
Planted forest	234	362	1.8
Mangroves	207	95	−2.4
Forest stocks (million cu. mtrs.)	261	135	−2.6
Forest biomass (million tonnes)	703	370	−13.3
Living forest biomass (million tonnes)	330	174	−2.5
Production forest ('000 hectares)	708	471	−1.6
Multiple use forest ('000 hectares)	1599	785	−2.8
Biodiversity conservation ('000 hectares)	220	216	
Removals (million cu. mtrs.—u.b.)	**1990**	**2011**	**Average: 1990–2011**
Wood	23.66	32.66	27.0
Woodfuel	21.04	29.66	30.1
Forest damage—land area burned ('000 hectares)	**2000**	**2004–12**	
	200	3,300	
Forest ownership (million hectares)	**1990**	**2010**	**Period growth rate, %**
Public	1.67	1.11	−33.5

(continued)

Table 6.1 (continued)

Private	0.86	0.57	−33.7
National forest management plan	None		
Sustainable forest management (SFM) policies	Yes. At the national level in public and private forests		
Supporting legislation and regulations for SFM	None		
National platform for stakeholder participation	None		
Stakeholder involvement in public forests: planning, operations, evaluation	None		

Source FAO (2015)

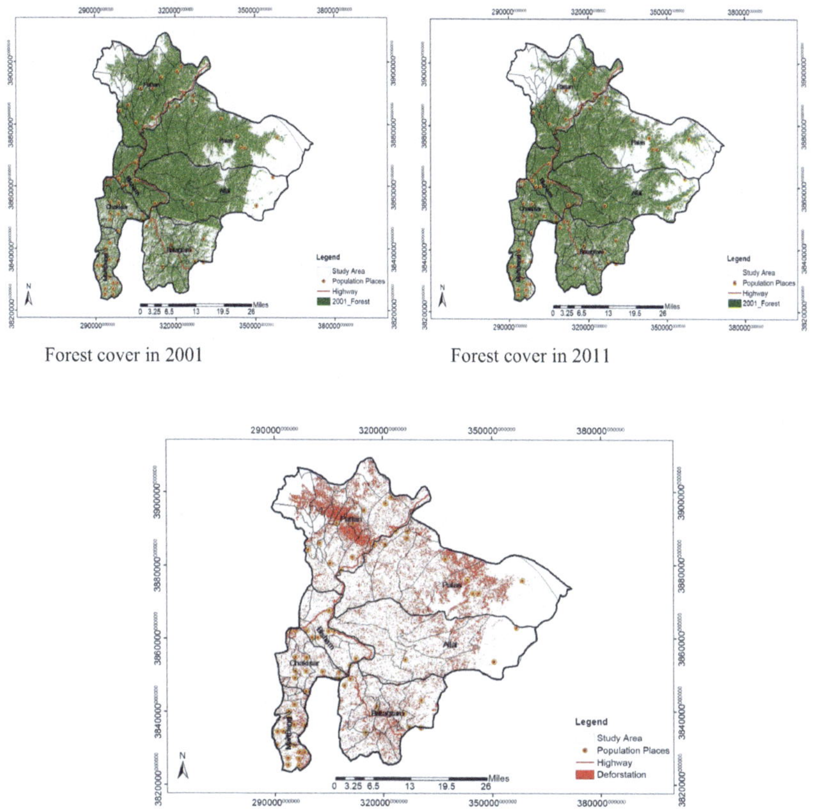

Fig. 6.1 Comparative forest data for the KPK province (*Source* Khalid et al. 2016)

a billion trees in both deforested and new areas across Pakistan. The program was launched in 2014 in KPK and, according to the government, had already achieved its target in 2017. However, independent assessments dispute this claim. They concede that 75% of the target was met but attribute 65% of newly planted area to natural growth. Even more serious concerns pertain to misgovernance and transparency in the program.

First, only the lower staff of the FD monitored the plantation followed up by minimum maintenance of the young trees. Second, the price for purchasing saplings from nurseries was considerably higher than the open market rates, especially for bulk purchases—the saplings being purchased directly rather than through open tender. Third, the distribution of saplings was biased in favor of large land owners whose sanctions far exceeded the mandated maximum (100,000 saplings). Subsequently, after receiving the funds they contrived to receive far fewer saplings retaining the difference.[8] Finally, a dissonance has been noted in many sites between the species planted and their ecological suitability with adverse effects on wildlife. We turn now to forest management in the KPK province demonstrating that continued deforestation stems from legislative changes, the lack of policy planning, and a regulatory hiatus, underpinned by a dismantling of community resource entitlements.

Forest Management in the KPK Province

The Ethnic, Environmental, and Socio-Economic Context

The three main ethnic groups in Dir-Kohistan and Swat-Kohistan in the Malakand Division are the *Kohistanis*, the *Pathans* and the *Gujjars*.[9] These upper valleys, where most of the conflicts around forest resources have occurred, have a predominantly *Kohistani* population. In the lower valleys of the Mata and Shangla districts, the major ethnic groups are the *Pathans* and *Gujjars*, with a relatively small indigenous *Swati* population. In the Kaghan valley, in the Hazara Division, the dominant ethnic groups are, in numerical order, *Gujjars*, *Swatis* and *Syeds*. The *Swatis* migrated from Swat during the extended Yusufzai invasion in the seventeenth century.

The upper valleys of the Malakand and Hazara Divisions are the least developed areas of the country, with limited physical infrastructure, social services, and economic opportunities. Land holdings are small and climate conditions limit crops to one or two a year. While the lower lying districts are relatively better off, poverty is still high in absolute terms. Natural resources; the forests, arable and grazing lands constitute the most important source of livelihoods in these areas. Subsistence involves making use of the different ecological niches: sustainable livelihoods depend on a careful husbanding of these resources. But these are areas where evidence of the poverty–environment nexus, the downward spiral of poverty and environmental degradation, is also the most visible.

Resource Management in Historical Perspective

The major changes in forest management systems in KPK correspond with four distinct stages: the era before the *Yusufzai Pathan* invasions, the post-invasion era, the colonial transformation, and the post-colonial era in which forest management broke down.

The Pre-invasion Era: Customary Law-Based Resource Rights

Sultan-i-Rome (2016) provided a comprehensive historical overview of forest management in the Malakand Division. Pre-colonial Indian states favored benign forest policies. They did not subject the forests and the forest users to the kind and scale of control exercised by the British later, which altered land-use patterns, property rights, and tenure systems. The occasional control was limited to extracting dues on certain animals and plant species, or to maintain hunting reserves. Substantively, the communities managed the forests and cultivable land.

Customary law defined a hierarchy of use rights rather than an absolute notion of private property. These rights were diverse enough to allow a variety of groups like livestock owners, animal trappers, shifting cultivators, and itinerant communities to make use of the land. The fluid order allowed an extensive variety of land-use systems to survive and flourish. Such diversity also allowed multi-species forests to exist, catering to a wide variety of ecological uses. From nomads herding livestock to the tribal people engaged in seasonal (*sweedon*)[10] agriculture, all were able to meet their subsistence needs collectively from the forests. The pristine condition of the forests in this era was the antithesis of what is described as scientific/conservation forestry. Hence Knudsen (2011) argued that "this conservation narrative has had a long lasting and, often devastating impact on forest resources."

The Post-invasion Consolidation Period

In mid-seventeenth-century Swat and Dir-Kohistan,[11] the invading *yusufzai pathans* diluted the customary law-based rights to natural resources.[12] Sheikh Malli, a *yusufzai* notable and revenue expert, introduced a system known as *garzinda wesh*; translated literally, it means moveable distribution. The rationale was that as land differed in composition, accessibility, fertility, and availability of water, it was necessary to ensure equal sharing of its best and worst features. Land allotments were by village and re-allotments, by ballot, were carried out every 5, 7, or 10 years, as agreed mutually between the villages. The land allotments included a mix of agricultural land, forest (*zangal*), pasture (*warshoo*), and wasteland. Essentially, the system assured socio-economic justice across villages.

In time, intra-village inequity and ethnic bias crept into the system. The *yusufzai* tribal elders began to assert private ownership rights to agricultural land (*dawtar*), claiming such entitlements as leadership prerogatives. They linked access to common property (*shamilaat*) resources—forests, pastures, rangelands, and water, proportionately to the size of private land holdings. Also, the more affluent villagers increased their private holdings through land purchases. In this way, the differentiated *dawtar* shares and the associated common property entitlements became increasingly unequal.

The non-*dawtaris,* comprising of the other ethnic groups *kohistanis, gujjars,* and *swatis*, were given use rights to common pool resources. In return, they were required to provide unpaid labor (*begar*) and pay a grazing tax (*qalang*). Tenants working on private farms paid the owners an agricultural tax (*ushr*).[13] As such, the resource rights regime differentiated clearly between the rights of owners and users.[14]

The Colonial Transformation

The colonial administration was driven by the need to protect their commercial interests, and accordingly passed various acts. The Hazara Forest Conservancy Rules in 1857 and the Forest Act of 1865, followed by the 1927 Forest Act, declared all forests the property of the government. The amended Hazara Forest Regulation Act was enacted in 1873, creating a new category, the "*guzara*" (communal or regulated commons) forest. Although, ostensibly, returning large tracts of forest, grazing, and wasteland back to the communities, the management of *guzara* lands continued to reside with the FD (for orderly exploitation) which, furthermore, extracted seigniorage from any proceeds generated through sales of forest products. A hybrid category, the "protected" forest also emerged as a compromise due to difficulties of demarcation (Azhar 1993). Communities were allowed open access to resources in these forests, except for specific uses proscribed by the government. This was essentially intended to arrest the growing trend toward encroachments.

When Swat and Dir-Kohistan states came into existence in 1917 during the British colonial era, the rulers (*Wali* in Swat, *Nawab* in Dir-Kohistan) claimed ownership and custodial rights over the forests. They established a FD to manage the forests and sanctioned a 10% royalty from the commercial proceeds of timber, paid in accordance with *dawtar shares*. The rulers also instituted two types of timber quotas. The local quota was meant for local residents requiring timber for domestic use. In addition, they were allowed to collect fuelwood, fodder, and medicinal plants. The *qaumi* (people's) quota applied to residents of areas where natural resources were not found in abundance. It was also used to acquire timber for public schemes. The *wesh* rotations were abolished, locking in private and common property entitlements spatially and in terms of shares. The other aspects of the old rights regime remained intact, namely the practice of charging *begar*, *qalang* and *ushr*.

The Hazara Division narrative was basically similar. Before the *Durrani* invasion in the mid-eighteenth century, communities enjoyed free access to forest resources. However, post-invasion the *Durrani* tribal rulers established control over these resources, without the benefit of a phase-in that their counterparts had allowed in Swat and Dir-Kohistan via the *wesh* system. But the outcome was the same. Communities could access forest resources, but in return for taxes and timber. In the early nineteenth century, the Sikhs seized control of Hazara Division but followed much the same pattern; forest resources could be used if communities paid the rents.

In 1926, Swat and Dir-Kohistan states and the colonial administration of the Government of India entered into a formal agreement to manage and conserve forests. The agreement transferred administrative authority of these forests to the Government of India under the 1927 Forest Act. However, key statutes in the Act were held in abeyance as *de facto* control and management remained with the states. While the rules and regulations were drawn up by the colonial government, the rulers continued to exercise effective jurisdiction over the forests.

The independence of Pakistan in 1947 and the subsequent signing of the instrument of accession had no significant impact on natural resource management in the states. Resource rights remained unchanged for both owners and users. There were no efforts from either the Pakistani government (with whom the states had not merged at the time) or the rulers to undertake any forest or land settlements.

In the Hazara Division, the forest policy was more stringent compared to its hybrid counterpart in Swat and Dir. The colonial government passed the Hazara Forest Act almost ten years after the overarching Forestry Act of 1927. A key feature of both acts namely the classification of forests into reserve, protected, and *guzara* forests—held in abeyance in Swat and Dir, was implemented in Hazara. Reserve forests became exclusively the state's property while communities had limited use rights in protected forests. Even in the largely denuded *guzara* forests, the state's presence was visible; an especially punitive enactment was the clause regarding *deodar* (cedar) trees in the Kaghan valley: these trees were declared state-owned even if located on communal property.

A change in management practices came about after Swat and Dir State merged with Pakistan in 1969. The forests were declared provincial subjects under the sole jurisdiction of provincial governments. In 1975, the provincial government declared forests as protected, and converted them into state property. The local and *awami* (people's) quotas continued; the latter were determined solely by the FD. Under the new system, traditional owners were to be compensated by providing them a share in royalties for timber extraction.

Post-colonial Forest Mismanagement

Good governance characterized autonomous rule in the post-colonial era in that enforcement was both strict and fair. Communities perceived customary law in a positive light as being conducive to sustainable resource use. This was largely a result of the clarity of established norms, ownership, and close monitoring of natural resources, which held despite the fact that customary law put no limit on the use of resources for subsistence.

Shahbaz et al. (2006) reviewed the various forest policies (1955, 1962, 1975, 1980, 1988, 1991, 2001) issued by the Federal Government of Pakistan which constitutionally has policy jurisdiction (while provinces have the implementation authority). The management approach has been top-down and autocratic with a focus on conservation, expansion, and revenue enhancement with little regard to sustainable livelihood of local stakeholders. Even though there finally was an acknowledgment of local stakeholders due to donor influence by the turn of the century, in practice little changed and the increased enforcement authority of FD guards nullified even the lip service to local livelihoods.

After the dissolution of the states and the subsequent take over of the forests by the Government of Pakistan, governance failures became endemic and forests degraded due to increasingly murky property rights (Azhar 1989). State forests are either "reserve" or "protected." Reserve forests carry community rights of water, passage, grazing, and fuelwood collection. Protected forests carry, in addition, the rights to fuelwood, fodder, and timber for house building, agricultural implements, funeral needs, graves, and communal buildings like mosques. *Guzara* forests, originally classified as wasteland, allowed virtually unlimited access. In addition to the rights indicated above, these included even commercial logging for a fee collected by the FD, harvesting timber to allay debt burdens and to meet schooling needs, and even cultivation in cleared patches. The tussles between rights holders[15] and the state have been on-going and this has included difficulties the state faces in demarcating the boundaries between state and *guzara* forests. As *guzara* forests were decimated, the pressure on state forests increased.

Ill-defined property rights in part led subsequently to community and timber contractor inroads—the latter aided in no small part by FD officials and local elders (Pellegrini 2007). When communities saw norms that protected resources their livelihoods depend on violated at will, they had no incentive to preserve the norms and a free for all or open access (tragedy of the commons) resulted.

While customary law continues to define resource rights in Dir, Swat and Hazara, these rights are increasingly subject to statutory oversight. Intrinsically this is because forest ownership, originally vested in the communities, has in time been transferred to the state. While communities continue to retain rights (see above) in the forests the FD's legal term for them is now "concessionists" rather than rights holders. The transition from community to state ownership has engendered conditions detrimental to the forests and turned harmonious relations between communities and the state into exploitative and conflict-ridden ones.

Statutory forest laws have restricted subsistence access to forest resources (fuelwood, timber, fodder, and other non-timber forest products). Commercial benefits to communities have been reduced to a minimum thanks to coalitions between the timber "mafia"[16] and the provincial FD. Community resource rights are both subsumed under statutory law, or reduced to paper rights. In other word, subsistence rights under customary law now defer to statutory law.

Forest royalties, to which legal rights holders are entitled, are largely appropriated by influential coalitions. The top-down approach to forest management has driven a wedge between communities and their birth right by denying them a say in its management and subjecting them to legal process, which is often arbitrary.

Unprecedented levels of degradation of forest resources has its roots in a management system unable to cope with the multiple and often conflicting interests of commercial loggers, private developers, government and military agencies, hunters and impoverished communities. The FD tends to choose the path of least resistance, coming down with a heavy hand on the disempowered communities and colluding for personal gain and profit with vested interests.

Rising prices of timber, fuelwood and forest products, low salaries and an erosion in the standard of living of the forest custodians, fines and penalties that are selectively applied and fail to match the nature of the transgression, and royalties that are appropriated by the rich and powerful, have combined to create a complex of perverse incentives antithetical to both conservation and equity.

The irony is that on the one hand key inroads into forest resources have been made by commercial and development groups which the FD colludes with. On the other hand, it targets communities, whose needs are of an essentially subsistence nature. If community rights and traditions were honored, they could collaborate with the authorities in the sustainable management of forest resources. However, the FD has chosen a path that has resulted in severe degradation of the forests.

Such marginalization of communities also reflects a historically ethnic bias. Thus, the *gujjar* communities across the board have the least rights and entitlements to grazing and forest resources, followed closely by the *kohistanis.* While this is a historical bias, it is compounded by institutional arrangements which align themselves with large forest owners and the timber mafia, who also are predominantly *pathans*. However, *pathans* also number significantly among small owners, rights holders, and non-owners who are at the receiving end of institutional biases.

The interrelationships of statutory and customary law and the complex and conflicting system of resource rights has created are another source of forest degradation. The deteriorating state of resources other than the forests, such as grazing lands, pastures, and fisheries present an equally dismal picture. In sum, the combination of predation, selective enforcement, illegal gratuities, and the induced raiding mindset among forest-dependent communities has made sustainable forest management next to impossible.

The brief segments in the text box below highlight the ineptness of the FD in facing external threats, its willingness to collude with various entities for profit and to circumvent forestry reform efforts.

Box 6.1: Pakistan Forest Department Mismanagement

The Taleban incursions

The Taleban overran Swat in 2007, subjecting it to their vicious brand of tyranny, until the Pakistan army dislodged them in 2009. Much like the drug trade, Swat's forests became another lucrative source of finance for their terrorist operations. The Taleban chopped down trees indiscriminately. Rodriguez (2010) wrote "employing termite-like efficiency, the militants felled and carted away vast swaths of Himalayan cedar, blue pine and oak leaving mountainsides dotted with stumps". As much as 15% of Swat's forests were wiped out during these two years. With the FD helpless, the timber mafia saw an opportunity to accelerate its felling operations, paying the Taleban for unrestricted access to the forests. During this short period, both actors converged to exacerbate the widespread deforestation already underway. They are largely to blame for the devastating impacts of the 2010 monsoon floods on Swat's population and its natural resources.

Trampling community rights in the guise of carbon trading: reducing emissions from deforestation and carbon trading

In 2011, Merlin Woods, a London-based company, signed a memorandum of understanding (MOU) with the KPK Forest Department for a 40-year project for forest protection and afforestation of over 300,000 acres of KPKs forests to be leased out to the company. Merlin Wood undertook to pay the KPK government $20 million as grant in aid for this REDD (Reducing Emissions from Deforestation and Forest Degradation) project and, subsequently, split the carbon trading proceeds with the government in an 80:20 ratio. The REDD-Monitor, a monitoring website based in Jakarta, raised a number of concerns about the project after consulting with SAFI (Lang 2012). The key concern was that the owner of Merlin Woods, a large forest owner in the province representing 22 other large forest owners, had secured the FD's sanction for the project without involving communities in the negotiations. Since communities had, variously, ownership, access and royalty rights in the two categories of forests (reserve, protected), excluding them was legally indefensible. This led to other concerns, namely: the lack of open bidding; the company's thin finances; no prior experience with REDD-type projects; the lack of a project feasibility study and a credible plan to trade carbon certificates. It was not difficult to conclude that Merlin Woods would primarily be involved in mining timber in leased forests and paying off its obligations to the forest department with the proceeds.

Forest royalties

Forest royalties were instituted by the nawabs, walis and maliks during the post-invasion era. They were meant to compensate communities for the transfer of forest ownership and management. Originally, the royalties were fixed at 10% of the proceeds from timber sales by designated contractors—a polite euphemism for the timber mafia. Over time these royalties increased to 60% primarily as a result of pressure by large forest owners in the protected and guzara forests. The nexus between the FD, the timber mafia and large forest owners, documented in detail by Pellegrini and Kruseman (2008), ensured that communities received little or no part of the royalties even though they are legally entitled to them. The ensuing, often violent, conflicts over these royalties were documented by Khan et al. (2004).

"Constructed social capital": Intent versus reality

As part of the donor-supported forestry reform process, the provincial FD established, variously, joint forest management committees, village development committees and women's organizations aimed at participatory forest management. Several studies were carried out to evaluate these committees. They concluded that the formation process was top-down and arbitrary, involving little or no social mobilization. The primary intent in forming these committees was to facilitate timber harvesting, community participation being a legal requirement. In effect, they morphed into forest harvesting societies, nominally empowered, but with little or no authority or management responsibilities which the FD was unwilling to devolve. Frustrated in their efforts to devolve such management to the communities, the donors stopped funding the initiative three years after its inception.

Spontaneous Collective Action for Royalties[17]

Matiullah (2004) noted that it is a great injustice that in an area rich in commercially viable forests, the majority of the people live in extreme poverty. This is in no small part a result of the current system under which the timber trade is conducted. In the protected forests of Dir and in *guzara* forests located in Dir-Kohistan's "Malakand Civil Division," timber harvesting is currently carried out by the Forest Development Corporation.

Although various organizational (direct contracts, Forest Development Corporation) and financial (fixed price, 'net-sale') arrangements have been tried over the years, these have, without exception, limited the community share in revenues to a minimum. Under the fixed-price system, for example, which was in use until 1981, rights holders were paid a predetermined amount per cubic foot of harvested timber (Knudsen 1996). This system was clearly exploitative since it allowed the government rather than the communities to benefit from rising timber prices.

Subsequently, a "net-sale" system was introduced, whereby harvested timber was auctioned and net proceeds from the sale (less marketing and administrative costs, and other overheads) were divided between communities and the government according to a set formula (Knudsen 1996). In theory, this entitled communities to receive a more equitable share of the income from the timber trade. In practice, however, this proved not to be the case.

For Dir, the net-sale system was never actually implemented and royalty payments continued to be based on the fixed-price arrangement. In some areas (not in the study area), royalties were paid before harvesting operations commenced, and profits and losses that occur during the extraction processes were shared by the government and the communities (Matiullah 2004). This arrangement in principle does appear to allow communities to share in profits that might accrue when the timber is sold in the market. However, this system did not take into account other chronic problems in the timber harvesting system, such as prolonged delays in disbursement and the involvement of the timber mafia.

Forced to wait for years, if not longer, for their share of royalty payments, individual rights holders were often compelled to sell their claims at highly discounted rates to forest contractors (Knudsen 1996; field interviews 2003). This entailed contractors procuring documents, in collusion with local leaders and FD officials, granting them power of attorney to appropriate the bulk of the royalties (Khan et al. 2004).

Even where communities did not sign over their rights to collect royalties, contractors had in many cases managed to appropriate the share of genuine rights holders. In the villages of Gawaldai, Kalkot, and Lamotai, for example, which are home to some of the richest stands of conifers in the country, residents claimed that royalties of up to Rs.195 million were appropriated by forest contractors.

No verifiable information exists on exactly how this was achieved but it is possible that in such cases contractors made a partial payment in advance, with the promise that a further share from the royalties would be paid to communities as and when the monies were released by the government. The system was clearly exploitative, and government delays in disbursing the amount due to communities only served to encourage these and similar practices. In many areas, meanwhile, local communities were also embroiled in court cases related to accumulated royalties and the method of payment.

But perhaps an even greater cause for concern is the fact that many communities with customary claims in forest areas were denied the right to royalty payments altogether. Their exclusion owes largely to the fact that no means existed to verify their claims. The land grants were awarded by the *nawabs* to their favorites and later provided statutory cover in the Dir State constitution. These grants became a key source of tension because claims to forest royalties were asserted based on them. This caused resentment and disaffection but not open conflict. However, violent conflict occurred over the issue of forest royalties against the state.

There have been at least two such cases in the Dir valley. The first episode occurred in 1976, five years after the government declared Dir's forests to be protected under statutory law. In an attempt to secure higher royalties and to curb the inroads into forests by contractors, local people (all ethnic groups) staged a protest against the government at Sheringal, the largest town in what is today the district of Lower Dir. The government initially deployed the Frontier Constabulary to control the unrest but as tempers flared and the situation turned violent, the military was called in. The disturbances were eventually handled by resorting to aerial bombing (field interviews 2003).

Coming as it did less than a decade after the dissolution of Dir State when its residents were drawn under the mainstream administrative aegis of the Pakistan government, there is no doubt that this incident sowed the seeds of distrust and paved the way for repeated bouts of anti-government violence in the decades to come. Following the bombing atrocity, the then prime minister visited the area and announced that royalties would be increased. By means of a notification issued on March 14, 1977, the community share in royalties was raised from 15 to 60%.

Certain tribes, who bore the brunt of the government crackdown and sustained the heaviest number of casualties, received a larger share of 80% (field interviews 2003). And here the matter could have ended.

It did not take long for local communities to realize that while their share of forest royalties may have been substantially increased, the system of extracting timber remained unchanged. Exploitative contractors had been a feature of the timber trade since the time of the *nawabs*, when such contractors were employed by the state to extract and transport timber from Dir's forests. This situation after accession to Pakistan was no different. Social resentment erupted into violence yet once again.

In 1993, in the wake of massive floods that had occurred the previous year, the government banned logging activities in the area to allow the forests to regenerate (Dawn 2005). No restrictions were, however, placed on the movement of timber down-country. The logging ban created a windfall for timber contractors, who had in many cases already paid communities meager sums of money for large volumes of cut timber. Even though the ban imposed in 1993 remained in force at the time of our fieldwork, illegal felling in these forests continued (Dawn 2005).

Social resentment boiled over again and manifested itself as unilateral collective action by local youth in the town of Kalkot, Upper Dir. They set up a checkpoint to stop all movement of timber outside the valley, and both the written and spoken rhetoric became confrontational. Scuffles broke out as forest officials attempted to dismantle these checkpoints. The situation was eventually brought under control and in March 1997 the government ordered an inquiry.

The inquiry commission, which submitted its report in June 1997, vindicated the communities' stance and advised payment of royalties in full (Khattak et al. 1997). It also recommended that the funds plundered by contractors be recovered and paid to rights holders. The recommendations were not implemented and agitation continued. The communities staged protest demonstrations on a regular basis and went on hunger strikes. In addition, they organized a "long march" to Islamabad.

Finally, in 2000, a second inquiry was commissioned which submitted its findings in October 2000. This time, however, the commission observed that it would be difficult to recover the looted money at this late stage. Not surprisingly, public agitation continued. Eventually, a *jirga* (assembly of male community leaders) was constituted which, in 2000, negotiated with the government on behalf of the communities. A portion of the accumulated royalties was released for distribution to rights holders through designated elders and the down-country movement of timber resumed in 2002. During the fieldwork period, rights holders had yet to receive their full share of royalties. Some in any case had refused to accept the decision of the *jirga* and the issue continued to fester (Dawn 2003).

Sarhad Awami Forestry Ittehad (SAFI)[18]

Origin[19]

SAFI originated during the Forest Sector Reforms Process in 1997 and the organization registered in 2008 under the Social Welfare Act 1961. SAFI believes that large-scale deforestation took place due to the top-down forest management regime that served vested interests with political support. This deprived forest-dependent communities of their rights and damaged the forest ecosystem.

As earlier mentioned, after the devastating flood in 1992, the Government of Pakistan imposed a complete ban on timber harvesting and initiated a legal and institutional reforms process in the forestry sector. In this context SAFI emerged with the active support of civil society organizations[20] to mobilize community resistance against the excesses committed by the large forest owners, contractors, and the FD and to convert such mobilization into a critical mass for policy advocacy for people-friendly forest sector reforms.

Its mission is to represent and protect the interests and rights of its 5,000 members (as of end 2019) which include forest owners, right holders, users and grazers and all those that are associated directly or indirectly with the forests of KPK. It purports to be transparent, accountable and rights based as well as pro-people.

Organization and Focus

SUNGI organized public meetings in a number of villages in the area to develop a strategy centered on community-based forest management which could protect the forests, ensure their sustainable use, and safeguard the rights and entitlements of poor forest-dependent communities. Immediately, a consortium of large forest owners and timber contractors, with covert support from the authorities, launched an intimidation campaign against SUNGI.

It became evident that SUNGI needed to organize the small *guzara* rights holders and other forest-dependent communities as a collective advocate for preserving community livelihoods and engage in the forestry reform process. Initially, loosely knit and Hazara specific, the movement eventually metamorphosed into SAFI, with a provincial mandate. Cross-province networking by SAFI was a key factor in awareness creation and exchange of information. It ensured location-specific concerns were disseminated widely which, in turn, built up into a critical mass for organized resistance.

SAFI had three broad objectives. The first was to mobilize community resistance against the excesses committed by the large forest owners, the contractors and the FD—excesses which resulted in both deforestation and economic disempowerment. The second objective was to convert such mobilization into a critical mass for policy advocacy. Campaigning for community rights in Dir-Kohistan can be viewed as reactive advocacy, while engaging in the more complex forestry reform process connotes proactive advocacy. The third objective was to promote community-oriented management interventions within the FD.

The organization's structure is four-tiered, as illustrated by Fig. 6.2.

The village level of organization is the SAFI basic unit. It consists of a general body of elected members. Each basic unit elects an equal number of its members to the higher *tehsil* tier. Similarly, each tier at the tehsil level selects an executive body from within its members for the divisional level body. The two divisional bodies (Hazara, Malakand) send nominees to the provincial executive committee, as do the southern districts and FATA. The present organizational structure emerged out of a long process from original conception of such an organization in the

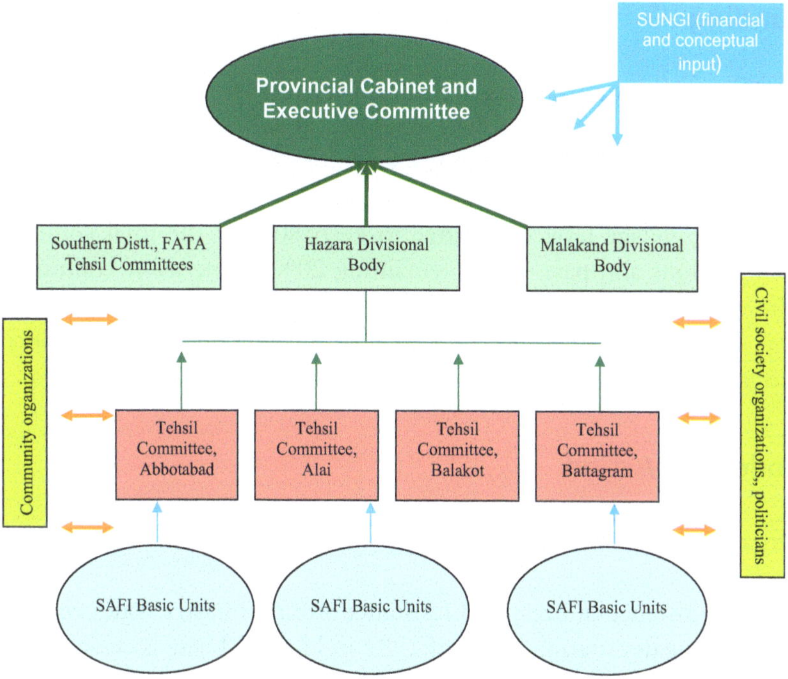

Fig. 6.2 SAFI organizational structure (*Source* https://safi.org.pk/)

early 1980s, progressing to membership drive, coalition building, and networking and eventually on to organized resistance and policy advocacy. In a relatively short time, it developed a distinctive pulse with two striking features being transparency and a strong resolve.

Scope

In the Malakand Division, SAFI's sphere of influence extends to the upper Dir-Kohistan and Swat-Kohistan valleys, as well as embracing Matta and Shangla districts. In the Hazara Division, SAFI has been active in the Mansehra district, especially the Kaghan Valley. In FATA, SAFI's focus is in the Southern District and Kurram Agency.

Funding

SAFI is at an important cusp with self-reliance as its next major goal. SAFI is not yet a fully evolved people's organization that can sustain itself with member contributions. It continues to draw heavily on foreign and local (NGO) donor support. The organization's financial structure allows the village level committee to keep 80% of the total voluntary contributions and pass on the remaining 20% to the *tehsil* committee. The *tehsil* committee in turn gives 30% of its share to the division level committee, which provides 50% of this amount to the provincial executive committee.

Collective Action

Organized Resistance

The first instance of organized resistance around forestry issues was triggered by the devastating floods of 1992 in Hazara. There is evidence that these floods were at least partially caused by widespread deforestation in which timber contractors played a key role (Rodriguez 2010). Specifically, there were polarized interests: at one end were arrayed the timber contractors, the FD and the large land owners, sometimes acting alone, more often in concert. At the other end were the disempowered small forest owners, non-owners, rights holders, and livestock owners. While small owners had property rights and some sense of security, the other groups merely had entitlements and concessions and even these tended to be ignored.

An important example of spontaneous collective action is demonstrated in the case of the Dir-Kohistan royalty issue. After the rich forests were declared state property the communities were promised a 15% share as royalty in the income from the forests. Commercial logging began on a large scale. Initially, this was done through contractors, who cut more trees than the legal limit, did not share the proceeds and went so far as to disallow communities their traditional subsistence rights. Discord began as early as the 1970s, erupting into outright violence (see above), when authorities resorted to force and shot dead a number of community leaders. This led to the abolition of the contractor system, which was replaced by the Forest Development Corporation. The community share of the royalties was increased to 60%. This was an enormous windfall, provided the communities were given their due share.

While communities were entitled to a substantial share of revenues (royalties) from the logging in *guzara* (community) forests, active collusion between the large property owners community leaders, contractors, and the FD officials results in appropriation of the bulk of these royalties. The local youth of Kalkot banded together to form the Youth Welfare Society for the Protection of Forest Kalkot (YWSPFK) to agitate against this exploitation. The society succeeded in persuading the government to form an enquiry commission[21] to look into the matter; in addition, they blocked the movement of timber by setting up a locally manned check post. While the commission recommendations weighed in favor of the communities they were not implemented. The YWSPFK then turned to SUNGI and SAFI for help. Subsequently, there followed a sequence of investigations and mass campaigns in which SAFI members from other divisions and districts of the KPK province participated. The outcome was encouraging; royalties were distributed to the communities and the movement of timber down-country resumed.

Proactive Advocacy

In the early 1990s, concerned donors initiated a forestry sector reform process in the NWFP in an attempt to arrest deforestation.[22] A key aim of the reforms was to introduce inclusive systems, which ensured an effective voice for forest-dependent communities in forest policy and management. It was recognized that if forests were to be preserved and used sustainably, communities needed to be involved in their management and community ownership and access rights defined clearly.

SAFI aimed to provide disadvantaged groups with a voice honed by social movements and also hoped that this would evolve into a movement for advocating issue-based politics. The expectation was that a peoples' movement could neutralize the strong institutional resistance to the reforms and ensure that the process remained on track.

The disconnect between the participatory objectives of the reforms and the insular manner in which they were formulated was a key concern for SAFI. The donors, the FD, and consultants were the key players in shaping strategies, policies, and legal frameworks. Civil society representatives were granted token (observer) status at best. But the intended beneficiaries, the marginalized forest-dependent communities, were kept at arms length, even as their self-appointed representatives sought to articulate a role for them in forest management. SAFI was able to bridge this divide and give a coherent voice to the community in the reform process and enabled them to engage with the decision makers as an organized lobby.

Specifically, SAFI's process achievements are in the area of community mobilization, coalition building, and networking. It has created widespread awareness about the forestry reforms, engaging with communities, and other stakeholders (NGOs, donors, the FD, politicians and the media) in consultations and discussions.

It has engaged in provincial and divisional level conferences, assemblies, and workshops.[23] In conjunction with SUNGI and other civil society organizations, SAFI has used these fora for policy advocacy—facilitating constructive policy dialogue between local forest communities and the NWFP government, to articulate community concerns at a higher policy level. At the *tehsil* level it has held several conventions and conducted planning workshops and seminars. Translating the forest ordinance into Urdu, Pakistan's *lingua franca*, has been a great help in the consultations.

Given the scale SAFI has attained, it has access to politicians that would not otherwise have been possible. For example, Malik Amirzada, a member of the KPK Provincial Assembly, supported SAFI's position on the Forest Ordinance, participated regularly in SAFI conferences, arranged meetings interviews with ministers, and gave interviews for the papers. Thanks to his efforts, SAFI met with Siraj-ul-Haq, the then senior KPK minister, and shared concerns regarding the Forest Ordinance and the Dir-Kohistan royalty issue.

Again, scale has enabled it to secure press coverage. The leading English (Dawn, News, Nation) and Urdu (Jang, Nawa-e-Waqt) papers have reported SAFI's activities widely via press conferences and events reporting. SAFI has employed several media channels including press conferences, media seminars, press releases, involving journalists in major events, building linkages with journalists, and organizing site visits for media persons.

Reciprocally, the media contributed to SAFI's movement gaining momentum. It enhanced the awareness of SAFI members, elevating their zeal and participation in its activities. Its key contribution was to highlight SAFI's policy concerns and advocacy initiatives, thereby giving the movement a more prominent profile among stakeholders and communities. It also provided a vital means to SAFI to hold those in authority and power accountable to those they are meant to serve.

The key concerns expressed at these various forums regarding forestry reform included reducing the arbitrary punitive powers of the FD and the need to institute penalties according to the gravity of the crime. In other words, it argued that illegal cutting for commercial gain is a more serious offense than forest encroachments for subsistence purposes. The NWFP Forest Ordinance, 2002, actually increased the policing powers of the FD; for instance, empowering them to shoot presumed malefactors on sight.

SAFI sought to improve forest royalty mechanisms and include women as royalty recipients. The existing royalty system lacked transparency and excluded women on religious/cultural grounds. Rights holders were deprived of their royalties by a coalition of large forest owners, the timber mafia and FD staff. The system needed to be made more accountable and innovative—innovative in the sense that royalties need to be linked with forest stands rather than trees cut.

It advocated for lifting the harvesting ban and to ensure marking and cutting was implemented according to the working plans. The ban on timber harvesting instituted in 1992 had many internal fault lines, the most prominent one being its almost complete lack of observance. Thus, the FD continued to mine timber resources to generate revenues; the timber mafia extracted timber on the flimsiest of pretexts, namely, that the trees were wind fallen or dry standing; in turn, this triggered infractions by the communities. SAFI stressed the need for a judicious, well-informed, institutionally supported, and time-defined program for removing the harvesting ban.

SAFI sought to activate the Forestry Commission (FC), a high-level forestry advisory body, as per the legal mandate (the FC Act was passed in 1999) and to ensure an equal balance between government and civil society membership. The FC had not been activated despite the legal mandate. Also, the nominees to this important advisory body had consisted entirely of government officials, either in-service or retired.

It sought to decentralize forestry roundtables (think tanks for the FC), and ensure they were broad based (representation of all the stakeholders) and accountable. As envisaged, the proposed forestry roundtables were limited in number and excluded key stakeholders, such as civil society and community representatives. SAFI advocated for broad-based representation in the roundtables as well as decentralizing them to the district level, in order to be able to capture local ecological and livelihood characteristics.

Among its achievements,[24] SAFI lists the following on its website:

- Mobilized, organized and empowered forest owners, rights holders, and non-owners for the rights struggle and influencing policy reforms.
- Replaced the colonial forest management regime with participatory Joint Forest Management, the New Forest Policy and the Forest Act (Ordinance 2002).
- New forest rules were enacted. Now more than 300 joint forest management committees are established.
- After a long struggle, the conflict between forest contractors and rights holders was resolved. People of a village (Kalkot, dir Kohistan) who were deprived of Rs. 200 million[25] by the contractors were compensated.
- Provincial Assembly of NWFP (now KPK) passed a resolution granting equal rights to all rights holders. For the first time in the history of a district of NWFP—now KPK (Dir-Kohistan)—an equal share from forest royalty was given to women.
- Recognizing SAFI, a representative body of forest peoples, the Government of NWFP awarded it membership of the Forestry Roundtable (a policy think tank).

- SAFI successfully lobbied for making some amendments in new forest rules: 18 *qaumi* (peoples) forest check posts were established in different parts of NWFP now KPK, to stop illegal timber trafficking.

Based on our fieldwork, we view these claims to be entirely credible.

Management Interventions

SAFI's increasing role in forest protection and management reflected another facet of its persona, which entails utilizing existing policy spaces. During our fieldwork we encountered two mindsets within the FD. Predominantly, the respondents were still locked into colonial, anti-community attitudes and took a skeptical view of the forestry reforms—especially those aspects pertaining to community forest management.

A smaller group was more open to change. Members of the group conceded the high incidence of degradation, and that existing management systems were unable to cope with the emerging pressures on the forests—both of a commercial and subsistence nature. Particularly in those areas where forest demarcations or land settlements had not been carried out, such as Dir, Swat and Indus Kohistan, the FD's ability to monitor, enforce, and undertake silvicultural activities was curtailed severely. Evident was the growing recognition that partnerships with communities offered prospects of protecting the forests and using them sustainably.

Attitudinal change was most evident in the Malakand Division. As tangible evidence of this, the FD had responded to SAFI's requests to change forest demarcations to improve access to FD offices; community check posts had been set up to interdict illegal timber movements—one of them (the Jery checkpost) in close proximity to the FD check post. Forest Protection Societies (FPS) had been formed to assist FD activities in the more remote areas which FD staff could not monitor easily. SAFI formulated a manifesto and constitution for the Qaumi Jungle Bachao Committee (national forest protection committee), an overarching forest protection body. One of the elected members of this committee was involved in silviculture activities in the forest near his village and was a vociferous opponent of land-use change.

In effect, the FPS's complement the activities of the FD. The latter continues to support FPS but prefer that their working agenda remains in line with the FD work plan. Members of SAFI have also assisted FD staff in apprehending culprits involved in illegal cutting. One constraint in this regard is the lack of integration between SAFI activities and the FD. As a specific example, the working of check posts could be much more efficient if community check posts and FD check posts could be placed at the same spot so that they could work together. Such integration was lacking during our fieldwork.

Summary and Conclusions

The creation of the Pakistani state was not a boon for Pakistan's forests which have become severely degraded. Indigenous property rights that provided a measure of protection based on common property management underpinned by customary law had already been threatened by historical changes based on pre and post British colonial incursions. However, some measure of acknowledgment of common property rights that had survived were undermined as a part of modern state formation.

Customary law transitioned to statutory law as part of this process. The creation of a modern state FD and its collusion with the larger property owners/community leaders and predatory timber mafia resulted in outright theft and disregard for local rights. In Dir, violent conflict resulted from the social resentment sparked by denied royalties as in the 1970s. Broken promises, royalty delays and denial and continued predation resulted once again in violent conflict in the form of spontaneous collective action in the early 1990s.

Matters also came to a head in the early 1990s in the broader region due to deforestation and the consequent flooding and soil erosion since natural protections provided by forests had been decimated over time. SAFI emerged from a people's movement and subsequently as an organization to fight for social and environmental justice. This once again represented spontaneous collective action but with a difference since it sought to harness the social resentment for sustained and meaningful forestry reforms. In this regard, it welcomed the capacity-building efforts of SUNGI, a development NGO that specializes in capacity-building of community-based organizations.

The SAFI initiative provides reason for optimism. In a relatively short time, the organization managed to achieve tangible gains. However, it has its work cut out for it. Attaining well defined property rights that harmonize customary and statutory law and ensuring sound administration that avoid delays and predation requires major changes in the political economy that can harness vested interests.

From the perspective of our conceptual framework, we view SAFI's work as an example of a mixed form of collective action. SUNGI, a development NGO, assisted the collective action and gave shape to it with financial and conceptual support. However, success was based on the fact that the initial impulse came from the grassroots and the initiative remained at the grassroots and so we refer to it as a mixed or hybrid form of collective action to distinguish it from the purely spontaneous collective action that occurred in Dir, or the RSP initiated induced collective action discussed in Chapters 4 and 5.

Notes

1. KPK is one of Pakistan's four provinces. It is situated in the north of the country at the base of the world's highest mountain ranges including the Karakoram.
2. These events occurred, respectively, in Azad Jammu and Kashmir and in Swat district, KPK.
3. https://www.fao.org/tempref/docrep/fao/005/AC921E/AC921E08.pdf, consulted November 4, 2020.
4. Nazir and Olabisi (2015).
5. FATA borders the KPK province.
6. Divisions are the administrative tier below provinces followed by districts, *tehsil*, union councils and villages.
7. Khalid et. al. (2016) provided more recent spatio-temporal maps showing deforestation over a ten-year period.
8. In early 2018, the National Accountability Bureau (NAB) formally launched an investigation following allegations of corruption and embezzlement in the program.
9. Livestock herding is a prominent occupation of the *Gujjars*.

10. The 'sweedon' system refers to shifting cultivation in the forests but under regulated conditions which did not degrade the forests.
11. Swat and Dir-Kohistan are a part of the Malakand Division.
12. Natural resources embrace forests, cultivable land, rangeland, pastures and wasteland.
13. The non-*dawtari* occupations were tenant farming, livestock grazing, and providing unpaid labor and artisanal services.
14. In exceptional cases where the *non-dawtaris* were allowed to buy property, their use of common pool resources still remained subject to the *dawtaris*' permission and was taxed.
15. These rights are inherited in an open-ended fashion across generations and so rights-holders increased dramatically with rapid population growth.
16. According to Shahbaz and Ali (2009, p. 14), this refers to a network of various actors including political leaders, some state forest officials, influential locals, businessmen (contractors), transporters, and police. We refer separately to the contractors, large landowners, and FD officials.
17. Much of this narrative, unless otherwise referenced, is based on personal communication with Waseem Ahmed Shah, Staff Correspondent, *Dawn*, Peshawar Bureau.
18. Literary this translates into Northern People's Forestry Union.
19. Drawn from https://safi.org.pk/.
20. SUNGI (Friend), a rural development NGO, was prominent in providing conceptual and financial support.
21. The Zia-ud-din Enquiry Commission, 1997.
22. The reform was initiated by the Dutch, Swiss, and Norwegian governments and by the Asian Development Bank, a multilateral aid agency.
23. These in chronological order were: The Forestry Conference, Abbotabad, 1997 (The Sarhad Forestry Working Group was established at this conference, which began to lay the groundwork for SAFI. The forestry working group comprised of five members, SUNGI, Sustainable Development Policy Institute, Hayyat Welfare Association, Environmental Protection Society, and Kurram Rural Development Organization), The Second Provincial Forestry Conference, Abbotabad 1998, The Second Forestry Strategic Planning Workshop, Mingora 1999, The Sarhad Peoples Forest Assembly, Pakistan Forest Institute, Peshawar, January 2000 and The Malakand Divisional Forestry Convention, Mingora 2002.
24. In Bakote district, SAFI district president, Chaha Abdul Latif, received a 'conservation award' from WWF in recognition of his long-term association with forests and the related conservation work.
25. One US$ was worth about 60 Pakistani rupees (Rs.) in 2002.

References

Azhar, R.A. 1993. Commons, Regulation, and Rent-Seeking Behavior: The Dilemma of Pakistan's "Guzara" Forests. *Economic Development and Cultural Change* 42 (1): 115–129.

Azhar, R.A. 1989. Communal Property Rights and Depletion of Forests in Northern Pakistan. *Pakistan Development Review* 28 (4): 643–651.

Dawn. 2003. Forest Royalty 'Embezzled'. May 1, check archives, dawn.com.

Dawn. 2004. Women Qazis for PATA appointed. June 6, check archives, dawn.com.

Dawn. 2005. Call to Lift Ban on 'Commercial Harvesting of Trees'. September 30, check archives, dawn.com.

FAO (Food and Agriculture Organization, United Nations). 2015. *Global Forest Resource Assessment.* Rome. https://www.fao.org/3/a-i4808e.pdf, downloaded December 11, 2019.

Government of the NWFP. 1997. Provincial Forest Resource Inventory. GAF AGA Consultants.

Jafrey, S. 2001. Deforestation: Present and Future Perspective. The Veterinary News and Views. https://www.slideshare.net/princesssania7/deforestation-21st-march-forest-day, consulted December 1, 2019.

Khalid, S.R., et al. 2016. Spatiotemporal Monitoring for Deforestation and Forest Degradation Activities in Selected Areas of Khyber Pakhtunkhwa (KPK). *International Journal of Geosciences* 7 (10): 1191–1207.

Khan, S.R., S. Bokhari, and M.A. Cheema. 2004. Resource Rights and Sustainable Livelihoods: A Case Study of Pakistan's Dir-Kohistan Forests. Sustainable Development Policy Institute-International Union for the Conservation of Nature, Islamabad.

Khan, S.R., M. Yusuf, and R. Ahmed. 2006. Anatomy of a Peoples' Rights Movement: A Case Study of the Sarhad Awami Forestry Ittehad (SAFI). Sustainable Development Policy Institute Working Paper Series No. 103 Islamabad.

Khan, S.R., S. Bokhari, and R. Matthew. 2009. Livelihoods, Security and Conflict: Dir Kohistan, Pakistan. In*Sustainable Livelihoods, Environmental Security and Conflict Mitigation*, ed. P. Moore. Final Report. Gland, Switzerland: International Union for the Conservation of Nature.

Khattak, Z., M. Iqbal, and J. Khan. 1997. Report of the Enquiry Committee on Determination of the Right of Forest Royalty of the Inhabitants of

Gawaldai, Kalkot and Lamotai of District Upper Dir. Government of the NWFP, Peshawar.

Knudsen, A.J. 1996. Deforestation and Entrepreneurship in the NWFP, Pakistan. Chr. Michelsen Institute (CMI) of Development Studies and Human Rights, CMI Working Paper WP 1996:11, Bergen.

Knudsen, A.J. 2011. Logging the 'Frontier': Narratives of Deforestation in the Northern Borderlands of British India, c. 1850–1940. *Forum for Development Studies* 38 (3): 299–319.

Lang, C. 2012. Merlin Wood's Mysterious REDD Projects in Pakistan. Posted on www.redd-monitor.org.

Matiullah, S. 2004. Mechanism for Improved Forest Management, Reduction in Timber Conversion Waste and Increase the Timber Outturn Percentage. Final Report. Consultancy # 22. Available online at https://www.palasvalley.org/reports/con22.pdf.

Nazir, N., and L.S. Olabisi. 2015. Forest Area and Land Use Change in Pakistan: A System Dynamics Approach. https://www.systemdynamics.org/conferences/2015/papers/P1296.pdf, downloaded November 18/2017.

Pellegrini, L. 2007. The Rule of the Jungle in Pakistan: A Case Study on Corruption and Forest Management in Swat. Nota Di Lavoro 91, Fondazione Eni Enrico Mattei, Milan. https://www.feem.it/Feem/Pub/Publications/WPapers/default.htm, consulted December 3, 2019.

Pellegrini, L., and G. Kruseman. 2008. Institutions and Forest Management: A Case Study from Swat, Pakistan. Nota Di Lavoro 2, Fondazione Eni Enrico Mattei, Milan. https://www.feem.it/Feem/Pub/Publications/WPapers/default.htm, consulted December, 2019.

Rodriguez, A. 2010. Pakistan Flood Crisis Blamed Partly on Deforestation. *Los Angeles Times*, October 13. https://www.latimes.com/archives/la-xpm-2010-oct-13-la-fg-pakistan-logging-20101013-story.html, consulted 12/2/2019.

Shahbaz, B., and T. Ali. 2009. Donor-Driven Participatory Forest Management and 'Local Social Realities': Insights from Pakistan. *Pakistaniaat: A Journal of Pakistan Studies* 1 (2): 35–59.

Shahbaz, B., T. Ali, and A.Q. Suleri. 2006. A Critical Analysis of Forest Policies of Pakistan: Implications for Sustainable Livelihoods. *Mitigation and Adaptation Strategies for Global Change* 12 (4): 441–453.

Sultan-i-Rome. 2016. *Land and Forest Governance in Swat: Transition from Tribal Governance to State of Pakistan*. Karachi: Oxford University Press.

7

Reversing Unsustainable Policies and Practices in the Fisheries Sector: A Chronology of Collective Action by the Pakistan Fisheries Forum

Introduction

The rapid decline in marine fisheries is a global phenomenon. Pauly and Chuenpagdee (2007) explained why the size and quantity of catch was decreasing globally even as subsidized capacity was increasing. The reasons include overfishing based on evolving fishing technology, associated increased capacity, and environmental degradation. For example, Hutchings and Myers (1994) showed overfishing to be the cause of the much-studied collapse of the Atlantic cod. Salayo et al. (2008, p. 692) reported that, due to overfishing, coastal fishing stocks in South and Southeast Asia had been depleted to between 5 and 30% of unexploited levels.

Data from Pakistan also reveal fishery degradation. Appendix Table 7.1 shows an increase in fishing vessels of all kinds between 1993 and 2003 in Pakistan's two coastal provinces (Sindh and Balochistan). We updated these statistics to 2014 using Food and Agricultural Organization (FAO) statistics (Appendix Table 7.4). The one-year overlapping in the numbers (2000) shows a massive fleet understatement in the Government of Pakistan source by about a third (21 rather than 34 thousand).[1] Also,

S. R. Khan and S. R. Khan, *Social Capital and Collective Action in Pakistani Rural Development*, https://doi.org/10.1007/978-3-030-71450-5_7

FAO statistics reported in Appendix Table 7.4 suggest a decline in fleet subsequent to 2010; from 34.1 to 31.6 thousand in 2014.

Appendix Tables 7.2 and 7.3 show trends in marine fish catches in coastal waters and the Exclusive Economic Zone (EEZ), which extends up to 200 miles from the coast. Increased catches initially were due to greater ingress by foreign trawlers, facilitated by both a change in zoning policy and the liberalization of licenses. However, despite the increase in vessels, there was a decline in catches across the board between 2000 and 2003 from 438 to 402 thousand metric tons (tonnes). This decline seems to have continued; on April 21, 2010, the director general of marine fisheries reported to a prominent daily newspaper that sea food catches had declined by 29% over the last decade.[2]

More recent data on marine catches were reported by the FAO and are presented in Appendix Table 7.4. There are a few years of overlap between Government of Pakistan data and those reported by the FAO and there is correspondence between the two unlike in the case of the number of vessels. The story evident in the last years of reported government data in Appendix Table 7.2 is confirmed by the more recent FAO data. The peak of marine catch of 487 thousand metric tons was in 1993 and there was a downward trend after that to 363 metric tons in 2018.

Not only have stocks fallen radically, some species of fish have been wiped out entirely, such as *gallo* and *kalaki* fish in Pasni, Balochistan Province, *zardum*, *paplet*, and *kalgun* in other areas of Balochistan and *palla* in Sindh Province. The size of fish has also become smaller. Our field research indicated that an Indian mackerel from Sindh, where overfishing was much more intense, was much smaller in size than the one found in Balochistan.

Resource degradation in Pakistan's coastal fisheries sector has two interrelated dimensions. In an overarching context, the increasingly commercial orientation of federal fishing policies has both reduced fish stocks and degraded fish habitats. Such degradation is visible across designated zones. Of particular concern to coastal fishing communities (artisanal fishermen) in Sindh and Balochistan are the provincially administered coastal waters. Not only are their catches reduced thanks to trawler ingress in these waters, their poverty-induced vulnerability makes them prone to degrade the very source of their livelihoods. A term commonly used to explain such unsustainable practices is the poverty-environment nexus. We argue that this nexus reflects an induced response, one that is triggered by the appropriation of their traditional fishing grounds and by imperfect credit markets.

The Pakistan Fisherfolk Forum (PFF) was formed in May 1998 to address the threats to livelihoods of local fishing communities. It is a representative body of fisherfolk working in the coastal areas of both Balochistan and Sindh. It is actively engaged in awareness raising, mobilizing, and organizing the communities for the protection of their livelihoods and sustainable management of fisheries much as SAFI is doing for forestry, as reported in Chapter 6. The PFF aims to restore fisherfolk open access rights via policy advocacy and community activism. We document the advocacy role of the PFF. In the context of the conceptual framework identified in Chapter 2, we classify the activity of the PFF as autonomous collective action.[3]

The chapter starts with a review of the state of marine fisheries and policy in Pakistan. Following that, the literature on sustainable community fishery management, which we view as important for ensuring sustainable livelihoods for fishing communities, is reviewed. This complements the literature review on social capital and collective action in the conceptual framework (Chapter 2). Next, we indicate how we gathered information on which the qualitative analysis reported in this chapter is based. We present our fieldwork findings next presenting institutional and policy information that explains the plight of vulnerable fisherfolk. This sets the stage for our discussion in the last section on the collective action engaged in by the PFF.

Marine Fisheries in Pakistan

The FAO[4] reported that in 2014 marine coastal fishing employed over 194,420 people directly and indirectly impacted—if one includes dependents—close to 1.3 million (assuming an average household size of 6.7)[5]. Fishing communities, whose way of life has survived for generations, are dispersed along a 682-mile coast line, lying between Sir Creek in Sindh Province and Jiwani in Balochistan Province, respectively, (Fig. 7.1).

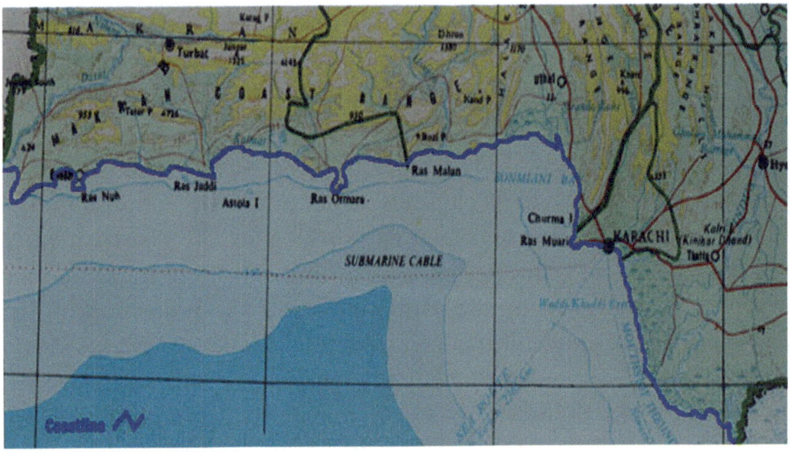

Fig. 7.1 Coastal map of Pakistan (*Source* Government of Pakistan [1997])

Balochistan has 477 miles of the coast line and the remaining 205 miles are in Sindh. The latter has 17 large and hundreds of small creeks (Fig. 7.2), which are branches of the larger creeks. Some 30 aggregations of fishing communities live along this coast line. A few of the large aggregations are permanent; the smaller groups come together during the beginning of the fishing season and vacate their habitations at its end.

Four harbors and nine important landing sites and jetties are situated along with the Sindh—Balochistan coast (for more details, see Birwani

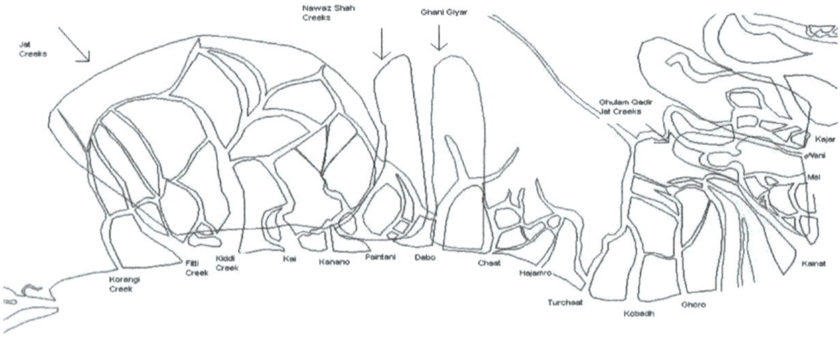

Fig. 7.2 Sindh coastal creeks (*Source* Pakistan Fisher-folk Forum, map drawn during fieldwork, September 2004)

et al. [1999]). The bulk of the fishing population resides in Karachi, Sindh Province. Karachi is also Pakistan's largest industrial city, with an estimated population according to UN estimates of about 16 million. The other concentrations are in Thatta, Sindh, and Gwadar and Pasni, Balochistan.

The FAO reported close to 10,000 powered boats operating in Pakistan's marine coastal waters in 2014. Our field research revealed that vessels of various sizes engaged in fishing; small and medium-sized boats, large launches, and trawlers. The small boats were between 18 and 25 feet in length and used to fish the coastal waters. Medium-sized boats ranged in size from 25 to 35 feet in length. Almost one-third of these vessels were shrimp trawlers; the bulk of them were owned by investors outside the community. Boat and shore fishing were practiced in creeks and within the 12-mile territorial limit, which falls under provincial jurisdiction. The larger launches went farther off shore into deeper waters on extended fishing excursions, some ranging as far as Somalia's coast.

The increasing poverty of fishermen is linked in important ways with the deprivation of their resource (open access) rights. Federal Government fishing policies indirectly affect artisanal fisherfolk by reducing the overall fishing stock and fish breeding runs. Directly, trawler ingress into territorial waters impacts their livelihoods. Provincial jurisdiction over these waters, which could potentially protect local fishermen, is undermined by the presence of Federal Agencies which override their jurisdiction and openly or covertly support commercial fishing. Also, territorial waters are encroached upon by feudal lords arbitrarily citing land acts in a classic illustration of resource capture. Such policies and forced acquisitions compel poor fisherfolk, striving to make a living, to resort to unsustainable fishing practices. Another source of unsustainability via poverty-induced practices is imperfect credit markets and associated distress pricing (see below).

Pakistan's deep-sea fishing policy was formulated in 1982, in the wake of the UN Convention on the Law of the Seas. For the first time, the convention defined territorial and exclusive economic zones for all states in the world. The fishing waters of the Sindh and Balochistan coasts were divided into three zones. The waters beyond the buffer zone and up to 200 nautical miles were designated as the exclusive economic zone

(EEZ), and are fished largely by deep-sea trawlers. The continental or buffer zone, falling between 12–35 nautical miles, was established to protect fish stocks in territorial waters. Both the EEZ and the buffer zone fall in the Federal Government's policy remit. The territorial waters (also known as the coastal zone) extend up to 12 nautical miles and come under provincial jurisdiction. However, in addition to its control over the EEZ, the Federal Government also maintains a strong presence in territorial waters through various Federal Agencies of customs, immigration, maritime security, shipping, and ports. This presence was reinforced with the creation of the Fishermen's Cooperative Society (FCS)[6] and Maritime Pollution Board (MPB).

The Federal Government's key policy thrust has been on the commercial aspects of marine fishing with the aim of boosting exports (see Appendix Table 7.4). Consequently, it allowed joint ventures between foreign and local investors. Little attention was paid to the concerns of local fishing communities or to the sustainable management of marine fisheries as demonstrated by arbitrary changes in zoning laws as well as weak enforcement. In 2001, the Federal Government abolished the buffer zone and, subsequently, trawlers began to ingress into territorial waters. Commercial fishing operations were allowed up to the 12-nautical mile (NM) limit but transgressions into coastal waters and into the creeks were reported frequently. The local fishermen pointed out that the trawlers denuded fish stocks by intercepting the inbound fish spawning runs, and degraded the ocean habitat with their drag nets.

There have been token policy changes in the past. The policy was amended in 1989, permitting only Pakistani flagged vessels. This failed to restrict foreign trawlers as local feudal lords and investors began to front for them. The deep-sea fishing policy of 2001 was purportedly more inclusive. It referred to the "human dimension" and described the "socio-economic uplift of the small-scale fishermen" as one element in its two-pronged strategy to rejuvenate the sector. However, various stakeholders that we interviewed expressed disappointment that there had been no substantive implementation of the range of proposed measures.

The extant marine fisheries policy of 2007,[7] formulated between 2004 and 2006 with ostensible consultation with all stakeholders, and drafted by the FAO, in principle recognizes the rights of local fishermen.

However, the policy is vague and contradictory. While the rights of the vulnerable (presumably local fisherfolk) are to be protected, an enabling environment is to be created to allow private sector initiatives to thrive. It is left to the private sector as a key partner to "be the sustainable vector of economic and social development." This is in keeping with the top policy priority of the marine fisheries policy of encouraging economic growth.

While there is lip service to sustainability or sustainable production, these concepts are not fleshed out. The targets and focus really are on the private sector and export growth. Thus, notwithstanding the stakeholder dialogues, local fisherfolk are once again given short shrift except in the rhetoric. The need to really heed to local fisherfolk remains. Over the years, it is they who have developed techniques based on local knowledge that can maintain ecosystem balance.

The FAO reported that regulation on the control of the use of harmful gear has been improved including, for instance, the ban on the use of purse seine and trawl nets. However, there is still no regulation limiting the number of fishing boats in small-scale fishing, as this remains open access. There is some attempt to regulate capacity in industrial fishing such that licenses are issued on the basis of vessel gross registered tonnage and aimed to allocate different-sized vessels to various zones of the EEZ, but of course the problem is implementation.[8]

The seasonal ban (June–August) to protect spawning fish coincides with the monsoon squalls and makes fishing difficult. In this case, nature comes to the aid of policy. We observed this in the shape of empty fish auction halls, inactive processing plants, and grounded fishermen repairing boats and nets. While the ban applies to sea-going vessels, it does not prevent shore fishing by locals, including in the shrimp breeding grounds.[9]

Participatory (Community Based) Fisheries: Literature Review[10]

The three related themes in this review are the state's commercial fishing policies that undermine the livelihoods of artisanal fishermen; the importance of using local stakeholder knowledge and; the need to empower fisherfolk communities whose livelihoods depend on the resource that needs to be sustained through some form of participatory governance. The activities of the PFF are assessed in relation to these criteria below.

The opening up of deep-sea waters to commercial fishing is fairly recent in South Asia. Sann (1997) assessed the consequent threats to fishing communities and documented the marginalization of traditional fisherfolk. Among the reasons for the degradation of fisheries globally and in Pakistan is the pressure to boost exports. Despite the decline in marine fish catch production in Pakistan, FAO statistics, reported in Appendix Table 7.4, show a continuous rise in exports from $50 million in 1981 to $459 million in 2018.[11] Using peak marine capture production in 1993 as the base, there was a decline in catch of 24% from the base year to 2018. However, exports increased from the base year to 2018 by 168%.[12]

Ibarra et al. (2000) and Thorpe et al. (2000) discussed overcapitalization and overfishing in Latin America, as driven by neoliberal export promotion. Young (2001) recognized in this context that the state pursues conflicting aims of short-term growth maximization and long-term resource conservation. It is of course the latter which maximizes the net present value by making fisheries sustainable, but the state deviates from such policy of conservation due to short-term pressures to secure foreign exchange or political collusion with vested interests. Young (2001, p. 284) cited the concept of the "tragedy of incursion" as being more relevant for resource degradation than fisherfolk-induced "tragedy of the commons" when referring to state-induced outside encroachment on local fishing grounds.

Recognizing the threat that commercial fishing policies pose to the biological stock Federal Governments have, in parallel, tried to institute top-down regulations aimed at conserving biological stock.[13] Beddington and Rettig (1983) argued that such regulations would not address complex socio-economic problems of those dependent on fisheries. Similarly, Aguero and Costello (1986) noted that the problems associated with fisheries are seldom solved by focusing simply on fishery management plans.

Ostrom (1990) argued that conservation of natural resources was easier when local communities were actively involved in the process (also see conceptual framework, Chapter 2). Similarly, Bromley (1992) argued that individuals cooperate to conserve an open access resource (OAR) when they are able to design, monitor, and enforce rules regulating how members utilize and allocate natural resources. Tokrisna and Duangsawasdi (1992, p. 537) viewed the communities as:

> [having the] necessary information on the resources and their exploitation such that, within the rights they have been granted, they can perform the necessary management functions such as limiting entry, fishing gear regulation, collection of resource rent, and benefit distribution.

The various readings compiled by Neis and Lawrence (2000) discussed integrating local knowledge into science and management in various contexts. The benefits they identified include anticipating and preempting stock declines rather than merely explaining them ex post.[14] An example of the successful working of a local Customary Marine Tenure (CMT) system for conservation was documented by Hviding and Baines (1994). Notably, the system in Marovo, Soloman Islands, provided for "stock rotation, periodic reef closures, community involvement, group control, stock monitoring, ecological knowledge and understanding, and owners involved as managers" (p. 32). The authors also documented how adaptable these local systems are.

Another example of a successful CMT in Papua New Guinea was provided by Asafu-Adjaye (2000). He argued that research by social anthropologists showed that, like the societies from which they come, these systems are highly adaptive and that they thrive on local environmental knowledge amassed over a long period of time. These systems not only control access to resources, but also include policing and monitoring.

Satria and Matsida (2004) documented that a local institution and monitoring and policing based on that was effective in overcoming destructive fishing practices like blast and poison fishing in a coastal region of Indonesia. However, the authors pointed out that this devolution of authority to the local level was by chance rather than by design because of a governance vacuum. Nonetheless, this success made the case for community management of fisheries.

Involving communities in participatory governance can take various forms including community-based governance and co-management. Pauly and Chuenpagdee (2007, p. 178) acknowledged that the virtual consensus on community-based management is based on solid reasoning and evidence but sounded a word of caution. They argued that without formal property rights, fisherfolk behave as do owners of large fleets that are run according to maximization principles.[15]

Kalikoski and Allison (2010) suggested that co-management is likely to be more effective if the approach is adaptive, builds on social integration, is sensitive to local power structures to prevent capture and devolves power in addition to responsibilities. Bene (2009) suggested, based on a review of two decades of participatory initiatives in fishery management in Sub-Saharan Africa, that the real issue was "downward accountability" without which participatory approaches were meaningless.

Much of the literature assesses success based on stock conservation. If stocks are sustained, this also enhances fisherfolk well-being in the long run. Schons et al. (2020) viewed the household as the unit of analysis for a cost–benefit study. They assessed the success of collective action for individuals based on fisherfolk time saving in the floodplains of the Amazon river in Brazil. While the property rights of communities were of late well-defined, there was no state enforcement and hence the need for community accords for resource conservation. These accords established rules associated with restrictions on fishing gear, catch quantity and size, and/or fishing seasons and defined punishment measures for those who violated agreements. Their quantitative findings showed that while in the short run there was a cost in terms of participating in enforcing accords, in the long run this freed up significant time on average for the households since more robust stocks resulted in less time spent in attaining success in fishing. The time saved could then be used for other, including income earning, activities.

The issues identified in this brief literature review play out in this study of fishery degradation and echo the literature review on participatory development in Chapter 2 (conceptual framework). They also play out in community-based fishery in Pakistan as indicated in the account of the state of marine fisheries in Pakistan above and the account of Pakistan Fisheries Forum (PFF) below. We turn now to a review of our research method.

Research Method

This chapter draws on qualitative information gathered on site in July 2005. Our instruments included a semi-structured household survey, focus group discussions, stakeholder interviews, participant observation, and interviews conducted by one of the authors with officials of the relevant agencies charged with managing fisheries. The household survey gathered information on income, assets, credit, indebtedness, technology, marketing, and other local institutions. The fieldwork was conducted in fishing villages in Karachi (Sindh) and Gwadar and Pasni (Balochistan).

The fishing villages selected in Karachi were Ibrahim Hyderi and Rehri Goth. The selection was made on the suggestion of the Pakistan Fisherfolk Forum (PFF), which considered these two adjacent villages ideal for the type of information we were seeking. Both villages combine to form the largest marine fisherfolk settlement in Sindh. Similarly, the majority of Balochi fishermen live in Gwadar and its surrounding villages/towns of Pasni, Surbandar, and Jiwani, and hence we selected this area for study. Our guides classified fishing households by income and we interviewed ten low income, ten middle-income, and four high-income households in each of the two provinces, for a total of 48.

Six focus group discussions (FGDs) were conducted; the provincial distribution was four in Sindh and two in Balochistan, with the size of the groups varying from 10 to 15. The villages were in Mubarik, Hawks Bay, Ibrahim Hyderi, and Rehri Goth in Karachi District and Surbandar and Pasni in Gwadar District.

Twelve stakeholder interviews were conducted, including with representatives of the fishing communities, *moles* (auctioneers), PFF, Fishermen Co-operative Society (FCS), Balochistan Coastal Development Authority (BCDA), Marine Fisheries Department (MFD), Balochistan Planning and Development Department (BP&DD), fish processing units, Societe Generale de Surveillance, the policy community, and academics.

Findings: Sources of Vulnerability for Fisherfolk

The information on traditional fishing methods is drawn mostly from interviews with representatives of the Pakistan Fisherfolk Forum (PFF), members of the fishing community, and fisheries department staff.

Unsustainable fishing methods/technologies[16]

A stated reason for unsustainable harvesting was the rapid influx of new fishing methods and technologies which began to replace traditional practices. This influx reflected a policy-market nexus as well as livelihood concerns. Efforts to maintain livelihoods in the face of indebtedness and declining catches appeared to force local fishermen into using inappropriate methods.

Traditional fishing methods were environmentally friendly, defined as not harmful to the ecosystem or sea beds and also sustaining species stocks. Nets, made of *resham* (silk) or *latha* (a cotton variety), were used for stationary fishing and had a sufficiently wide mesh (2.4–6 inches) to release the small fry. These materials were also used for the *thukri*, a shrimp net used in small boats (18–25 feet), and those for hand casting. A similar type of net and one used for the same purposes was called *phat*. Another type of casting net was called the "bin" net. This net was used to catch fish along the coastline. The *dori* was used for creek fishing. *Rach lara, lathay ka ban* (gill net) was used on medium-sized boats (25–35 feet) and launches which fished the buffer zone (between 12–35 nautical miles). Yet another type of environmentally friendly net, the *jhaari*, was no longer in use. In addition, fishermen used the common hook and line method, i.e., a baited line with a single, a few, or many hooks.

Environmentally harmful nets were inducted in an effort to increase fish catches. These were made of nylon, had a fine mesh, and caught small fry. The translucent nylon allowed fishing both by day and night time. These nets were prone to rip off coral that subsequently washed up on the beach. The mechanization of boats and launches permitted mobility and the increasing use of winches accelerated the pace of fishing and encouraged the use of bigger nets.

Examples of the destructive nets being used include the *bhulo gujja* (tidal trap net) which was a fine mesh cone net made of nylon with the mesh getting finer toward the cone. The net was tied by wire cords to two iron rods, which were embedded in the creek mouth. While the net was meant for shrimp, small fry got trapped in the fine mesh and decomposed. The net was introduced by migrant Bangladeshi fishermen but the uptake by local fishermen was rapid. A variant was the *chappal gujja*, which was tied along the seashore near mangroves and caught juvenile and small shrimp. The *dooboo* fishing method, whereby fish was caught during the time of day they breed and feed, led to hampering the growth of stock.

Launch *gujja* was a larger version of the *bhulo gujja* and was used on medium size and large boats and launches (35 feet and beyond). It was a drag or trawling net made of thicker nylon but the mesh was still fine and trapped fry. The net scraped the ocean floor and damaged the fish habitat. According to Mohammad Ali Shah, Chairman PFF, this net was first introduced in 1951 but had begun to rapidly replace the gill net. The use of these nets and winches earned these traditional launches the pseudonym of "mini deep-sea launches." *Qatra* (fine mesh net, also referred to as a wire net) was used in medium and large-sized boats and launches to catch trash fish, mostly sardines, which were converted to chicken feed. This was also a factor in fish stock depletion because sardines were a source of food for larger fish.

"Plastic nets" is the term used for fine mesh nylon nets used in Balochistan. They came in all sizes and were used in small and medium-sized boats. They were originally introduced at the turn of the century by the migrant Bangladeshi community, working under contract to the processing plants to catch Indian mackerel, ribbon fish, and sole for export largely to the Far East. In time, they were adopted more widely.

Our interviewees informed us that deep-sea trawlers use a variety of nets including trawl liners, bag type trawl nets, and hooked rope nets (used by long liners). Foreign trawlers were issued licenses by the Federal Government to fish beyond 12 nautical miles offshore. The combination of wire nets and winches to carry out bottom dragging for up to a month at a time destroyed coral reef systems and marine life on the sea bed. After indiscriminately catching all species, since bottom dragging does not allow for targeted fishing, only the desired fish (often those not subject to duty) were kept and the rest (up to 90% of the total catch) thrown back into the water.

Poverty-Resource Degradation Nexus

As indicated in the introduction, poverty is viewed by some scholars to contribute to resource degradation and vice versa. This vicious cycle is referred to in the literature as the poverty-environment nexus in the context of resource degradation and is viewed as also applying to the behavior of poor coastal fishing communities (Cavendish [2000] and Dasgupta, et al. [2005]). We explain below that this nexus is complex and emanates from local institutions of credit and marketing.

In the absence of readily available institutional credit, the fisherman's only recourse was the informal credit system. A combination of technology upgrades and rising costs made local fishermen increasingly dependent on loans to finance their capital expenditures (boats, launches, nets, and engines) and running expenses (boat maintenance, net and engine repairs, ice, fuel, and food). The loan repayment conditions required the fisherman to pay a commission on their catch until they paid off their entire debt. This commission did not result in a reduction of the principal, which was required to be paid separately.

This system had several variants, all of them exploitative but in differing degrees. The exploitation in this context had two components. First, it resulted from the interrelated imperfections in the credit and product markets. Thus, there was a differential between the interest paid on loans, because the credit market was imperfect, and the lower interest rates fishermen could get if there were more sources for loans—in other words, a more perfect credit market. Second, the market value of the fish was higher if the fisherfolk were not constrained to sell to creditors. The various credit arrangements are briefly explained below.

In the commission system, the *nakhuda* (launch or boat captain) owned his vessel and equipment (net and engine), but borrowed from the *mole* (auctioneer) or *beopari (middle man)* to meet running expenses. He was not compelled to sell to the same *mole* or *beopari* but had to pay interest (varying from 5% to 10% of the value of the catch) as repayment for the loan until the principal was paid off.

In the *gaatu* system the *nakhuda* did not own a fishing vessel and equipment or have funds for the running costs. He secured both through a loan from a *mole* or a *beopari*, who provide the upfront capital and loans for operating expenses. When a mole lent to a fisherman, the latter was constrained to auction his catch through him and pay him a higher commission (7%).

The *mole* also under-weighed the catch as explained by Brohi (2000). Baskets of various sizes were used for bringing the catch to the auction. It was up to the *mole* to guess the weight of the basket, which was subtracted from the weight of the fish auctioned. All this was done on the basis of a rough estimate. The fishermen complained that they sustained losses as a result of a deliberately faulty estimate.

In the *pati* system (*pati* means share), the *nakhuda* hired *khilasis* (fishermen) to assist him with various chores while out at sea, including rowing, steering, fishing, cleaning, and salting. The trips were sometimes short (a single day) or, in the case of large launches, extended up to two months. The net earnings (after deducting costs) were divided into *patis.* If the *nakhuda* was the owner, he got 4.5 shares (one for the boat, one for the engine, one for the net, and 1.5 for his expertise). If the boat was leased from an investor, the lessor got three *patis*, while the *nakhuda* got 1.5 *patis.* The *khilasis* got 1 *pati* each. The monetary value of the share naturally varied with the volume and price of the catch. The term for loss was *lada*. If, for instance, a trip costs Rs. 50,000/- and the catch sells for Rs. 40,000/- the lada amounts to Rs. 10,000/-.

Pathans (immigrants from North-West Pakistan) engaged in the practice of loan-sharking and charged extortionate interest rates (up to 10% a month) for running expenses, often deducting a portion up front as advance repayment. The loan shark was the lender of last resort, since rates were extortionate and repayments time-bound. Prevented from being market players, fishermen locked into this nexus of dependence got the lowest effective returns on their catch.

The situation in Sindh was more stressed than in Balochistan. Rising capital and running costs, and the increasing frequency of *ladas*, combined to create a situation where fishermen were unable to repay their running costs, with the result that their debts mounted. There was also a surge of investments in boats and launches, both by investors and local *beoparis*, which contributed to overfishing and losses.

The fish marketing system was complex, involving *moles*, *beoparis*, and fishermen. The process reflected the impact of the credit systems described above. It also varied by species of fish, type of net used, and whether the fish were exported, consumed locally, or both. Karachi is the main fish market in Pakistan, both for fresh and saltwater species, as well as the country's only legal export outlet. The Karachi harbor was inaugurated in 1951 and its marketing functions were handed over to the Fishermen Co-operative Society (FCS), which predated the harbor. The society introduced an auctioning system, to be managed by its designated *moles* registered with the FCS. The harbor had about 45 moles working full time. In order to regulate marketing, the system was made mandatory in both Sindh and Balochistan.

The Gwadar harbor had 11 active *moles*, but these fell under the jurisdiction of the harbor authority. *Moles* were present in smaller numbers at the jetties in the smaller coastal villages and they also played the role of salaried *munshis* (managers) for prosperous and influential individuals, referred to in local parlance as *seths* (businessmen, investors) or *waderas* (landlords). While the initial membership fee for a *mole* was nominal (Rs. 15,000), a sufficiency of capital was required to become a *mole* in order to provide loans to fishermen for their running expenses.

A *mole* was allotted a space in the auction hall where he auctioned the fish unloaded at the jetty by boats and launches. The *beoparis* bid for lots and could sell successful bids to the processing plants or in the local market to both retailers and wholesalers. The *mole* also doubled as a commission agent, collecting money from *beoparis* and paying it to the fishermen for a commission. In this regard, the *mole* could inject stability into the process by ensuring that fishermen got paid.

Other parallel marketing systems were also in place that bypassed the *mole*. In Sindh, a category of small *beopari* called *vichaatey* purchased fish directly from fishermen. The *vichaatey* worked on behalf of large *beoparis* who in turn supplied processing plants exporting fish and shrimp. Alternatively, they converted trash fish into chicken feed. The *vichaatey* charged the large *beoparis* a commission between 5% and 10%. In Gwadar, the processing plants designated *beoparis* who bought fish directly from the fishermen.[17]

The presence of these marketing systems suggested different pricing arrangements whereby exploitation varied directly with indebtedness. The *vichaatey* assured competitive prices by virtue of their numbers; our informants expressed no concern about price collusion. They charged their costs to the *beopari*—who they often worked for. This was the closest to a fair return to poor local fishermen. However, the *vichaatey* were illegal and their ability to operate depended on patronage.

The option of going through the *mole* was less preferred because of the mandatory commission and the delayed payments. Under the *mole* system, fair returns to fishermen were only possible for those who were debt free or able to repay their loans within the season. Indebtedness ensured a steady supply of fish for the *mole* since the fishermen were constrained to auction their fish through him. In this case, the fishermen got a lower actual price for the fish due to the deductions (commission and debt repayment).

Alternatively, fishermen took loans directly from the *beoparis* (back-stopped by the processing plants). In general, this was a preferred arrangement as it meant an avoidance of commission payments and also immediate cash payments to fishermen upon delivery. This practice was prevalent in Gwadar for fish that were frozen and exported to the Far East, including Indian mackerel, ribbon fish, sole, and crabs. As it was a "demand pull" arrangement, the *beopari* did not impose extortionate terms. However, this arrangement coexisted in an uneasy relationship with the mandatory auction system.

Fishermen became very vulnerable when the debt to the *mole* exceeded a certain limit because further loans could be discontinued. The fishermen then turned to the *beoparis*, who were still willing to provide loans but they ensured repayment through a lower price for the fish they purchased. This growing cycle of indebtedness and distress pricing was evident in Sindh, especially among the small fishermen, who were struggling to cope in a regime of declining fish catches and mounting debt.

There is an obvious empirical link between poverty and indebtedness. The debt to income ratios for the low, middle, and higher income groups in our sample were 3.27, 1.46, and 0.38, respectively. Even the smallest boats required substantial capital and running cost outlays. For example, the poorest fisherman, who owned a small boat, first spent Rs. 200,000/- to Rs. 300,000/- to construct the boat and spent Rs. 500–600 on every fishing trip. During the fishing season, he made at least 20 such one-day trips, averaging about Rs.10,000 per month. Rising costs and decreasing catches resulted in falling income levels and increased indebtedness.[18]

Overfishing in the Sindh coastal waters and the consequent fish stock depletion encourage local launch owners to intrude into the more productive Balochi waters. The Federal and Provincial maritime agencies and departments are known to collude in this practice by taking informal pay-offs (between US$500–650 per trip at the time of the survey).[19] Not only do these launches catch fish illegally, but their drag nets also cut the smaller stationary nets of the small boat fishermen.

On occasion, communities resorted to violent collective action to assert their resource rights. For instance, the Pasni fishermen first reported violations to the authorities. Absent a response, they took matters into their own hands and impounded the fishing nets of the Sindh launches claiming they were asserting their rights under customary law.

Existing fishing policies made matters worse for marginalized fisherfolk. The Maritime Security Agency required prior security clearances to allow fishermen access to waters around the port. Federal and Provincial fishing policies, through both intent (zoning lows) and default, supported commercial interests at the expense of environmental and livelihood concerns (see above).

Changes in fishing policy and practice also marginalized women. Previously they participated fully in the fishing activities of the community, thanks to the absence of imposed gender distinctions. When fishing was productive and catches were close to shore, women used to go out in the boats, fish, and return before nightfall. On occasion, they even camped overnight on the offshore islands. However, as the fertile fishing grounds were pushed further seaward, security concerns confined them to the shore. As traditional fishing methods gave way to mechanized ones, and transactions become commercialized, the women's role in making and mending nets, taking the catch to market, and other supportive functions were reduced.[20] Notwithstanding the adversity faced by the fisherfolk documented in this section, the resilience of fishing communities, to which women contribute enormously, was very much in evidence during our fieldwork despite the economic disempowerment of these communities.[21]

Apart from the poverty-environment nexus, there are other causes of fishery degradation resulting from policy failures that reinforce the vicious cycle of the nexus. These were discussed in some detail in Khan and Khan (2011) and included mangrove destruction due to fresh water capture (dams and barrages), unchecked oil spills, industrial, agricultural, and household effluents, and run-offs into the mangrove and coastal waters. The next section assesses the collective action of the Pakistan Fisherfolk Forum (PFF) in addressing the concerns of poor fisherfolk identified in this section.

The Pakistan Fisherfolk Forum

The PFF, founded in 1998, is a community-based organization which has engaged in numerous campaigns on behalf of fisherfolk interests. Its wide-ranging mandate has included fishery policy reform, agitation against both state-engineered processes of resource capture and direct appropriation by powerful interests, and promotion of participatory fishery management. On its website, it claims a membership of 100,000 (35% female), and an agenda pertaining to "policy issues relating to fishing rights, fish marketing & fish conservation, rehabilitation of the

Indus Delta, sustainable fisheries policy, abolition of the contract system over inland waters, historical fishing rights on entire water bodies for indigenous fishers, discouraging industrial fishing by deep sea trawlers, [addressing] marine pollution, [and] detention of fishermen."[22]

While some of SAFI's successes were widely acknowledged, it has been more difficult to access PFF's success. However, since PFF now has a membership of 100,000 compared to 5000 for SAFI, it has more potential street power to get its campaigns heard by the press and policymakers.[23] PFF has not been sparing in using this potential and many of its campaigns have got widespread press coverage. We note some of the prominent ones below starting with policy advocacy.

PFF's policy advocacy has centered around formulating a sustainable fisheries policy. It is the only comprehensive document of its kind that exists in Pakistan presently. The policy is based on local voices and is geared toward addressing the problems of local fishermen. This initiative on the part of PFF is also important as it represents a serious effort from civil society to improve governance and policymaking processes in the provincial government. The draft policy is broadly based on principles of sustainable ecosystem management. It envisages "to protect fisherfolk communities livelihoods resources in the country, bring sustainability in the fisheries resources of Pakistan for the present as well as coming generations and ensure complete protection and rehabilitation of the coastal as well as freshwater biodiversity." The proposed measures of the policy are reported in Appendix 7.1.

PFFs efforts to counter resource capture in its various manifestations confront almost insurmountable obstacles. These are posed by the formidable power nexus between foreign and domestic investors, real estate developers, feudal land owners, and the Federal and Sindh Provincial Governments, which inject legal legitimacy and provide administrative support for land and sea water encroachments by these entities. Notwithstanding these obstacles, PFF has pressed on with limited financial, legislative, and legal recourse. PFF advocacy takes the shape of research and documentation, seminars and workshops, media campaigns and protest marches.

A city plan, passed by the Sindh Assembly in the form of the Zulfiqarabad Development Authority Bill, 2012 and subsequently approved by the Sindh cabinet, entails building a megacity situated on four tehsils in the Thatta District deltaic region. Ostensibly the aim is to bring a vast acreage of barren land under cultivation, provide jobs for potential migrants to Karachi, and establish markets for agricultural produce from the hinterland and for sea food catches. In reality it amounts to a land grab by a cartel of Chinese investors and local real estate developers, backed by the Provincial Government. The proposed megacity will not only displace upward of 280,000 local residents but place their livelihoods derived from fishing at risk.

PFF rejected the Zulfiqarabad City Plan stating at the outset that it was developed unilaterally without consulting the potentially affected communities. Had such consultations taken place the PFF, as the community's representative, would have outlined the plan's ecological, economic, social and procedural anomalies. The precedent for such mandatory consultations is embedded in international conventions such as, among others, the International Bill for Human Rights and the ILO Convention requiring the participation of indigenous people in the formulation, evaluation, and implementation of national and regional development plans. Further, the city plan did not secure the approval of the Executive Committee of the National Economic Council (ECNEC) which is mandatory for projects costing more than half a billion rupees.

The PFF pointed out that over three-quarters of a million hectares of coastal land including mangrove forests would be affected and this would negatively impact carbon sinks and migratory bird habitats. This would be in direct violation of national forestry laws as well as international conventions such as the Convention on Biodiversity, Convention on International Trade in Endangered Species, the Ramsar Convention (on wetlands), and the United Nations Framework Convention on Climate Change. They also pointed to potential natural hazards in the proposed city site from seismic activity, flash floods, and cyclones, all of which had occurred with high intensity in the area in the last three decades. Finally, the PFF cautioned that not only would the planned city cause extensive ecological damage but it would engender large-scale displacements via property appropriation, forced evictions, coerced land sales, and, in the extreme, violence.

Another recent campaign (October 2020) involved a Federal Government Ordinance to develop two islands (with Chinese assistance) of the Karachi coast via a Presidential Ordinance. These islands, Bundal and Bhuddo, were previously under Sindh Provincial Government's jurisdiction. These islands are located at the mouth of Korangi Creek and are spread over 10,000 acres. The Federal Government aims to invest $50 billion in building a modern city that "would surpass Dubai." The islands are transit areas for fishermen heading out to sea and have become no-go areas, replicating earlier restrictions on access along the coast in Gizri Creek and Phutti Island, which have now become elite recreational sites.

The Presidential Ordinance resulted in a political uproar with Sindh based and other opposition parties opposing the move. PFF opposed the move because it views such development as a source of marine pollution and a threat to island mangroves. A 2008 WWF survey[24] recorded a mangrove cover of 3,349 hectares on the Islands. In addition, 96 fish and 54 bird species along with three species of marine dolphins and turtles are located in the Island sites. Not only would city development endanger these species and forests it would deprive almost 80,000 fisherfolk of their livelihoods, their access to already depleted offshore fishing areas, and destroy the islands' efficacy as buffers against sea intrusion and cyclones. The PFF launched the Save the Sea Islands Movement, and organized a flotilla off Bundal to protest the Ordinance.[25]

The head of the PFF also pointed out that it had successfully contributed to blocking the Federal Government attempts to develop the islands thrice in the past. Their legal case was that the islands are part of the Indus river delta on which construction is prohibited by the constitution. Also, the islands are within 12 miles of the coastline and hence fall under Provincial and not Federal jurisdiction. In 2000, a company from Thailand was given permission to build a town on an island but the plan folded after resistance. In 2006, Aamar, a company from Dubai, was hired by the Federal Government, but after protests, that plan was shelved again. In 2013, Bahria Town, a military construction company, was given permission to build a city on one of the islands but the Supreme Court revoked it.[26]

The PFF holds annual events on World Fisheries Day in concert with similar events launched globally. The event draws attention to overfishing, habitat destruction, and other serious threats to the sustainability of marine and fresh water resources. It also highlights the critical importance of water to human and other species. The event comprises seminars and formal and informal gatherings conducted across the affected districts of Sindh. The attendance at these events is invariably large and diverse, consisting of concerned government officials, civil society activists, NGO's, media representatives, teachers, advocates, and fisherfolk community. The themes vary every year; in 2016 the focus was on "action against ocean grabbing" and "illegal occupation of inland water bodies."

In 2017, the mobilization and awareness raising phase for the campaign started on February 10 and continued until March 6 and the PFF estimated having sensitized 20,000 people including fisherfolk, academics, religious leaders, government officers, and media personnel. The second phase of this campaign (March 7–March 14) started with a 100-person (50 females) caravan that marched across Sindh for awareness raising in fisherfolk and peasant communities where they received warm welcomes. The march culminated in a people's assembly of 5,000 PFF members on March 14, 2017, the International Day of Action for Rivers.[27] The main demand was for allowing more water to flow into the delta.[28] Action by civil society organizations, including prominently the PFF, has made building more dams difficult for the government.[29] The PFF believes that over the course of Pakistan's short history dating back to 1947, the government has built a series of dams and barrages. By doing so, it has diverted the natural flow of the River Indus, destroyed the rivers' ecology, and resulted in sea water intrusion and the destruction of mangrove forests and biodiversity since not enough fresh water flows into the delta. This dam and barrage construction has therefore displaced fisherfolk whose livelihood depends on the rivers and the delta.

In September 2020, twenty Chinese trawlers docked in Karachi harbor. The chairperson of the PFF, Muhammad Ali Shah, was deeply concerned that the Federal Government, beholden in many ways to the

Chinese government, was planning to grant deep-sea fishing rights to Chinese companies. This concern stemmed from his belief that these trawlers would destroy the livelihoods of almost two million coastal fisherfolk. In response, the PFF took the matter to court which in turn asked the government to take all stakeholders into confidence about the issue. Environmentalists supported the PFF and other fisherfolk associations confirming that the Chinese companies would deplete fish, shrimp, and other marine life and also damage the marine ecosystem.[30]

As pointed out above, the PFF is in no position to take on powerful vested interests (launch owners, land developers, feudal lords) backed by the Federal and Provincial governments. However, through its advocacy and awareness raising campaigns it strives to keep more forward-looking government officials, the donor community, and the media abreast of developments and depredations that affect the fishing communities. A notable achievement such events have triggered is donor/NGO-initiated mangrove plantations along the coast with its beneficial backward and forward linkages.

Summary and Conclusions

While the findings above suggest that poor fishing communities do degrade resources, we have demonstrated that this poverty-environment nexus is a response induced by policies and institutions. As we noted, Federal and Provincial fishing policies, through both intent and default, support commercial interests at the expense of environmental and livelihood concerns. Zoning laws, imperfect credit markets, and price manipulation by the processing plants, middlemen, and the sea lords lead to reduced catches and low returns on these catches. Consequently, poor fishermen resort to environmentally harmful technologies to sustain themselves.

This powerful motivation to do what is necessary, including destructive netting practices, to sustain families will remain. Policy needs to be tailored to this reality. Rather than arbitrarily banning the use of harmful nets, a ban which is more likely to be honored in the breach, a more promising alternative is state-supported, community-based micro-credit, whose uptake is rapidly expanding in Pakistan.[31] Once the credit and vulnerability issues are addressed, the imperfections in the product market can also be resolved. Monopsonistic market power results from credit dependency, and, once that problem is resolved, the institutions to ensure a fair market price are already present.

Via community mobilization, with the collective action efforts of the Pakistani Fisherfolk Forum, an accord could be reached with the fisher-folk that gives them a policing role to reverse unsustainable practices. As indicated in our literature review, communities are better able to police and sustain resources that their livelihoods depend on. Participatory approaches or co-management frameworks tapping local knowledge have been found effective in many countries.

While the poverty-resource degradation nexus is one source of the problem, others such as pollution, fresh water capture (via dams) and mangroves degradation, unsustainable foreign exchange-driven fishing policy, and jurisdictional overlaps (between the Provincial and Federal Governments) also need to be addressed. If these sources of fishery degradation are successfully addressed, it will also simultaneously attenuate the poverty-resource degradation nexus. The vulnerability of the Bangladeshi community also needs to be addressed. States have the right to check entry, but they should grant dignity and security and to those already present. Doing so in this case would remove another source of pressure on fisheries.

Acknowledgements This chapter is based on Khan and Khan (2011). Our thanks go to all the stakeholders we engaged with during the fieldwork. We are particularly indebted to the fishing communities for letting us into their lives and inspiring us with their courage in the face of adversity.

Notes

1. Since UN agencies like the FAO, rely on national government sources, the discrepancy is puzzling. We were unable to procure more recent government data.
2. Shahid Shah, "Pakistan's seafood catch has declined by 29 pc in a decade" *The News International*, April 21, 2010.
3. Mohammed Ali Shah, the founder of the PFF, was born to a poor fisher family, educated himself and mobilized fisher communities over a prolonged period during which he faced obstacles including imprisonment. For details, refer to https://www.thenews.com.pk/archive/print/105620-mohammad-ali-shah-voice-of-the-fishermen, consulted 11/10/2020.
4. http://www.fao.org/fishery/facp/PAK/en, consulted 10/20/2020.
5. https://dhsprogram.com/pubs/pdf/FR29/03Chapter3.pdf, consulted 10/20/2020.
6. The Fisherman Co-operative Society was founded in 1945, originally as the Karachi Fishermen's Cooperative Purchase and Sale Society Ltd. It is situated at the Karachi Fish Harbor. The objectives of the Society are to ensure the welfare of, and provide benefits to, the poor fishermen by supplying them with basic amenities (for example, nets) at cheaper prices. The society's board of directors consists of 15 directors, seven of whom are elected by members and eight are nominated by the government. Under the terms of the FCS agreement, moles (fish auctioneers) generally receive a 6.25% commission on the auction of the catch, half of which they pay to the FCS.
7. http://extwprlegs1.fao.org/docs/pdf/pak150786.pdf, consulted 10/20/2020.
8. http://www.fao.org/fishery/facp/PAK/en, consulted 10/20/2020.
9. Climate change seems to be negatively impacting marine fisheries given the increase in tropical storms and major floods in recent years. In this context, refer also to Pavithram et al. (2016) regarding the vulnerability of marine fisheries to climate in Kerela, India.
10. This review did not explore studies that quantitatively or qualitatively identified the determinants of Participation in community collective action for fishery conservation. Refer to Johnson (2001) for an example of one such qualitative study.

11. We assume the exports are in nominal terms since the FAO did not specify that they were real. Fishery exports from Pakistan amounted to about two percent of total exports in 2018.
12. The FAO statistics source cited in Appendix Table 7.4 indicates that, over the same period, per capita fish and fishery products in Pakistan declined from 2.7 to 1.9 metric tons despite the rapid increase in exports. Pakistan's population growth rate is much higher than comparator countries in South Asia. Based on the CIA factbook, Pakistan's population growth rate percentage for 2016 was 1.45 compared to 1.24 for Nepal, 1.19 for India, 1.05 for Bangladesh, and 0.8 for Sri Lanka, respectively.
13. Explaining this top-down approach a senior marine fisheries department official stated that artisanal fishermen degraded fish habitats via their netting practices.
14. While the focus of community fisheries in this chapter is on low- and middle-income countries, Wlatner-Toews et al. (2006) for example reflected on the case for, and method of, relying on local knowledge for fishery preservation in the context of a high-income country. Japan is known for local community involvement in marine fishery management and Yamamoto (1995) documented the evolution of this process.
15. Paul (2005) documented, based on a study of *kadakkodi* in Karela, India, challenges local institutions of fishery resource conservation and conflict resolution can face due to changes in resources, technology, and culture.
16. The practices referred to in this section have lasted generations and are likely to be extant. However, they have been referred to in the past tense since the fieldwork was not recent.
17. At Sorbandar, a fishing village in Balochistan, Iranian power boats entered Pakistani waters and bought fish directly off the fishermen at sea. This marketing phenomenon was an outlier. In this case the fishermen got a competitive price for their catch and were not required to pay a commission, but the volume of fish sold in this manner was extremely small.
18. Fisherfolk livelihoods were also threatened because of the lack of compliance of the final product with international food safety and sustainable harvesting standards. Food safety standards cover both pre-processing and processing activities. While processing plants tended to comply with food safety standards, primarily due to the threat of loss of market share, there was a lack of information and training provided to those further down the value chain. The EU banned seafood exports from Pakistan in April 2007 (delisted all 28 fish processing units). An EU mission was expected

November 16–27 to inspect the Karachi Harbor and consider lifting the ban but the visit was unexpectedly cancelled and the ban was still in effect at the time of our fieldwork. Shahid Shah, "EU team to inspect fish harbor in November," *The News International*, Saturday, October 31, 2009. The ban was finally lifted on March 12, 2013.

19. At the time of our fieldwork in 2005, one US $ was worth about 60 Pakistani rupees.
20. Mohammad Ali Shah of PFF documented how nylon nets displaced women's cotton net weaving and Bangladeshi labor displaced their post-harvest activities such as cleaning and drying, crab processing, and shrimp pealing, https://pff.org.pk/wp-content/uploads/2020/08/A-Bleak-of-Future-Women-in-Fishing.pdf, consulted 11/1/2020.
21. Globalization or commercially induced displacement of women in fishing activities is a common phenomenon in artisanal fisherfolk communities. There are several examples in a thematic issue of Development on gender and fisheries (Volume 51, Issue 2). In particular, Porter et al. (2008) documented how, in Tanzanian coastal communities, men took over octopus trapping from women as the commodification of a subsistence product made it more profitable.
22. https://pff.org.pk/about-pff/, consulted 11/1/2020. It has extended its mandate to include peasants and campaigns among other issues for land reform.
23. Of course one should not underestimate the public and policy attention that 5,000 *pathans*, willing to protect their interest militantly if necessary, can secure.
24. https://medium.com/panda-musings/building-a-paradise-f85f4859cfc0 and https://www.dawn.com/news/798984/wwf-concerned-over-island-projects, consulted 11/10/2020.
25. https://search-proquest-com.proxy.mtholyoke.edu:2443/abicomplete/docview/2450823491/4791F53381DD4A7BPQ/3?accountid=12605, consulted 11/2/2020.
26. https://search-proquest-com.proxy.mtholyoke.edu:2443/abicomplete/docview/2443863707/4791F53381DD4A7BPQ/6?accountid=12605, consulted 11/2/2020.
27. https://pff.org.pk/wp-content/uploads/2020/08/Caravan-Report.pdf, consulted 11/2/2020. This link documented the march with pictures.

28. As per the Water Apportionment Accord of 1991, Sindh demanded at least 10 MAF of water flow into the delta. Between the years 2000 and 2010, the highest number was 5.8 MAF in 2008–2009, with the lowest being 0.2 MAF in 2004–2005, https://www.dawn.com/news/1505725, consulted 11/2/2020.
29. The Kalabagh Dam, mooted for construction over four decades ago, has been indefinitely postponed.
30. https://search-proquest-com.proxy.mtholyoke.edu:2443/abicomplete/docview/2451138483/4791F53381DD4A7BPQ/2?accountid=12605, consulted 11/2/2020.
31. Khan and Ansari (2018) reviewed the literature and found interest-free loans, a microcredit variant developed by Akhuwat in Pakistan, very promising.

Appendix

PFF proposed fisheries policy

1. Determination of fisherfolks' rights
2. Fish stock survey
3. Rehabilitation of threatened species and heavily fished grounds
4. Introduction of sustainable fishing practices and fishing gear
5. Water allocation for biodiversity/fishing grounds
6. Water allocation for the Indus River delta
7. License system in fisheries livelihoods
8. Training and provision of alternative livelihoods
9. Improvements in marketing systems
10. Fish net manufacturing plants
11. Introduction of safety measures during fishing trips
12. Community-based sustainable aquaculture

13. Establishment of district-level fishermen cooperative societies
14. Registration of nets
15. Mangroves conservation
16. Alternative skill development training for fisherwomen
17. Ban on over fishing
18. Revision of deep-sea fishing policy
19. Proper implementation of ban on harmful nets
20. Representation of fisherfolk in the policy/decision-making bodies
21. Ban on the construction of new fishing boats
22. Rehabilitation of fishing communities affected due to large dams
23. Abolition of sea lords
24. Formation of trade unions and implementation of labor laws
25. Community-based natural resource management
26. Enhancing community participation and ownership
27. Reviving the institutional credit facility
28. Reduce and then eliminate by-catch practices

See Tables 7.1, 7.2, 7.3 and 7.4.

Table 7.1 Number of registered fishing vessels (1993–2003)

Vessels (Categories)	1993	1994	1995	1996	1997	1998	1999	2000	2001	2002	2003
Sindh											
Trawlers	2,028	2,245	2,252	2,310	2,427	2,522	2,564	2,570	2,611	2,677	2,702
Gill-netters	1,604	1,865	1,871	1,945	2,015	2,236	2,305	2,317	2,432	2,489	2,510
Motorized cum-sailing vessels	3,211	3,424	3,430	3,526	3,611	3,695	3,755	3,923	3,998	4,202	4,388
Sail boats (marine)	5,651	5,884	5,895	5,922	6,253	6,285	6,358	6,504	6,713	6,718	6,809
Total	12,494	13,418	13,448	13,703	14,306	14,738	14,982	15,314	15,754	16,086	16,409
Balochistan											
Trawlers	–	–	–	–	–	–	–	–	–	–	–
Gill-netters	765	860	941	1,019	1,111	1,162	1,295	1,329	1,389	1,680	1,508
Motorized cum-sailing vessels	3,313	3,552	3,826	4,022	4,195	4,250	4,279	4,314	4,372	4,227	4,463
Sail boats (marine)	142	89	23	26	39	39	25	29	34	33	25
Total	4,220	4,501	4,790	5,067	5,345	5,451	5,599	5,672	5,795	5,940	5,996
Total marine	16,714	17,919	18,238	18,770	19,651	20,189	20,581	20,986	21,549	22,026	22,405
Progressive addition		1,205	319	532	881	538	392	405	563	477	379

Source Government of Pakistan (2005)

Table 7.2 Marine catch by Province ('000 metric tons)

	1950	1960	1970	1980	1985	1990	1995	2000	2003
Sindh	26	46	102	175	229	260	281	294	271
Balochistan	11	16	37	58	94	107	123	130	127
EEZ	–	–	–	–	10	2	2	14	3
Total	37	62	139	233	333	370	406	438	401

Note EEZ = Exclusive economic zone
Source Government of Pakistan (2005)

Table 7.3 Declining yearly catch by fish species (metric tons)

Local Name	English Name	1993	1994	1995	1996	1997	1998	1999
Boi	Mullet	21,620	18,439	16,567	16,622	17,678	16,392	11,367
Tarli	Indian oil Sardinella	73,960	50,543	45,231	42,611	44,410	38,110	25,100
Padon	Thryssas	29,260	18,111	17,564	14,091	16,113	13,165	15,154
Palli	Clupeoidei nei	40,210	31,198	21,615	21,982	20,100	19,209	21,103
Kiddi	Kiddi shrimp	18,210	15,121	12,289	13,171	15,912	13,854	12,121

Source Government of Pakistan (2002)

Table 7.4 Update on Pakistani Fishery Statistics

	Fleet ('000)	Marine capture production ('000 metric tons)	Total exports of fish and fishery products (million $s)
1950	na	na	na
1960	na	na	na
1970	na	na	na
1980	na	215.5	50.0
1985	na	333.2	79.8
1990	na	350.6	93.5
1993	na	478.5	171.0
1994	na	400.5	152.0
1995	na	387.5	149.6
1996	na	376.7	131.6
1997	na	407.1	176.8
1998	na	416.6	135.2
1999	na	460.6	142.1
2000	34.1	422.3	149.8
2001	na	418.3	130.6
2002	na	420.6	130.9
2003	na	406.6	137.0
2004	na	401.1	152.4
2005	na	355.3	140.1
2006	na	366.5	196.1
2007	na	353.3	191.7
2008	na	362.7	193.2
2009	na	346.7	228.5
2010	35.2	340.2	265.9
2011	na	336.2	330.9
2012	35.8	356.0	331.9
2013	30.1	361.5	361.3
2014	31.6	351.9	382.4
2015	na	377.0	348.0
2016	na	379.5	352.0
2017	na	397.7	430.5
2018	na	363.6	459.0

Notes na = not available
Source FAO Fishery and Aquaculture Statistics, http://www.fao.org/fishery/facp/PAK/en, consulted 10/15/2020

References

Aguero, M.N., and G. Costello. 1986. Constraints to the Development of Effective Fisheries Management in the LDCs: Implications for Training and Research. In *Groupe d'etude des Resources Maritime, Proceedings of the International Conference on Fisheries*. Rimouski, Quebec, Canada: University of Quebec at Rimouski.

Asafu-Adjaye, J. 2000. Customary Marine Tenure Systems and Sustainable Fisheries Management in Papua New Guinea. *International Journal of Social Economics* 27 (7): 917–927.

Beddington, J.R. and B. Rettig. 1983. Approaches to the Regulation of the Fishing Effort, Fisheries Technical Paper. Rome: FAO.

Béné, C. 2009. Governance and Decentralization Reforms in Small-Scale Fisheries—An African Perspective. In *Fisheries, Sustainability and Development*, 253–266, Stockholm: Royal Swedish Academy.

Birwani, Z., A. Ercelawn, and M.A. Shah. 1999. *Sustainable and Just Livelihoods for Coastal Fisherfolk: Securing Rights in Environmental Law and Policy*, 1999. Karachi: Pakistan Institute of Labor Education and Research.

Brohi, S. 2000. Exploitative Nature of an Informal Credit System in Coastal Fisheries. *The Daily Dawn*, Karachi, October 7.

Bromley, D.W. 1992. The Commons, Property, and Common Property Regimes. In *Making the Commons Work: Theory Practice and Policy*, ed. D.W. Bromley, 3–15. San Francisco: Institute for Contemporary Studies Press.

Cavendish, W. 2000. Empirical Regularities in the Poverty-Environment Relationship of Rural Households: Evidence from Zimbabwe. *World Development* 28 (11): 1979–2033.

Dasgupta, S.U., M.C. Deichmann, and D. Wheeler. 2005. Where is the Poverty-Environment Nexus, Evidence from Cambodia, Lao PDR and Vietnam. *World Development* 33 (4): 617–638.

Government of Pakistan. 2005. *Hand Book of Fisheries Statistics of Pakistan.* Karachi: Marine Fisheries Department.

Government of Pakistan. 2002. *Handbook of Fisheries Statistics of Pakistan*, Vol. 18, Ministry of Food, Agriculture and, Co-operatives, Livestock Division, Islamabad.

Government of Pakistan. 1997. *Geological Survey of Pakistan*, 2nd edition, Islamabad.

Hviding, E. and G.B.K. Baines. 1994. Community-based Fisheries Management, Tradition and the Challenges of Development in Marovo, Solomon Islands. *Development and Change* 25 (1): 13–39.

Hutchings, J.A. and R.A. Myers. 1994. What Can Be Learned from the Collapse of a Renewable Resource—Atlantic Cod, Gaus Morhua of Newfoundland and Labrado. *Canadian Journal of Fish and Aquatic Science* 51 (9): 2126–2146.

Ibarra, A.A., C. Reid and A. Thorpe. 2000. Neo-Liberalism and Its Impact on Overfishing and Overcapitalization in the Marine Fisheries of Chile, Mexico and Peru. *Food Policy*, 25 (5): 599–622.

Johnson, C. 2001. Community Formation and Fisheries Conservation in Southern Thailand. *Development and Change* 32 (5): 951–974.

Kalikoski, D.C., and E.H. Allison. 2010. Learning and Adaptation; The Role of Fisheries Co-Management in Building Resilient Social-Ecological Systems. In *Adaptive Capacity and Environmental Governance*, ed. D. Armitage and R. Plummer, 69–88. London: Springer.

Khan, S.R. and Ansari, N. 2018. *A Microcredit Alternative in South Asia: Akhuwat's Experiment.* London: Routeledge.

Khan, Shaheen R., and Shahrukh R. Khan. 2011. Fishery Degradation in Pakistan: A Poverty–Environment Nexus? *Canadian Journal of Development Studies* 32 (1): 32–47.

Neis, B. and F. Lawrence. Eds. 2000. *Finding Our Sea Legs: Linking Fishery People and Their Knowledge with Science and Management.* St. John's, Newfoundland: Institute of Social and Economic Research.

Ostrom, E. 1990. *Governing the Commons: The Evolution of Institutions for Collective Action.* Cambridge: Cambridge University Press.

Paul, A. 2005.Rise, Fall, and Persistence in Kadakkodi: An Enquiry Into the Evolution of a Community Institution for Fishery Management in Kerala, India. *Environment and Development Economics* 10 (1): 33–51.

Pauly, D., and R. Chuenpagdee. 2007. Fisheries and Coastal Eco-Systems: The Need for Integrated Management. In *Sustainable Resource Management: Reality or Illusion?*, ed. P.N. Nemetz. Northhampton, MA: Edward Elgar.

Porter, M., et al. 2008. Globalization and Women in Coastal Communities in Tanzania. *Development* 51 (2): 193–198.

Salayo, N. et al. 2008. Managing Excess Capacity in Small-Scale Fisheries: Perspectives from Stakeholders in Three Southeast Asian countries. *Marine Policy* 32 (4): 692–700.

Sann, A. 1997. *A Livelihood from Fisheries: Globalization and Sustainable Fisheries Policies.* London: Intermediate Technology Publications.

Satria, A. and Y. Matsida. 2004. Decentralization Policy: An Opportunity for Strengthening Fisheries Management System? *The Journal of Environment & Development* 13 (2): 179–196.

Schonsa, S.Z.G. Amachera, K. Cobourna and C. Arantes. 2020. Benefits of Community Fisheries Management to Individual Households in the Floodplains of the Amazon River in Brazil. *Ecological Economics* 169 (March): 1–12.

Tokrisna, R. and M. Duangsawasdi. 1992. Thailand Experience in Fisheries Management. In *FAO/Japan Expert Consultation on the Development of Community-Based Coastal Fishery Management Systems for Asia and the Pacific*, FAO Fisheries Report No. 474, Vol. 2, 532–537. Rome: FAO.

Thorpe, A., A.A. Ibarra, and C. Reid. 2000. The New Economic Model and Marine Fisheries Development in Latin America. *World Development* 28 (9): 1689–1702.

Wlatner-Toews, D., L. Noronha, and D. Bavington. 2006. Science and Society in Place-Based Communities: Uncomfortable Partners. In *Interfaces Between Science and Society*, ed. A.G. Pereira, S.G. Vaz, and S. Tognetti. Sheffield: Greenleaf Publishing.

Yamamoto, T. 1995. Development of a Community-Based Fishery Management System. *Marine Resource Economics* 10 (1): 21–34.

Young, E. 2001. State Intervention and Abuse of the Commons: Fisheries Development in Baja California Sur, Mexico. *Annals of the Association of American Geographers* 91 (2): 283–306.

8

Defying the Military: Spontaneous Collective Action for Social Justice

Introduction

The Pakistani military[1] allots land near the Indian border to military personnel. The reasoning is that military personnel would have the capacity to be "first responders" as fighting men in case of enemy military action. This allocation includes non-commissioned soldiers and officers with allocations varying by seniority. While non-commissioned officers might settle on border farms, as was intended, senior military officers for the most part opt for various absentee tenure relationships in seeking the comforts of urban living.

Isolated stories started appearing in the press about these land allocations a few of which are introduced here. In Rakh (village) Azizabad and Rakh Sadiqabad (situated near Chowk (crossing) Munda, District Rajan Pur), 30 thousand acres of the land was allotted to in-service and retired military personnel in 2007. Many farmers had been cultivating this land for more than a century. The farmers reported that after the

This chapter drew on Khan and Akhtar (2014).

S. R. Khan and S. R. Khan, *Social Capital and Collective Action in Pakistani Rural Development*, https://doi.org/10.1007/978-3-030-71450-5_8

allotment military men accompanied by the police started to displace them. The farmers collectively resisted giving possession. Military officers who managed to occupy the land subsequently sold it. Other officers continued to try to occupy the land with the support of the police and met with much resistance and these protests were highlighted by leading newspapers (Daily Khabrain, Nawai-Wakt and Jang Multan, July 2, 2008; Daily Dawn March 20, 2009).

In Union Council Fateh Pur Air Force personnel were allotted 335 acres of mainly agricultural land in 2001. Without prior notice, the lands, houses, and shops of the local people cultivating and living on the land were bulldozed. People protested and took their complaints to the civilian officials but were not compensated for the land they had been cultivating for decades and those leading the protest were arrested.

In Rakh Kona, Tehsil Chobara, District Layyah, 20,500 acres of land was allotted to the military in 1982–1983 for a pittance of Rs. 146 per acre to be paid in installments over 20 years. In Rakh Jaded of the same Tehsil, 40,000 acres was allotted. The senior officers installed large boards as markers of ownership. Much of this land was subsequently contracted out for cultivation or sold at market prices. As usual, the land had been made cultivable by locals and their protests were unheeded.

The military is the most powerful and generally revered institution in the country. Indeed, given the long ongoing conflict with India, they are regarded as the saviors of the country and it is regarded as unpatriotic to write or speak against the army in particular and the military in general.[2] However, the perpetration of social injustice by the military led to spontaneous resistance on the part of the peasantry. We decided to explore the issue of military land allocations systematically and this chapter summarizes the key findings regarding social resistance to military high handedness.

In the rest of this chapter, we explain our research design and how it evolved. We discuss the institutional issues pertinent to our research including the conceptualization of the military land allotment scheme, the allocation process, legal issues including those pertaining to civil-military conflict and border Ranger[3] and police jurisdiction issues, and the scope of the border and non-border allocations. Next, we document the social resentment and spontaneous resistance to the military's land acquisitions. After that, we document peasant collective action that resulted in more organized resistance and some success in the fight for peasant rights. We end with an update on the most prominent of these social movements. In terms of the conceptual framework, Chapter 2, this chapter documents spontaneous collective action.

Evolving Research Design and Method

Before turning to documenting social resentment and resistance, our intention was to evaluate how productively the military farms were utilized relative to a control group. We originally intended to focus only on the border allocation scheme and to select a stratified random sample. The border allotments are made in a five-mile belt all along the Indian Pakistan border. In Punjab, this starts from Sialkot District in the north and ends with Rahim Yar Khan District to the south. The interim districts are Narowal, Sheikhupura, Lahore, Kasur, Okara, Bahawalnagar, and Bahawalpur. Not all land in this five-mile belt had been allocated at the time of our fieldwork and some of the land originally owned in this belt was under civilian ownership.

We expected to pick one district in Northern and one in Southern Punjab and subsequently randomly select tehsils, union councils, *patwari halqas*,[4] and finally farms as the unit of analysis. We hoped to get a sampling frame from the Border Area Committee (BAC) office that deals with border allocations. When the colonel who served as chairman of BAC blankly refused to provide any information, stating it was confidential, we ascertained that we could get this information from the copies of allocations retained by the Punjab Board of Revenue. However, here also we were not successful.

Not deterred, we decided to use a geographical map as the sampling frame. We expected to identify military farms and using a control group (non-military farm of the same size as close as possible), study issues of efficiency, tenure, treatment of cultivators, and possible asymmetrical access to and abuse of state resources. A pretest of instruments we went into the field with suggested that our quantitative focus was unlikely to yield much for both kinds of allocations.

First, each district has from two to six *tehsils*, each *tehsil* from four to six union councils, and each union council from one to five *patwari halqas*. Given our limited time and budget, we were unlikely to get many relevant farms in our sample from random selection. Second, not all *tehsils*, union councils, and *halqas* were relevant from the perspective of military allocations and our random selection may not have yielded much. Third, we discovered during the pre-tests that *patwaris* are not amenable to random selection. Securing information from them was a challenging endeavor and the recommendation of friends and acquaintances, preferably of those who have leverage, was often necessary. Fourth, and most important, many military men had either not claimed their land (below officer level) or sold it and those that had retained ownership were mostly contracting out on a fixed rent basis. Hence most of the tenure questionnaire and the access questionnaires we had developed were irrelevant.

We realized that we needed to maximize exposure to those areas in which allotments to military personnel had been made and land actually claimed. Thus, our focus shifted away from quantitative and comparative questions toward a more qualitative and suggestive study. In this vein, we also realized that exploring just the border allocations would be too limiting. We therefore broadened the scope of the research study to include all military land allocations in the Punjab.

It became clear within a fairly short period after we began our research that it was in non-border areas, particularly in southern and western parts of the province in which population density was lower and agricultural cultivation less intense, that the majority of new allotments were taking place. Allotments in highly arid, virtual desert zones such as Thal and Cholistan began in the 1950s and then intensified in later decades following the creation of the Thal Development Authority and Cholistan Development Authority, respectively. Allotments were being made in these regions because there was no longer that much available land in the canal irrigated districts of central Punjab.

Having started with a purist sample design constructed far from the field to yield statistically random data with which we would test economic hypotheses regarding farm efficiency (military vs. non-military), our methods and design changed considerably and the study became far more of an exploratory one.

In broad terms, we decided to explore social impacts and social responses to the military's land acquisitions and relate these to the themes of social justice. We added to these broad research questions in a spirit of "learning by doing" as our fieldwork progressed. For example, early on in the research process we found that paramilitary Rangers patrolling the border were an integral part of the military's burgeoning corporate empire and they had to be an important part of the story we were telling.

Thus, from structured and semi-structured questionnaires, our research method evolved to relying on key informant interviews and farmer and citizen group discussions. All the key informant interviews and group discussions were based on existing contacts; additional contacts were generated during the course of the initial meetings via a snowball method.

For the border allocations, we covered all the districts in the Punjab, though not all the *tehsils*. We used the same research method to explore non-border interventions and the military's collective allocations. In the case of non-border allocations, we cannot claim exhaustive coverage—we targeted what we thought were the most conspicuous examples in terms of scale as well as political controversy and social reaction generated.

Our pretest fieldwork spanned from May 31, 2010 to June 11, 2010. This included trips to the provincial capital for data and institutional information and the field test of instruments and exploration of data availability was done in Kasur District. By this time, we had determined what the substance of our research was going to be as explained above. The second intensive phase of the field work that included six field trips continued until July 21, 2010. The third and less intensive phase of the fieldwork continued until end of February 2011. In subsequent months we continued to follow media reports and also investigate interesting new leads wherever it was logistically feasible.[5]

Institutional Issues

Border Allocations

Army GHQ (General Head Quarter, Rawalpindi) manages border allocations with implementation assistance from the BAC located in the provincial capital (Lahore). BAC also has a field office in Bahawalnagar Tehsil, Bahawalnagar District, for operational assistance. BAC is headed by a serving colonel and it works closely with the Punjab Board of Revenue which makes the land available to the military for allocations. In fact, the offices of both the Chairman of BAC and the major serving under him are in a Board of Revenue building.

We acquired institutional information from the major because the head of the BAC was either late (arrived after 11:00 am) or absent from work on our visits. Apparently turnover is high in the BAC office and so institutional information is scarce. We did manage to glean some institutional information from lawyers working with BAC who we met in the Board of Revenue offices. No documents for any aspect of these allocations were made available to us, although they no doubt exist in GHQ in the form of confidential reports. Since we did not have access to those reports, we patched together the institutional information via discussions with government officials and concerned lawyers.

Conceptualization of the Border Allocation Scheme

The BAC was established in 1952 with refugee claims on the border under its purview initially. Only civil land ownership on the border established prior to 1952 was and is honored by GHQ and BAC. As indicated above, the border allotments are made in a five-mile belt along Pakistan's eastern international border with India. The idea was to have the barren land made fertile by the military personal settled there. More important, the retired military presence could facilitate the military in time of war. Instead of an unorganized exodus, there would be disciplined leadership managing the civilian population and interfacing with the military.[6]

In proportion to the agricultural allocations, land in *marlas* (30.25 sq. ft.) was made available in nearby towns to facilitate settlement. Initially, the agricultural land had to be retained for five years before it was eligible for sale and a no-objection certificate (NOC) had to be procured from GHQ in such cases. The major informed us that the 1965 and 1971 wars vindicated this border allocation scheme and the military found that their expectations were realized.

However, he also conceded that almost 90% of the allotted land had been sold. While it was impossible for us to verify whether the land in question had been sold before or after the two aforementioned wars, the high proportion of land allocations sold suggests that the border allocation scheme was a failure, at least in terms of its official stated purpose.

Land Allocation Process

If GHQ wants to make allocations, it seeks information about state land via the Defense Ministry from the relevant province. For Punjab, the Board of Revenue (BoR) reports on the status of available land and GHQ then makes the allocation informing BAC, which passes instructions down to the District Coordinator's Office and on to revenue officials starting with the Executive District Officer of Revenue (EDOR) and finally the *patwari* for registration of the plot.[7]

A Settlement Officer of the BoR coordinates with BAC and has an adjoining office. While information on allocations are considered highly confidential, we were informed by higher officials at the BoR that copies of allocations are maintained in the Settlement Office. We managed to secure a copy of allocations since 1999 in a few districts through a senior official in the BoR, details of which are provided in Khan and Akhtar (2014, Appendix Table 3.4). The said official meticulously ensured that the copy provided to us had his name removed from it. We were able to secure no more official records from the BoR.

Legal Issues

One of the BAC's functions is trouble shooting. For example, one plot of land can and has often been allotted several times by GHQ. The BAC investigates such problems and reports back to GHQ. Those who have a genuine prior allotment are not displaced and in cases where a plot of land is allotted more than once accidentally, GHQ makes a fresh allotment.

We consulted a constitutional lawyer on the issue of constitutional cover for the military border scheme and other land allocations and about which law has primacy if there is a conflict between military and civil law. His response was that the consensus view in the legal profession is that martial law is an aberration that suspends the Constitution. Martial Law Regulations, providing for such allocations, can be given constitutional cover via indemnity when civilian law is restored.

The BAC also functions as a court. Two army officers and a junior member of the Punjab BoR form the bench. For example, a plot of land might be sold without an NOC from GHQ and issues pertaining to that plot of land could be adjudicated on by BAC. In general, such land was reappropriated by BAC with a loss to the buyer and the land reallocated to military personnel. Lawyers were resentful that the Chairman BAC, who presides in the hearing, is high handed, "acts like a sovereign," and refuses to make relevant files available to litigants, and views civilian courts as "subject to approach" (corrupt).

Decisions of bodies such as the BAC, which have legal recognition, can in principle be challenged under Article 166 of the Constitution via a writ petition (when all recourse is exhausted), with petitioners having the right to seek legal counsel. Civil courts have rarely provided relief to ordinary civilians. In principle, writ petitions on BAC cases could eventually make their way up the civilian court system and be filed by litigants in the Lahore High Court. Two senior judges of the Division Bench hear the case.

Lawyers engaged in BAC litigation informed us that that the High Court often remanded (sent back) the cases to lower courts. If the civil courts did decide against retired military personnel selling the land illegally and if the sale was nullified, military personnel would in principle have to compensate the buyers for the amount taken. This rarely happened in practice as indicated above since the BAC did not recognize the jurisdiction of civilian courts and reappropriated the land and reallocated it.

All this is now moot since in 2008, the Supreme Court declared that an NOC is not required, unless the buyer is deemed by some competent authority to be an "undesirable." This has legally converted the Border Land Allotment into a welfare scheme like the non-border allotments—which it *de facto* was in any case.

More importantly, the very fact that the GHQ can arbitrarily demand information on available state land from the provincial authorities and then instruct the same authorities to simply allot this land to military officers without concern for what alternative uses may have been imagined by the civil authorities—including elected representatives—reflects just how much power the military exercises viz. a viz. other state institutions. Many of our informants expressed resentment at just how unashamedly this practice has become institutionalized and how little resistance there is to it on the part of other civilian state institutions.

A brief note is necessary here to clarify the legal status of the Rangers who figure very prominently on the border. The Rangers are the border guardians but do not have policing authority except on issues of border crossings and other "defense" concerns. However, since the police are obliged to accept the Rangers' view of matters on any law and order issue, the latter exercise considerable additional authority over locals beyond policing the cutting of trees that are deemed a defense asset (cover for tanks and other vehicles). Using raw intimidation and claims that "trouble makers" are Indian agents or "smugglers," the Rangers are able to block farming activity under these and similar pretexts which, generally, enables them to get their way.

Scope of Non-Border Allocations

Siddiqa (2007, pp. 174–182) reported that about 12% of state land is in military hands. The appropriations are based on the Colonization of Land Act, 1912, and made by the provincial governments on the request of the military via the Ministry of Defense. Almost two-thirds of all allocations are rural and 98.5% of total allocations are in private (retired military) ownership, both border and non-border. The rest include camping grounds, oats, hay, and dairy and stud farms.

As stated at the outset of this chapter, the information we gathered on border or non-border allotments is not exhaustive. However, while it is at least possible to identify the general contours of the border allotment scheme, non-border allotments are potentially much broader.

Allotments throughout the so-called canal colonies have been ongoing for the best part of a century. In traditional allotment districts such as Okara, Sahiwal, Khanewal, Faisalabad, Sargodha, and Multan there is now only limited land that remains to be allotted as mentioned above. Thus, it is in the (Siraiki-speaking) southern and western districts that most new allotments are taking place. In most cases, it is common land, or what are locally known as *rakh*—previously used mostly as grazing lands—that have been acquired by the state and allotted to the military (and other government) personnel. This practice is not necessarily new, but it is these lands which appear to have become the favorite target of GHQ allotment schemes in districts such as Layyah, Muzzaffargarh, Bahawalpur, and D.G. Khan.

While the lands in question are variously irrigated and rain-fed; it is largely in the districts of the Thal desert such as Layyah and Muzaffargarh that rain-fed lands have been allotted. At the time of our fieldwork, there were also a number of new mega water projects either in the planning or execution stages with command areas in the millions of acres. Crucially the main planning document (PC-1) that outlined the design execution plan of these projects—which included the Greater Thal Canal and the Chashma Right Bank Canal—left vague the question of who the beneficiaries of the newly irrigated lands would be. In both the case of the Greater Thal Canal (which had not been completed) and the Chashma Right Bank Canal (which was complete), we found plenty of anecdotal evidence to suggest that new colonists included a large number of military personnel.

In the Cholistan region, and most notably in Bahawalpur, where we found the most allotments, a number of trends could be discerned. First, there were substantial chunks of land that had been allotted that had no access to water at the time. We presumed that there was a prospective plan to provide water access to such lands in the future. Second, there were a number of allotments that appeared to have been made for urban expansion—so nominally rural (peri-urban) allotments in and around Bahawalpur would become subsumed into the cantonment area, a model of development with colonial roots. Third, military allottees had benefited from abuse of power to divert existing water sources to their lands.

Many of the irrigation initiatives undertaken by the state in the 1950s and 1960s, prior to the creation of the Cholistan Development Authority, were not perennial. In many cases those who came to the region as land allottees (and this included large numbers of east Punjabi and Urdu-speaking Partition[8] migrants along with civil and military personnel) were able to rely on only six months of irrigation water. Anecdotal evidence suggests that many of the more recent military allottees have been able to secure water from the older sources for much more than the typically allowed six-month period. In other words, they had essentially monopolized existing water sources and this had given rise to considerable conflict with the local population that did not have access to perennial irrigation.[9]

Finally, there were a number of different types of tenure arrangements operative. Aside from transfer of ownership to individual allottees, there were long-term leases, short-term leases, sublets (mostly illegal), and even blatantly illegal occupations. Details of some allotment in Cholistan to the military are provided in Khan and Akhtar (Appendix Table 3.5, a–e).[10]

Spontaneous Resistance

We concluded from our fieldwork that the farmers unanimously view the border allocation scheme to have been a failure since the military men did not stay on as they were supposed to and it was "the sweat of the local farmers" that ensured development of the local land. Households who had been relying on the public commons to meet their livelihood needs for decades had been unceremoniously evicted with the connivance of district administrations, including the police. The growing sense of injustice was compounded by the high-handed behavior of the Rangers. We formed the impression that farmers were initially willing to respect state allocated property rights, but that retrospectively the grievances inflicted on them resulted in the questioning of the injustice of these allocations and to growing social resentment that led to spontaneous acts of resistance.

During our research we observed and heard about spontaneous protests of various kinds in response to the injustices meted out to local communities by both Rangers and other military personnel. The majority of these episodes—a few are highlighted below—did not culminate in any major victory for the affected communities. However, the intensification of overt resistance over time despite the high costs does indicate the emergence of a new societal consensus against military excess. Perhaps foreshadowing the future, we document in the next section a more sustained collective action that has resulted in significant benefits accruing to local communities previously subject to blatant abuses of military power.

One of the recurring themes we encountered was of Ranger personnel violating established moral norms of rural Punjab. On a number of occasions, we found that local communities react vociferously to Rangers who openly or secretly spied on women who were active in household or other work. In Bhedian Kalan, a village six km away from the Ganda Singh border in Kasur, the local community's moral outrage was expressed in the form of a major protest on July 18, 2010. Incensed at Ranger personnel who had been ogling village women from the roof of a rented house, the local community blocked a main thoroughfare for many hours, raised slogans against the Rangers and demanded justice from the authorities. The event got media coverage (Daily Times, July 19, 2010) but there was no immediate action taken on the part of the *tehsil* or *district* administration.

In Rakh Azizabad and Rakh Sadiqabad near Chowk Munda in District Rajin Pur about 30 thousand acres of land was allotted to retired and serving army personnel in 2007. Farmers claimed that this land had been cultivated by their families for more than a century. Once the land was allotted, army men came with the police and started to displace them. Farmers decided to resist the occupation and a dispute ensued. Army officials who managed to gain possession sold it.

Another injunction against which there was a fair amount of overt protest pertained to the building of bypasses around cantonment areas which resulted in considerable cost and inconvenience to local communities. In Sialkot, the bypass around the cantonment forced ordinary civilians to travel up to 12 km to reach destinations which were less than 500 yards away. Already furious about this situation, local residents reacted strongly to an arbitrary Rs. 300 fees being charged by Rangers for a "sticker" necessary to pass through a designated check post. They undertook what was effectively a social boycott and pulled their children out of the Ranger public school. The Rangers backed down and relinquished their "sticker" contract, reportedly foregoing almost Rs. 20 million.[11]

One of the more interesting instances of resistance we came across was in Rahim Yar Khan. A colonel was awarded agricultural land that contained a heritage site in Pathan Hanara. The Buddhist Stupa was about to be bulldozed by the colonel to level the farm, but this was blocked at the last minute by concerned citizens who demonstrated against this action. The endangered site was taken over by the Ministry of Culture and Rs. 1.8 million awarded for its restoration.

During our visit to Bahawalpur City during fieldwork, we confronted a major traffic jam caused by road blockades resulting from a large demonstration of farmers protesting on water issues in front of the district government offices. We learned later that there the procession included about 2,000 farmers on motorbikes and 10,000 farmers including a large contingent of women. Women were active in confronting the soldiers trying to break up the demonstrations. The head of the *Kissan* (farmer) Board, the organization responsible for the demonstration, informed us that water was being diverted to the canal (Abasia) that served the military farms at the expense of the canal (Punjnad) that served the local farmers. The low water level in Punjnad resulted in few farmer outlets being served. Records were tampered with by the irrigation department officials to distort reality.

This collective action was successful in that the failure to disperse the demonstrators and the subsequent blockade and paralysis of a major part of the city resulted in the *Kissan* Board activists being invited for discussions. The executive engineer agreed to provide additions of 250 cusecs (cubic feet per second) water to Derawar sub-canal and 120 cusecs each to Dairy and Salary sub-canals, respectively, that served the farmers. He said this was the maximum he could do given his authority and that more could only be authorized by the chief engineer who happened not to be present on the day of the demonstration. The farmers agreed to disburse that day in view of the partial fulfillment of their demands, but the head of the *Kissan* Board was fired up and informed us that this was only the beginning of their fight for social justice in the form of "direct action." It became evident during our fieldwork that the chances of sustained and successful collective action were much more likely when embodied in organizational form.

Organized Collective Action

In Okara, the military farms are spread out over 17,000 acres and almost 20 villages. In June 2000, the farm management announced that the *battai* (crop sharing) arrangement for the Okara farms was to be replaced by a new contract system, under which the rent was to be paid in cash rather than by *battai*. According to farm officials and the military, this decision was taken to improve the revenue generated from these farms in view of the fall in annual farm income from Rs. 40.79 million in 1995–1996 to Rs. 15.87 million in 1999–2000 (Rs. 52 = US$1 in 2000).

Whereas these falling revenues were to some degree attributed to corruption within the military farm management, the bulk of the blame was put on the economic performance of the tenants.

This is difficult to sustain, given that it was the tenants who had consistently been receiving no more than between a third and a quarter share of the whole produce. Moreover, the chances of malpractice by tenants were next to impossible given the round-the-clock monitoring and supervision by the farm employees.

It seems more probable that the farm management itself was responsible for the embezzlement of income and under-reporting. According to some senior retired military officers, who had been posted in Okara during their years in service, the provision of milk, free of cost, to officers' households and even the presentation of farm animals from these farms as gifts or bribes to the officers was common practice.

Under the new contract system, tenants would pay a fixed amount of rent in cash per annum per unit of land leased. The lease period was originally set at three years, but later extended to seven years as a concession to the tenants. Seemingly generous, the contract duration was misleading, as the contract itself was subject to annual renewal on the basis of the economic performance during the previous year. The rent at which the land was to be leased out was set between a minimum of Rs. 2,200 and a maximum of Rs. 3,600 per acre. It was estimated that under this system the military farm authorities could earn profits between Rs. 28 and Rs. 46 million.

Tenants resisted this change mainly because they feared the threat of eviction under this new arrangement. Their fears were based on two clauses in the contract:

> Clause 11: If the land is required for defense purposes, the land is to be evacuated at six months' notice. In this case, the contractor will be refunded for the rent already paid by him in advance.
>
> Clause 25: The contractor cannot claim occupancy tenancy rights. Under no circumstances does the contractor possess ownership rights.

Furthermore, the timing of the introduction of this system coincided with the sudden inclusion of some land from Chak (village) 11/4-L in the area of military farms directly cultivated by the army and the Okara cantonment. As a result, some tenant families were dispossessed and displaced. This move by the army to repossess land by evicting those with usufruct rights only served to increase tenant mistrust of the military, and to confirm their worst fears about future developments of the same sort.

The new contract was also unacceptable to tenants on other grounds. For instance, clauses 10 and 13 prohibited the cutting or trimming of trees and digging of mud from a field without prior approval from the farm authorities. Clause 26 of the contract granted ownership rights to the lease-holder of only one in every ten trees that he would plant after July 2000, a sharecropping arrangement amounting to no more than a tenth of the produce.

These were important concerns for tenants who—in the absence of modern amenities such as gas—depended on the trees in their area for firewood for cooking purposes. Given their poverty, they also depended on the mud from these fields to plaster and repair their *kucha* (mud) houses from time to time. In spite of their long presence on the land, tenants were never allowed by the farm authorities to build any concrete or brick houses in these villages. All these factors, magnified by the threat of eviction, gave an impetus to the formation of a resistance movement as tenants perceived a serious threat not just to their well-being but also to their socio-economic survival as peasants.

While the movement initially started out as a rejection of the contract proposal, once aware that the army itself was neither the legal owner nor the lessee of the land (discussed below), it turned into a struggle for the ownership rights of the land itself. In a matter of months, it spread into nine other districts of the Punjab: Multan, Khanewal (Pirowal), Jhang, Sargodha, Pakpattan, Sahiwal, Vihari, Faisalabad, and Lahore.

All of the land in these districts—amounting to some 68,000 acres—was leased in the early twentieth century by the Punjab Government to various government departments, including the Ministry of Defense, and is spread over these ten districts (including Okara). The bulk of this land (38.6%) is under the control of the armed forces: it accounts for a total of 26,274 acres, corresponding to Military Farms not just in Okara (17,013 acres) but also in Lahore (6,659 acres), Sargodha (1,525 acres), and Multan (1,050 acres).[12]

In essence, the dispute over the land on all state farms boils down to the legal status of the state agencies administering the farms. The land for the military farms in Okara was given to the British Indian army for cultivation under a lease agreement in 1913. While the original lease document is unobtainable, a report by the executive district officer Okara to the Punjab Board of Revenue attests that the land in question was "transferred by the Government of Punjab to the Central Government (Ministry of Defense) on lease vide Memo No. 1844-S dated 9-8-1913 for a period of 20 years @ 15,000/- per annum for the entire land."

Although this lease was only extended for another five years after 1933, the Ministry of Defense (under British rule) continued to pay rent till 1943. Since the land was in the use of the British Indian army in 1947, its possession was automatically transferred to the Pakistan army under the new Ministry of Defense after Partition. Since 1943, the Ministry of Defense had never paid the annual rent to the provincial government.

Based on these arrears, on September 22, 2001 the executive district officer (revenue) for Okara wrote as follows to the secretary of the Board of Revenue: "The record of payment of rent/lease money is neither available in this office nor provided by the Military Authorities." Following this, the Board of Revenue asked the deputy director, military farm Okara, to provide proof of rental payment to the Punjab Government for the lease.[13] The failure of the farm management and the army GHQ to respond to this query, much less provide any evidence in this regard, further confirmed that after 1943 none of the rental payments due were actually paid to the Punjab Government.

These arrears also established that no attempt was made by the Ministry of Defense to renew its lease agreement with the provincial government. As such, the Board of Revenue held that the Ministry of Defense was in illegal occupation of the land in question, for it had neither renewed its lease since 1938 nor paid the annual rent to the Punjab Government after 1943. The legal situation obtaining on other farms is similar to that in Okara, in that the lease period under which these government departments were given the land for cultivation had long since expired. Thus, the attempt to change the rent collection system from *battai* (share) to contract status had no legal standing.

Faced with the prospect of being dispossessed, tenants initially attempted to negotiate their way through the crisis. After the repeated failure of the military farm management to reach an accommodation, tenants expressed their opposition to the unilateral attempt at changing the rent collection system by organizing a peaceful protest. On October 7, 2000 a rally of about a thousand people culminated in a four hour "sit-in" at the lawns of the deputy commissioner's office in Okara (Arif, 2002), an event that marked the beginning of the tenant protest movement and the formation of the Anjuman Mazarain Punjab (AMP, Tenants Movement of Punjab).[14]

Alarmed by this episode, two days later the deputy director of the military farms contacted the local police for assistance, alleging that villagers were not allowing the farm managers to take away the wood lying in one of the villages (Chak 10/4-L). As a result, the local police, accompanied by a heavy contingent of the frontier constabulary, an elite force, raided the village. Here they encountered resistance by women and children from the village, who formed a human barrier to protect their men. Armed only with their *thapas*,[15] these women succeeded in preventing the police from entering their village.

Following this resistance to police harassment, tenants' faith in social mobilization increased, and gradually they became aware of the fact that they could generate panic within the state machinery simply by virtue of the numbers involved in the movement. There were over 100,000 residents of Okara military farms, and typically the movement was able to mobilize between 30,000 and 40,000 people at any one time. This is despite the fact that less than half of the residents were landholding tenants, or those who were the principal losers as a result of the change in tenure. In other words, wage laborers were just as active a participant in the movement as the tenant. This was true of other farms as well, where mass mobilization included many non-tenants who participated actively.

Six people were killed by the authorities in the first five years of the movement, and only two were actually tenants, while the others were wage laborers. These deaths took place in direct confrontations with paramilitary forces. The military also deployed the Rangers, who besieged the Okara area for extended periods of time, most notably in

August 2002 for around three months and in May 2003. The Pirowal farms also suffered similar treatment. There were hundreds of criminal cases lodged against the tenants, some on trumped-up charges of anti-state sedition and terrorism. Dozens of activists and their supporters were jailed and many continued to suffer through the ignominy of regular court appearances long after.

Thus, many of those who were not tenants nevertheless shared with the latter the full effects of state repression. Non-tenants living on the farms were severely restricted by the siege of the farms conducted by the state, and their livelihoods were correspondingly undermined. As a result, those in this particular category also supported the collective action, seeing it as a method of restoring the stability and social mobility that the actions of the state had made impossible. Another reason why the non-tenants established solidarity with farm tenants, to the extent of sharing a common political consciousness with them, was due to the presence of socio-economic networks within the villages, i.e., linking social capital (Chapter 2).

Given the response by the state to peaceful protests by the tenants and non-tenants, it is not surprising that the movement had to rely on civil disobedience, the object being to generate public support by underlining the repressive nature of the state. Tactics included hunger strikes in urban centers, appeals to international networks and even foreign missions.[16] The use of social mobilization to protest peacefully against the state machinery was remarkably successful, both in attracting public attention and deterring the state from using further coercion to force the tenants into relinquishing their control over the land.[17]

The collective action was successful in securing its immediate objective: retaining control over the land and maintaining economic security. Tenants stopped surrendering harvest shares to the authorities since the beginning of the conflict. Many laborers, who were part of the collective action, started working on the lands of tenants as opposed to private farms and received a higher wage than they previously earned.

Non-tenants—including wage laborers—took advantage of new economic opportunities generated by the enhanced purchasing power of tenants.[18] Many of those who were not themselves tenants and who earned significantly from off-farm employment—including overseas remittances—rented land from existing tenants who had larger plots, and were unable to cultivate the land with family labor, or no longer had access to inputs from the state.

Tenants and non-tenants alike concurred that they were clearly economically better off than they had been prior to the revolt. Their mutual bond was strengthened by the fact that both groups were beneficiaries of an overall improvement in the village economy. As expected however, tenants experienced a much more significant improvement in their material standard of living. There was also a newfound sense of dignity and self-respect among the residents of the farms that came from frustrating the military's numerous attempts to enforce a draconian tenure system that peasants were convinced would lead to eviction.

The successful collective action in Okara inspired other farmers to organize in two areas close to the Okara military farms. Indeed, in both of the cases documented below, local farmers directly affiliated themselves with the organization founded by the Okara military farms tenants. In *tehsil* Okara, land in seven villages of the so-called Coleyana estate—named for the British Colonel Cole who was allotted 365 squares in the late nineteenth century—was allotted to ex-servicemen as well as serving military officers, as well as junior commissioned (JCOs) and non-commissioned officers (NCOs).

In 1957, in the initial phase of the General Ayub Khan land reforms, the entire estate land was awarded to the *mazareen* (tenants) who had worked the land under the original British allottees. This award was rescinded in 1960 and the land was then allotted over the next eleven years to military officers. Land awards were in direct proportion to rank: JCOs were awarded one square (25 acres), majors and colonels four squares, and brigadiers and above ten squares. After 1994, the bulk of the remaining land was allotted to JCOs and NCOs.

All the land was awarded on ten-year leases under the *ghori pal* (horse nurturing) scheme, although many officers were able to get extensions from conversion. Tenants who became owners of the land in 1957 were once again relegated to tenant status in 1960. These farmers had been working on the lands for generations and this change in status was a bitter pill to swallow. The military men were expected to manage the land themselves but more than 90% of them rented out their allotments.

The resistance over the military allotments started soon after the reallotment process began and many court cases were initiated but in vain. To add insult to injury, tenants were also confronted with high rents, and arbitrary police mistreatment and evictions when they resisted. In the wake of the successes of the Okara military farms tenants, a new wave of resistance began. The leadership of Okara military farms tenants met with and directly facilitated the Coleyana Estate farmers. The organization subsequently established was able to sustain collective action in the form of a struggle for farmer rights.

Prior to this collective action, farmers who resisted demands for higher rent ranging from Rs. 30,000 to Rs. 40,000 per acre, were subject to police evictions initiated by the District Coordinator Officer. The formation of the union stopped these evictions and rents were reduced to from Rs. 10,000 to 15,000 per acre, with some farmers refusing to pay even that. As is always the case with collective action, there was some free-riding such that those not part of the union also benefited from reduced rents. Others, who felt intimidated by the state or worried that there would be future consequences continued to pay the higher rents.

The results above were not easily achieved and the struggle for farmer's rights is an ongoing one. Organizing initially met with brutal state force and in one such brutal action on March 6, 2009, three farmers were killed and 27 wounded resisting evictions. Agent provocateurs continued to try to undermine the social organization by playing both sides and trying to create discord and we were told that the leadership received death threats on their cell phones from "numbers unknown."

Yet, the farmers were determined in their resistance. The organization elected its office bearers and collected dues from all members and maintained a strike fund. It covered expenses such as those associated with court cases imposed on farmers, newspaper advertisements for events, support for the lowest income farmers, and solidarity events. Women had separate committees and they were the fiercest participants in the collective action by immediately mobilizing and confronting police with sticks along with the men. In case "thugs" were used to enforce evictions, farmers armed themselves. In confronting force, they resorted to putting up road blocks by using tractor trolleys.

As in the case of the Okara military farms, prior to the contemporary wave of resistance, farmers were treated with disdain by the military landlords and their henchmen and women were harassed and did not feel safe. However, since the formation of the union the tenants demanded to be treated with respect and received their due. The farmers claimed to have popular support in their struggle even among middle-income groups in the adjoining towns. Conversely, the military's goodwill was severely eroded.

A similar resistance struggle emerged on the Boyle Gunj Military Stud Farm in *Tehsil* and District Pakpattan (which borders Okara district). Here too the military controlled the 147 squares of land on the stud farm for over a century, subjecting the tenants who tilled the land to semi-serfdom. The tenants refused to pay rent or surrender harvest shares on 142 of the 147 squares. The more enterprising claimed a larger share of this land. Both police and Rangers tried to evict the farmers unsuccessfully and the latter retaliated by destroying the military's greenhouses.

The stud farm was leased from the Government of Punjab by the army at the rate of Rs. 110 per acre for 99 years in the second decade of the twentieth century. Initially, sharecropping was the norm, but, rather than sharing revenue as is conventional in such contracts, the army insisted on first netting out its expenses from revenues before a division was made and there was often little left for farmers. The disaffectation of the tenants led to a rental contract at Rs. 3,200 per acre in 2003. However, the tenants also found this to be very steep at the time. Many had been evicted from the land in 1972 when the army tried to manage the farm using wage labor. While the old tenants were allowed back after protests, they asserted historic rights, dating back to British times, as cultivators of these lands and that these rights exceeded those claimed by the military.

Update on the Okara Military Farms Collective Action

In the nineteen-year-old struggle, 13 tenants at the farms lost their lives in the farmers' social movement for the ownership of land their families had been cultivating for over one 100 years. Around 1,900 tenants were jailed over this period, including over 200 peasant women. Three of the main leaders of the *Anjuman Mozareen Punjab* (AMP—Punjab Tenants Association) were in jail, including AMP general secretary Mehar Abdul Sattar, who is serving a 10 years jail sentence on fake cases. Sattar is also joint secretary of Pakistan *Kissan Rabita* Committee, a network of peasant organizations in Pakistan. The false police charges include murder, attempted murder, dacoity, theft, terrorism (anti-state activities), and blocking public roads. Despite the brutal repression of the AMP, only 10% of the tenants agreed to pay rent.[19]

In 2016, an investigative committee was set up by the National Human Rights Commission of Pakistan to look into the conflict in Okara. In its interim report, it deemed the restrictions imposed on the peaceful gatherings of the AMP by local authorities as "arbitrary and unconstitutional." It decried the use of the Anti-Terrorism Act against the AMP members and leaders as draconian, and criticized the excessive use of force reflected in the use of heavy military vehicles (including tanks) and weapons against citizens.[20]

On December 31, 2018, the Okara military farms commandant Brigadier Rana Mohammed Fahim told a hearing of the National Commission for Human Rights that the Punjab government owns the Okara military farms, vindicating the position of the Government of Punjab and the tenants. The National Commission for Human Rights stated: "It has been principally decided that criminal cases registered against the tenants will be withdrawn. *Batai*, which existed prior to the year 2000, will be restored and tenants would start giving 50 per cent of their production to the army or the government. Tenants would not get ownership rights, but no one will harass them in future and they will not be dislocated." The army stated that it will waive off the dues owed by the farmers which had accumulated over the past 18 years and will begin paying rent to the Punjab government after the *battai* system is restored. Since peasants did not secure land to the tiller, at the time of writing (December 2019) they sought an adjournment of the proceedings until January 17, 2020 in order to arrive at a consensus regarding further course of action.[21]

Conclusion

We document cases of spontaneous collective action in this chapter but these mostly dissipated. However, organized collective action enabled peasants to successfully take on the military, the most powerful state institution of the country. A sympathetic press, broader media attention, civil society, and public support certainly helped the cause. However, most helpful was the ability of indigenous leadership to tap indigenous social capital to organize for collective action. "Urban activists" facilitated the organizational activity.

Okara farm tenants secured political attention because of numbers. In the past they had been politically exploitable and this led to lessons learnt. Political naiveté continued even after the social movement began. First, tenants were promised ownership rights by two federal ministers on the condition that they voted for General Musharraf in the highly suspect presidential referendum of April 2002, which they did. Second, similar promises were made by an influential Okara landowner Rao Sikander Iqbal in the lead-up to the October 2002 general election. Following his success, he became Federal Minister of Defense and proceeded to suppress the social movement with greater force than was previously the case.

Because of these experiences, tenants ceased to place their trust in the political process. Alienation from the political process facilitated the development of a distinct consciousness among peasants on state farms. Many leaders of the revolt revealed that while conflicts on the basis of primordial identities (*qaum* (caste), *biraderi* (clan), *religion*) were not uncommon prior to the revolt, they almost ceased during the course of the social mobilization.[22]

The success of the Okara farm collective action inspired other social movements in nearby locations among farmers in similar situations. In fact, the Okara social organization was able to facilitate these movements by providing advice and guidance. In general, the political process can be an avenue for social change when there is a considerable vote bank involved as in the case of Okara peasants. However, when the poor are taken for granted and promises made but not delivered on, social capital-driven collective action can be an effective tool to attain social justice and perhaps the only alternative.

Notes

1. The army is the largest component of the Pakistan military and this is generally the case. While the land allocation scheme discussed in this chapter is administered by the army, our reference throughout the chapter is to the military since during our fieldwork, we did find other forces to be part of the scheme administration.
2. The Prime Minister Imran Khan at the time of writing (2020) made a statement to this effect that was reported in most of the prominent daily newspapers on November 3, 2020.
3. The border Rangers are a paramilitary force policing the borders and under the command of the army.
4. *Halqas* are lands under the jurisdiction of particular *patwaris* (revenue officers) that they maintain records for.
5. The list of districts and tehsils visited for border and non-border allocations is provided in Appendix 3.1, the list of persons consulted and interviewed in Appendix 3.2, the list of group discussions in Appendix 3.3, an example of recent military allocations made by the Punjab Board of Revenue in Appendix Table 3.4, examples of non-border allocations made in Cholistan in Appendix Tables 3.5, a–e, and a map indicating our coverage in Appendix 3.6 of Khan and Akhtar (2014).
6. There appears to be a historic precedent for such border allocations ranging back to Athen's conflict with Sparta. For details refer to Mitchell (2000). Thanks to Zulqarnain Dogar for pointing this out to us.
7. The local government field hierarchy under the EDOR is District Officer of Revenue (DOR), Deputy District Officer of Revenue (DDOR), *tehsildar*, *naib* (deputy) *tehsildar*, *qanoon go*, and most critically the *patwari* who registers the land and maintains the record. The *patwari* possesses immense power despite being on the lowest rung of this hierarchy. It is common knowledge across Pakistani society that *patwaris* take great liberty in manipulating land transactions.Indeed, in some cases lands being allotted to military personnel do not fall into the category of agricultural land. For example, right alongside Grand Trunk Road near Pirowal in

Khanewal district, approximately 8000 acres of land in the possession of the Punjab Forest Department was handed over to GHQ.

8. The reference is to the partition of the Indian subcontinent into India and Pakistan in 1947.
9. Intriguingly in some cases these newer conflicts have led to considerable reordering of earlier political alignments. For example, tensions between Urdu-speaking settlers and the local *Siraiki* population persisted for a number of decades after Partition. However, Urdu-speakers have tended more recently to ally themselves with *Siraikis* in opposition to newer Punjabi settlers.
10. All of this information was obtained from the personal records of Dr. Ayesha Siddiqa, whom we wish to gratefully acknowledge.
11. One US$ in July 2011 was the equivalent of about 90 Pakistani rupees.
12. Some of the other government departments administering these state farms include the Punjab Seed Corporation (in Pirowal, Khanewal), the Maize and Cotton Research Departments (in Sahiwal), the Rice Research Department (in Lahore and Faisalabad), and the Livestock Department (in Sargodha and Sahiwal).
13. This memorandum was dated October 4, 2001.
14. The role of "urban activists," was important to the formation of the AMP and the social movement.
15. These are small, blunt wooden sticks used to wash clothes. They quickly evolved into the symbol of the movement.
16. In many respects, the same tactics deployed by the Zapatistas in Chiapas after the peasant uprising of 1994 ensured their survival when confronted by the Mexican state and its army (Solis, 2007).
17. Human Rights Watch (HRW, 2004) condemned the state repression against the tenants in a damning report. Two follow-up HRW dispatches in 2016 on the state of peasant struggle in Okara and high-handed treatment meted out to farmers by the Rangers are posted on the HRW website, https://www.hrw.org/sitesearch?search=okara, consulted 11/5/2020.
18. These included small mechanic shops for which demand increased as more tenants started buying machinery—including tractors and motorcycles.
19. Farooq Tariq, Saturday 5 January 2019, http://internationalviewpoint.org/spip.php?article5875, consulted 12/28/2019.
20. Tanupriya Singh, January 07, 2019, https://peoplesdispatch.org/2019/01/07/after-decades-of-farmers-struggles-pakistan-army-admits-farm-land-is-not-owned-by-them/, consulted 12/28/2019.

21. Ibid.
22. Aasim Sajjad Akhtar noted the resurfacing of these identities once the social movement gained some success. "When a Movement Stops Moving: The Okara Peasant Struggle Twenty Years on," https://criticalasianstudies.org/commentary/2019/11/19/201923-aasim-sajjad-ahktar-when-a-movement-stops-moving-the-okara-peasant-struggle-twenty-years-on, consulted 12/28/2019.

References

Arif, M. 2002. *Jaag Utha Kisaan (The Farmer has Awoken).* The Network: Islamabad.

Human Rights Watch (HRW). 2004. Soiled Hands: The Pakistan Army's Repression of the Punjab Farmers' Movement. New York, https://www.hrw.org/report/2004/07/20/soiled-hands-pakistan-armys-repression-punjab-farmers-movement, consulted 11/5/2020.

Khan, S.R. and A.S. Akhtar, with S. Bodla. 2014. *The Military and Development Denied in the Pakistani Punjab: An Eroding Social Consensus.* London: Anthem Press.

Mitchell, K. 2000. Land Allocation and Self-Sufficiency in the Ancient Athenian Village. *Agricultural History* 74 (1): 1–18.

Siddiqa, A. 2007. *Military Inc: Inside Pakistan's Military Economy.* Karachi: Oxford University Press.

Solis, D.V. 2007. Rural Chiapas Ten Years after the Armed Uprising of 1994. In *Rural Chiapas Ten Years after the Zapatista Uprising,* ed. S. Washbrook. London: Routledge.

9

The Allai Valley Earthquake and COVID 19: Collective Action Undermined

Introduction

On October 8, 2005, an earthquake measuring 7.6 on the Richter scale (Mercalli intensity of 8) struck parts of northeast and northwest Pakistan. The areas severely impacted were in Indus Kohistan and Azad Jammu and Kashmir. The human and economic damage was high: at least 73,000 people were killed, another 40,000 injured, and 2.8 million left without shelter and susceptible to further injury. Most of the deaths and injuries occurred in the 1–20 age group comprising mostly school-going children crushed under stone and concrete structures.[1] The estimated damage in dollar equivalent terms amounted to US $5.5 billion (about 5% of Pakistan's nominal GDP in 2005).

The proportion of women dead and injured exceeded men, more so in the case of deaths than injuries. This was because the earthquake

This chapter draws on "Environmental Degradation, Social Marginalization and the Institutional Dynamics of Vulnerability in the October 8, 2005 Pakistan Earthquake: A Case Study of the Allai Valley in Indus-Kohistan." It was written by Shaheen Rafi Khan as the principle investigator on behalf of the Sustainable Development Policy Institute, Islamabad. It was funded by International Development Research Center, Canada.

S. R. Khan and S. R. Khan, *Social Capital and Collective Action in Pakistani Rural Development*, https://doi.org/10.1007/978-3-030-71450-5_9

struck in the morning when women were at home while the men had left for work. Building debris and landslides caused the bulk of the predominantly spine, chest, and bone injuries.

The focus of our study was the Allai Valley in Indus Kohistan (see Appendix Fig. 9.2). In this chapter, we first particularize the conceptual framework introduced in Chapter 2 to the context of dealing with natural disasters. This highlights the social and institutional context of vulnerability. Next, we briefly describe the research method and respondent socio-economic characteristics. We relate the erosion of community property rights and how this set up the accentuation of the potential impact of natural disasters and then describe the actual damage to the community from the earthquake. Finally, we describe the institutional barriers that impeded the collective action that could have enhanced coping and recovery. To illustrate the limits of spontaneous collective action, we also explore a case study of a community in another locality attempting to deal with COVID-19.

The Social and Institutional Context of Resilience and Vulnerability

At least three elements in particular contribute to the resilience of individuals and a community. First, there is the ownership of assets and the legal and customary rights to exercise command over the necessities of life. Thus, if people are endowed with land, capital, and labor and property rights are secure, they can trade during times of crises for food and other items they need to survive. Second, each community develops an ability to cope and even poor communities can develop defense mechanisms against hazards. Finally, ecosystems ability to bounce back after natural disaster to its original state after a shock and how well depends on how humans treat them.

The three elements come together in what is referred to as coupled human–environment system. The term “coupled” recognizes the interface between communities and their environment.[2] A negative interface could be due to poverty and has been referred to in the literature as the poverty–environment nexus (Chapters 6 and 7). Poverty may cause communities to not be in harmony with their environment resulting in a vicious cycle of further poverty, environmental degradation, and more poverty. Consequently, the system vulnerability to natural hazards increases since even endowments and coping capacity are negatively impacted. The disharmony is often created by external factors as explained below.

If communities do live in harmony with their environment, that is often the result of enabling external as well as indigenous factors. Enabling external factors are supportive institutions, which recognize resource rights, establish appropriate economic incentives, and manage natural resources collaboratively with communities. A key internal enabling indigenous factor is strong social capital.

Autonomous social capital is defined in Chapter 2 as the mutual trust and social interactions that enable communities to cooperate and engage in spontaneous collective action for mutual benefit. Mutual benefit can embrace resilience to and coping with disasters. At a minimum, this requires norms (including sanctions), rules, and procedures for informal networks and collectives.

Vulnerability is a complex and evolving multidimensional concept where social, economic, institutional, and environmental factors come into play when assessing the impacts of a natural disaster. In Fig. 9.1, we depict a disaster as affecting two communities with equal intensity and both suffer damage. However, the damage varies. The circle represents the mediating mechanisms includes social, cultural, and institutional variables as mentioned above: their interplay determines a community's

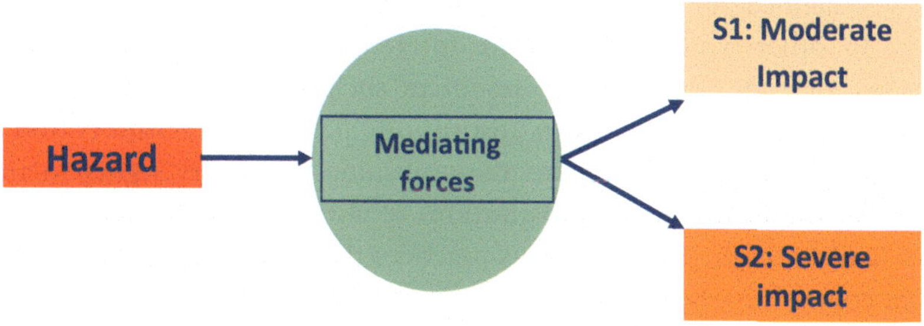

Fig. 9.1 Varying impact of natural disasters by community

vulnerability and resilience in the face of shocks. In a mutually reinforcing capacity, they can moderate the severity of impacts caused by such shocks and enhance coping capacity. Conversely, when at odds with each other, they increase the community's vulnerability and diminish its coping capacity.

Elaborating further, two aspects of institutions and their interface with autonomous social capital come into play. One aspect comes into play *ex ante*; it pertains to customary laws/rights of communities to own land and capital and to exercise command over their own labor. Such laws/rights have relevance in as much as they ensure sustainable use of natural resources which, in turn, can mitigate hazard impacts. Rural livelihoods are intertwined with the commons (forests, grazing lands). Customary rights underpin prudent use of the commons, ensuring their resilience in the face of external shocks. By contrast, a mountain slope with denuded forest cover is more likely to trigger a landslide when a tremblor occurs, endangering settlements, and cropped land in its proximity. This is the sense in which vulnerability can be an evolving concept.

The second aspect comes into play in an *ex post* context and relates to the effective coping capacity of communities embodied in norms, rules, and regulations that enable communities to cooperate and engage in spontaneous collective action for mutual benefit. The enabling organizational forms for such collective action include mutual aid, participatory decision-making, and dispute resolution. In fact, trust-based norms, rules, and sanctions underpin both customary law and informal networks and collectives.

Well-defined resource rights regulate the community resource interface. In other words, they ensure intra-community accord regarding the use of communal natural resources such as forests, grazing land, and water. The interface with institutions pertains to statutory forest laws and management systems that subsume customary rights to the commons, informal (tribal) institutions of authority that relate to labor and land use rights and; religious practices that govern intra-family and intra-community behavior.

The benign confluence of the social and institutional interface represents vibrant social capital embodied in functioning networks and collectives that yield spontaneous and effective collective action. When the two are at odds, social capital is degraded, the informal networks and organizational forms become ineffectual, and positive collective action does not ensue.

Thus, when statutory law governing the use of forest resources infringes on community resource rights (Chapter 6) it triggers a process referred to above as the poverty–environment nexus. This is a downward spiral of poverty and environmental degradation where poor communities deprived of their resource rights prey on these resources making them vulnerable to external shocks. At the ex post level, when informal (tribal) institutions of authority and religious diktats subvert or undermine community networks and collectives they weaken community coping capacity, including to natural disasters.

In the analysis that follows we will demonstrate the processes including elite capture that led to a breaking of the social and institutional interface. This exacerbated the earthquake's impacts and rendered informal networks and collective action incapable of coping with its aftereffects.

Research Method

The research team made a preliminary reconnaissance visit to the Allai valley in Indus Kohistan in the late spring of 2007. During this trip, the team identified and interviewed key informants among government agencies, non-governmental organizations, and communities. They provided substantial background information on rural livelihoods and the social and political dynamics in the study area.

The team divided the study sites into three eco-zones—upper, mid, and lower. After selecting villages, it conducted 149 household surveys distributed equally across the eco-zones as shown in Table 9.1.

Household sampling was random in each location and the response was quite good. The surveys provided information that allowed the establishment of a vulnerability profile across the study area including

Table 9.1 Villages by eco-zone and distribution of households in Allai valley

Eco-zone	Village	No.of households
Upper	Gangwal	48
Mid	Biari	50
Low	Thalus	42
	Biari	4
	Total	144

Source Author survey

household demographics, resource endowments, labor practices, and the damage communities suffered in the earthquake.

In addition, the team sought information regarding the causes of vulnerability, the sources and types of relief and recovery aid received; their perception of the effectiveness of community social institutions; their expectations of help from their leaders and the government; changes in environmental quality and resource endowments over time; and actions they had taken to protect themselves against future disasters.

The research team supplemented the surveys with a smaller number of in-depth, semi-structured interviews in select households. These were meant to qualitatively probe issues addressed in the household surveys and focused on the factors contributing to vulnerability and the community's capacity to effectively address them. While the women were unwilling, for cultural/religious reasons, to interact individually with the team they were more amenable to participating in focus group discussions (FGD).

The discussions aimed to provide an independent forum in which women could talk about the conditions that created vulnerability. In particular, the women identified pre-earthquake conditions that made them more vulnerable to the immediate effects of the earthquake; factors that made it difficult for them to respond to and recover from the earthquake; and problems that continued to confront them in its aftermath.

The team completed the fieldwork component of the study between May 2007 and May 2008. The final field component of the study involved unstructured interviews with representatives of government, inter-government, and non-government agencies involved in earthquake relief, and recovery. These interviews, conducted in July of 2008, sought to identify the extent to which earthquake relief, rehabilitation, and reconstruction efforts responded to local conditions in a participatory locally relevant form of post-disaster planning.

Respondent Socio-Economic Characteristics

The respondents were mostly between 20 and 60 years of age and surprisingly highly educated. The gender disparity in education was however large. Among men, the *Swati* and the *Mada Khel* ethnic groups were the most highly qualified. These groups formed the most politically influential and economically powerful constituency.

While the majority of agricultural land holdings were small (between 1 and 10 kanals),[3] a substantial number of households also had larger holdings (between 11 and 30 kanals). The bulk of the land was inherited. Land transactions were insignificant, reflecting the traditional attachment to ancestral property. Share cropping was an established practice although, surprisingly, its prevalence was not as marked as one would have expected. The perception was that the khans have eminent domain over natural resources and lease out farming land to their tenants. However, we also gleaned in conversations that perceptions have shifted over time, as successive generations continued to till the same land and acquired informal proprietary rights over them.

The dominant land use was agriculture but horticulture and livestock rearing were also important. Households also had entitlements in common property resources, such as forests, pastures, wasteland, with such entitlements varying in proportion to the size of agricultural land holdings. Further, such entitlements were also ethnically delineated.

The crops were primarily rain-fed, to a limited degree perennial streams were diverted into man-made channels, which irrigated fruits and vegetables and propelled rudimentary grain crushers. The upper and mid eco-zones allowed only summer (*kharif*) crops, with the harsh climate preventing winter (*rabi*) planting. The cereal crops were maize, wheat, rice, and barley. Maize and wheat were also grown in some of the low-lying areas of Allai during the *rabi* season.

Livestock ownership (cows, buffaloes, goats, poultry) was depleted as, over time, livestock prices, fodder, and maintenance became unaffordable for many families. While most of the fodder was supplied from their own lands, the diminishing size of land holdings placed an upper limit on the number of livestock that a household could sustain. The earthquake caused high livestock fatalities and, in most cases, households had not been able to raise funds to replace their dead animals.

Communal grazing was limited to nomadic pastoralists (*Gujjars*), who travel in the spring with their herds and flocks to the high alpine pastures and paid *qalang* (grazing tax) to the communities and the khans for rights to graze their herds.

Livelihood opportunities were limited with the size of landholdings supporting subsistence agriculture. Similarly, the small livestock numbers per family did not go beyond meeting household needs for meat, dairy, and poultry products. The picture was one of overarching and extreme poverty, which was exacerbated by limited off-farm employment opportunities and low earnings.

Among the 144 households interviewed, only 82 family members indicated they had jobs, whether permanent, casual, or self-employed. Annual income from livestock ranged roughly from Rs. 220 to Rs 3,700[4]; the incomes were skewed toward the lower income bound. Asset ownership was difficult to pin down. While the respondents confessed to having very few assets, they reported asset losses due to the earthquake well in excess of what they admitted to owning.

The Environmental Consequences of the Attrition of Resource Rights

Chapter 6 provides a detailed historical account of the attrition of community resource rights. This is summarized here in the specific context of Allai extending over three periods as narrated in Chapter 6. The first period was before the khan era when communities owned and managed natural resources under their own traditional arrangements for sharing common property.

The khan era culminated in them having complete control over natural resources. However, despite appropriating large tracts of arable land, pastures, and forest, the khans could not completely proscribe community resource use rights. Instead they conditioned them on various imposts, such as *begar* (forced labor) and *qalang* (grazing tax). More pernicious were the various sharecropping and land tenancy arrangements which locked generations into feudal subservience.

In the third, extant, period Allai was integrated into the state and the forests, in particular, were declared protected and managed by the Forest Department (FD). The new dispensation freed communities from their fiscal obligations to the khans and the practice of *begar* stopped. The tenancy and sharecropping obligations became more attenuated with the khans' weakening hold on subjects. Resource rights to forests are, in principal, encumbered within an elaborate system of fines, penalties, and permits. However, absent the means of enforcement, communities have virtually free access to the forests.

Recall from Chapter 6 how the timber contractors, village elders, large forest owners (including the khans), and the forest department manipulated the system to deny poor communities royalty payments from commercial logging. In survey responses, the FD was viewed as controlling, corrupt, and unduly constraining access to resources that the community has rights to. Such misgovernance was an inducement for the communities to flaunt regulations and extract timber covertly. The communities felt quite unequivocally that the misapplication of statutory law was the source of forest degradation.

The environmental consequences of transiting from khans/community to state management and the consequent lack of any community incentive to protect natural resources are captured visually in photographs contained in Appendix 9.2. These photographs depict landslides that occurred during the earthquake, precipitated by the extensive deforestation underway when forests became the state's remit. The impact on proximate dwellings is also visible. Another contributing factor was land-use changes, specifically the conversion of forest land to terracing for crop cultivation (also shown).

Earthquake Damage to Communities

Allai is highly prone to natural hazards with the community recall primarily being of floods and earthquakes. There was a high incidence of floods during 1991 to 1997. The earthquake in question disproportionately impacted poor households which generally meant women-headed households, large households, and households comprising mainly of elders. The high levels of vulnerability among women, children, and the elderly persisted up to six months after the earthquake. During this period, the lack of shelter, food, and medicines, in that order, were the key deprivations the poor in the communities faced.

The land losses were quite uniform across the eco-zones. The poor farmers (those owning arable land in the 0–10 kanal category) suffered the highest losses. Also, agricultural land was the most severely affected in relation to other land categories for the smaller holdings. Primarily, this was a locational/poverty-determined phenomenon; the smallholdings fell in the ecologically marginalized, erosion-prone areas. Annual maize harvests (the main staple) fell substantially as a result of land loss/degradation.

Households lost almost 50% of their livestock and were able to replace only half of their losses due to funding constraints. This had adverse implications for nutrition, home insulation, and soil supplementation. Again, this impact was disproportionately harder on economically impoverished households. The loss of land and livestock also had negative income spin-offs sourced in these losses.

In order of ranking the key assets lost were principal dwellings and outbuildings, agricultural implements, and food stores. The damage percentages were high with most assets being completely destroyed. In Gangwal, a village in the high zone, the traditional (*dhajji*) structures remained intact, in stark contrast to the more costly stone houses which were destroyed (see picture in Appendix 9.2).

Almost three-fourths of the key assets were replaced as indicated in Table 9.2.

The three key sources of financing were self-financing, the government, and NGOs. The primary reason for the high self-financing was that the Earthquake Relief and Rehabilitation Agency (ERRA), and its

Table 9.2 Key assets lost in earthquake and replacement rates

Productive assets	Lost	Reconstructed/replaced	%
Agr. Implements	83	80	93
Food stores	72	43	59
Outbuildings	79	51	64
Principal dwellings	134	113	84
Shops	3	3	100
Trees	6	4	66
Total	406	297	73

Source Author survey

outsourced partners, provided selective financial assistance and attached stringent conditions with disbursement.

The earthquake also had other resource impacts. The time taken to collect water increased as a result of earthquake-induced drying up of water sources. Households collected dung primarily for manure and secondarily for fuel, which was produced in the form of dung cakes. The reduction in quantity produced after the earthquake reflected the loss of livestock due to the earthquake. All in all, the earthquake had a devastating impact, particularly for the most vulnerable, and this was intensified by the institutional barriers that retarded collective action.

Institutional Barriers to Collective Action

Allai Valley

Autonomous social capital in Allai consists of informal groupings and spontaneous assemblies of local communities around social events. Respondents agreed that social events were a binding force among communities. The key events were weddings, funerals, and *khatums* (post-funeral events). These events were important for strengthening family and social relations. Communities participated in these events voluntarily rather than from a fear of social sanctions. The significance of these events had not abated over time.

The institutional barriers to collective action were two-fold. The direct barriers were hereditary and religious authority. In turn, over time these barriers weakened the traditional authority structures, namely, the *jirgas*. *Jirgas* represent the assembly of local notables (such as the khans), *pesh imam* (clerics), local teachers, revenue officials, and locally elected officials. They make decisions by consensus. The veneration in which these decisions are held, based on a track record of impartial justice, means that no enforcement authority is needed. The *jirga's* traditional functions were mediating disputes between and among families, and between villages, adjudicating on crimes (theft, murder), protecting resource rights, encouraging social cohesion, and confronting incursions from outsiders. The *jirga* is a fluid construction in that once the issue that caused its constitution is resolved the *jirga* disbands. The communities prefer *jirga* justice because it is swiftly dispensed compared to extended court cases.

Potentially these *jirgas* could be viewed as structural social capital, which, in conjunction with cognitive social capital, could have leveraged substantive and focused relief and rehabilitation responses from the government, donors, and NGOs. Instead, communities were left to their own devices in providing mutual relief assistance which, at best, was minimal. The question we needed to explore was why the *jirgas* lost their traditional relevance.

Primary leadership resides in the hereditary khans where lineage is accepted as the most important requisite for leadership. By the same token, the excesses committed by the khans, evident in interviews, undermined their social acceptance. With the exception of the *numberdar*, a government (revenue) official, other government officials, village elders, and elected leaders, khans, religious leaders lost respect and legitimacy.

The khans were completely ineffectual in addressing community needs immediately after the earthquake. They went to the extent of claiming compensation from ERRA on grounds that the devastated houses of community members were constructed on their lands and, as such, they were entitled to the compensation.

Interestingly the respondents were generally silent about the clergy which exerts spiritual authority. The omission in our view suggests fear rather than goodwill. From the press and various other sources, we learned that the clergy was the direct cause of distress to communities by denying them permission to move to safe refugee camps down-country. The refusal stemmed from religious prejudice against allowing women to mingle with outsiders.

The *jirga* we gleaned morphed into a handmaiden of the khans and religious clerics and therefore represented vested interests rather than community concerns. On substantive property disputes, the *jirga* favored the khans and looked the other way when forest royalties meant for the communities were misappropriated. In particular, the *jirga* became notorious for condoning, even mandating, honor killings of women, and for overtly exhibiting ethnic biases, for instance against the poor herding communities (*Gujjars*). The proliferation of honor killings reflects more recent infusions of *Taleban*-inspired fundamental religious dogma compared to a softer cultural practice of religion among the *Pukhtuns*.

While autonomous social capital shaped mutual support within the community, the collective impulses did not translate into substantive relief efforts which were primarily driven by development agencies and NGOs collaborating with official relief agencies and the military.[5]

Notwithstanding the discordance between the social and institutional interface, the community came together to ensure mutual aid and participation in earthquake-related responses. The source of such assistance was mostly relatives, neighbors, and friends. Most of the loans taken post-earthquake were for house construction. The primary loan sources were relatives and shopkeepers who responded to the emergency by providing such loans on concessional terms.

Migration was another coping strategy. Migration peaked during the earthquake, triggered by the shortage of food and funds and the need for medical assistance. While a substantial number of migrants moved into relief camps, the majority of them went to nearby towns, to rented houses, or to their relatives' houses. This reflected partly a cultural predisposition not to expose family members to strangers and partly the injunctions of the clerics. Most of the migrants returned to their homes after six months.

Union Council (UC7) Pind Begowal, Islamabad: The Impact of COVID-19

The case of UC7, Pind Begowal, presents another case study of a disjuncture between autonomous social capital and spontaneous collective action but with some additional twists. In this case, the disconnect stems from the inherent nature of autonomous social capital with inbuilt characteristics that, depending on the nature of the event—in this case COVID 19—can invert and turn collective good into collective harm. It illustrates how the heterogeneous nature of autonomous social capital can create internal divisions. In an interesting development, in the conflicting environment created by the pandemic, an organization specializing in constructing social capital and inducing collective action was called into reinforce the positive forces in autonomous social capital and to contain its harmful tendencies.

The *rajas* are the dominant clan (*biraderi*) in Pind Begowal. The Union Council (UC), the local government administrative unit, primarily includes members of the clan, including the UC Chairman, a forward looking, progressive, and dynamic individual. His enlightened vision, aimed at service of and the uplift of the rural poor, embraces free education, affordable and accessible health care and rural infrastructure. The clan network provides the administrative, logistical, and advocacy back-stop for service provision. Funding for such services is provided in equal measure by foreign and local donor contributions and government funding. Foreign donations are both agency-sourced and individual contributions.

The more traditional aspects of autonomous or latent social capital (i.e., village events, social gatherings, weddings, funerals, *khattams* (commemorating completion of readings of the Holy Qur'an), *barsis* (commemorating death anniversaries), mosque congregations and council of elders) are venues where community needs are highlighted, problem-solving approaches developed, and differences resolved. The following provides a flavor of the development and social achievements accomplished to date via spontaneous collective action:

The House of Light School, a brainchild of the UC Chairman and his German expatriate friend, provides free co-education, lunch, and transport for classes 1 to 10 for poor children, selected on transparent poverty criteria. A major part of the school infrastructure was funded by the Japanese government while local teacher salaries are financed by individual and NGO contributions. A combination of progressive teaching methods and sound local teacher training has produced impressive results in the National Board exams for classes 5 and 10. A private variant of this school, run on identical management principles and charging a nominal fee, was established to cater to the growing demand overload for those with means.

The UC has leveraged its contacts with private individuals and the local government to fund the establishment of a hospital, dispensary, and the purchase of two ambulances to serve the local communities. With the onset of the pandemic, the dispensary provided free testing facilities—both mobile and onsite—and the results were published on a designated website. A combination of website and team advocacy relayed pertinent information on social distancing, required precautionary actions and the avoidance of social ostracism of infected persons.

The pandemic rendered jobless or reduced the incomes of earning family members—daily laborers, taxi and van drivers, restaurant staff, plumbers, auto mechanics, electricians, construction workers, among others. The UC deployed the *biraderi* to package and distribute food rations, funded by private contributions, to impoverished families. In addition, it facilitated recipients of the Federal Government's *Ehsaas* (one-off cash distribution) program in securing the cash payments.

For a decade, a bridge on a key road artery remained in a potentially dangerous state of disrepair due to vehicle weight overload. Because of the convenience, heavy vehicles made short shrift of barriers put up to prevent ingress onto the bridge. The local government and the Capital Development Authority regularly hived off responsibility on each other when approached to repair the bridge. Finally, taking matters into its own hands, the UC mobilized *biraderi* members to block traffic access from both sides of the bridge while repairs were underway. With technical input from a civil engineer the bridge was sustainably repaired, with immovable blocks placed on one side to block heavy traffic and drainage created to divert water inflows and standing rainwater into the stream below. The financial contributions for undertaking repairs came entirely from the community.

The above are select examples of autonomous social capital making broad-based and substantive contributions to community well-being via collective action. However, the advent of the pandemic, created internal rifts in the community whereby members embodying the more traditional manifestations of autonomous social capital come in direct confrontation with its more secular and well-informed members.

Many community members ignored lock-down injunctions and safety messages when such injunctions and messages interfered with their ability to participate in traditional events referred to above. These events form an integral part of their lives, aspects that they refused to forego even at the risk of becoming infected. A combination of fatalism, extant low infection rates, and a faith in local remedies sustained such self-destructive behavior. Efforts by the UC Chairman and more informed members of the *biraderi* made little headway. While conservative community members were made cognizant of the potential danger that their behavior posed, they in turn viewed religion, culture, traditions as sacrosanct and inviolable.

The UC Chairman called in the services of the National Rural Support Program (Chapter 3) to help design an information and advocacy campaign aimed at behavior modification. It presented an interesting example of the conjunction of autonomous and constructed social capital designed to moderate the formers' more harmful manifestations. Unfortunately, at the time of writing (Spring 2020), not much headway has been made in the midst of the first wave of the pandemic, when there was no sign that the infection rate had flattened in the locality.

Conclusion

Vulnerability to natural hazards is a complex and evolving phenomenon. It encompasses social, cultural, and institutional variables that, in a mutually reinforcing capacity, can alleviate disaster impacts. Conversely, when the social and institutional dimensions are at odds, the community's vulnerability is enhanced and its coping capacity is diminished.

Thus, when statutory law governing the use of forest resources infringes on community resource rights it triggers a process referred to as the poverty–environment nexus. This is a downward spiral of poverty and environmental degradation where poor communities deprived of their resource rights prey on these resources making them vulnerable to external shocks. At the ex post level, when informal (tribal) institutions of authority and religious diktats subvert or undermine community networks and collectives they weaken community coping capacity, in this case its ability to cope with the after effects of an earthquake.

Structural social capital in Allai consisted of *jirgas*, an assembly of leaders and elders that made decisions by consensus. However, the legitimacy of these assemblies was undermined as they morphed into institutions representing vested interests rather than community concerns. This undermined their ability to institute collective action. Potentially these *jirgas* could have leveraged substantive and focused relief and rehabilitation responses from the government, donors, and NGOs.

While autonomous social capital shaped mutual support within the community, the collective impulses did not translate into substantive relief efforts which could have been leveraged by organized community effort. The communities were reduced to providing mutual relief assistance which, at best, was minimal given their limited resources.

Another case study also showed that autonomous social capital that drove successful indigenous collective action with initiatives in education, health, and infrastructure was ineffective when it came to coping with COVID-19. Local institutions (norms, cultural practices) that reinforce autonomous social capital were at odds with the need to contain infection rates. An attempt to draw in a national organization adept at constructed social capital and induced collective action had little success in overcoming entrenched cultural practices.

Notes

1. The schools were not designed to withstand severe tremors in earthquake prone areas The school buildings suffered far more damage than the old, more earthquake-resistant, colonial structures.
2. Practitioners of disaster mitigation object to the use of the term "natural" associated with disaster because they view this as understating the impact of humans in bringing about and accentuating the disaster. For example, they view land erosion and flooding as resulting from deforestation rather than a heavy rain episode.

3. There are eight kanals to an acre.
4. One US$ was roughly Rs. 78 in 2008.
5. The flaws in these relief and rehabilitation efforts are documented in Khan (2006).

Appendix

See Figs. 9.2 and 9.3.

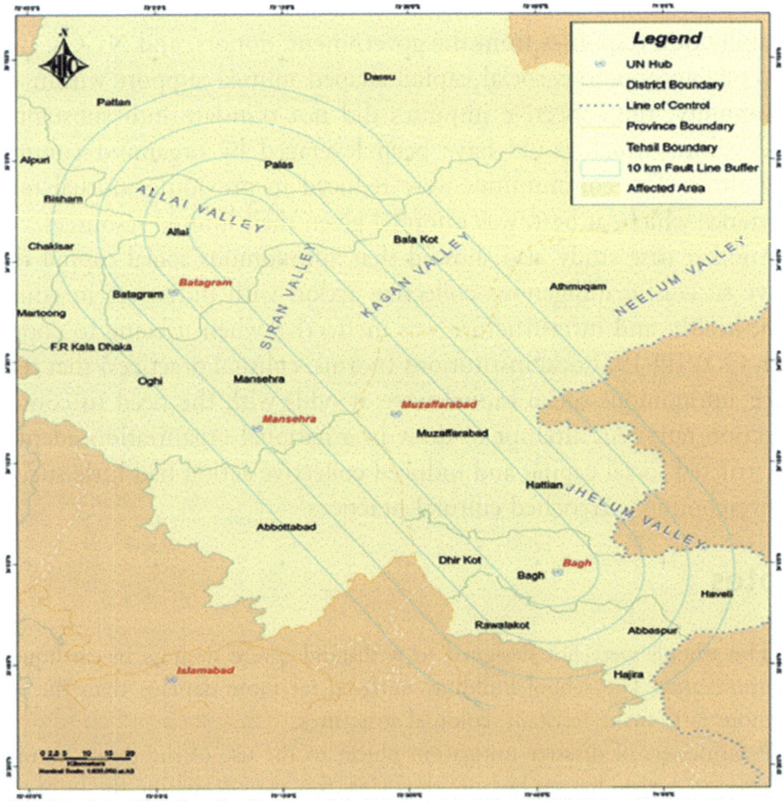

Fig. 9.2 Allai Valley (*Source* Geological survey of Pakistan)

Fig. 9.3 Deforestation, land use changes and earthquake destruction

Deforestation increases vulnerability to landslides and earthquakes

Fig. 9.3 (continued)

Land use changes

Fig. 9.3 (continued)

Earthquake induced destruction

Fig. 9.3 (continued)

Reference

Khan, Shaheen R. 2006. *The Role of the Military in Humanitarian Assistance: Bridging the Gap*. Sustainable Development Policy Institute, Islamabad, prepared for ActionAid.

Part IV

Conclusion

10

Summary, Conclusions, and Recommendations

As stated in the introduction, this book distinguishes between indigenous and constructed social capital and the associated spontaneous and induced collective action for rural development.

Collective action often pertains to the micro or meso (between micro and macro) levels. It rectifies the shortcomings of the mainstream neoliberal approach to development which, despite lip service to poverty alleviation, has in practice exacerbated it according to many critics.[1]

The focus of this book is to complement macro heterodox development approaches like new developmentalism or political economy of development (Khan, 2020), at the micro or meso levels with cost-effective, community-centric and empirically grounded initiatives that can lead to broad-spectrum development outcomes, economic, social, and environmental. This point regarding its complementary role needs emphasis. As indicated in the introduction and Chapter 2, social capital induced collective action is no panacea or substitute for approaches that address broad-based structural transformation while addressing issues of asymmetrical power and equity.

S. R. Khan and S. R. Khan, *Social Capital and Collective Action in Pakistani Rural Development*, https://doi.org/10.1007/978-3-030-71450-5_10

One form of constructed social capital and induced collective action we explored in Chapters 3 and 4 has resulted from the work of a network of development NGOs referred to as Rural Support Programs (RSPs) in Pakistan. This takes the form of apex organizations referred to as Local Support Organizations (LSOs). These multi-tiered organizations (community, village and apex) are in principle an exit strategy for RSPs so that these development NGOs could move on spatially to other areas for social mobilization and social capital construction.

Based on our fieldwork, we think that much more hard work was needed to ensure that the LSOs were on firm foundations so that they could take over and indeed excel at the work RSPs were doing. LSOs have a comparative advantage in doing development work, given that they are rooted in the community and that they embody the social capital that can be tapped to make collective action work for communities of which they are a part and that they represent.

They also have the major advantage of possessing local knowledge. However, the localism could also be a disadvantage, and RSPs will need to be wary when that is the case, in order to offset potential negative effects. For example, as our brief historical review demonstrated, local governance in most parts of Pakistan emerges from a tradition of ruling rather than serving. This was reinforced by colonialism, and the post-colonial experience further entrenched autocratic and hierarchical governance that represents an obstacle to the attempts to institute participatory governance. RSPs need to intervene in a diplomatic manner particularly in cases where hereditary governance trumps newly initiated participatory norms. It is tempting not to rock the boat, and that is the approach often adopted in government-supported initiatives.

RSPs have traditionally bypassed rather than taken on entrenched rural elites and that may be sensible. However, the clout that they possess as semi-government organizations can be put to good use in running interference where needed to ensure that LSO democratic governance and accountability mechanisms are in place.

Another problem is lack of an effective communications strategy as part of the exit strategy, since perceptions in such social endeavors can create reality. In some cases, we sensed a high level of dissatisfaction at the grassroots level with the board, executive body, and general body of

LSOs, and much of this could be attributed to a lack of awareness. The concept of an executive body distinct from the management committee is a sophisticated one, even for the NGO sector in urban areas. However, given the much greater level of sophistication, this practice has been understood and is now entrenched in that sector. A much more effective communications strategy is needed in rural areas to attain a similar comfort level at the grassroots level.

RSPs also need an inward communications strategy. While the RSPN and the top RSP leadership were fully aligned with the exit strategy being implemented, there was a lack of complete buy-in lower down the hierarchy among those actually charged with implementing the strategy. One manifestation of this disconnect was the reluctance to bow out gracefully. RSPs continued to be perceived by communities as the weighty partner. Until the communities perceived the baton to have been transferred, they continue to look to the RSPs for support. A dependence mentality is the opposite of the participatory approach that the RSPs have worked so hard to cultivate.

In some cases, this will mean withdrawing from spaces that the LSO has the competence to take over. We found that in Punjab and Haripur, RSPs ran parallel programs, such as in microcredit, which were competing with and infringing on LSO space. RSPs need to concede space so that the LSOs are center-stage in community perception and reality.

Timing, of course, is of the essence, and this is an art, not a science. Some internal maturity indicators can help, but this decision can never be mechanical. Wrong decisions are inevitable, and are something to learn from. But the extremes of premature abandonment or of an unwillingness to concede space should be avoided. Also, institutionalizing follow-up and capacity-building once space has been conceded is still needed.

Our fieldwork demonstrated a wide diversity, complexity, and richness in grassroots institutions. In keeping with our recommendation for establishing firm foundations for LSOs, RSPs need to be more sensitive to the indigenous social capital that already exists in communities and build on that rather than have one common approach to institution construction. This would be more in keeping with the essence of the participatory approach that the RSPs have instituted with considerable success.

As the RSPs make clear when introducing themselves to communities, participation means involvement in all aspects of a project from needs assessment and conception to maintenance. In cases where there was a disengagement of the executive committee from projects, which were contracted out, participation was not achieved. Local participation and ownership require a full engagement with all stages of the project including implementation and monitoring. We were surprised to come across projects in which the communities even questioned the validity of the site.

The RSPs also need to make clear to the LSO leadership that the onus of attaining full participation is on them. For LSOs to blame communities for desultory participation, as was sometimes the case, is simply to demonstrate a lack of understanding of the process in which they are engaged. We do not view a paid, rather than a voluntary, managerial staff as a problem per se. RSP staff is paid and yet also had the privilege of working for organizations that do good, and so this should not be any different for LSO managerial staff working in very remote locations in difficult conditions. They too have the privilege of working with and for their own communities, but the incentives need to be right. Failing to recognize this reality is to set the organizations up for high turnover; and without the active labor market that now exists for the broader development NGO sector, turnover imposes a very high cost in remote rural locations.

The main issue is establishing a sustained revenue stream (possibly in part forthcoming from an endowment fund). The communities are currently too poor for a 'pay for service' model to work. Ultimately, the LSOs are delivering services that the state should provide (constitutionally and as citizen rights) but does not have the capacity to do so. Essentially, the state needs to view the LSOs as complementing it, but it must provide the revenue stream for capacity-building and service delivery. Even as higher-level RSP leadership continues to press for this, building the infrastructure of sustainable apex organizations at the grassroots level needs to continue to persuade the state that effective organizations of the people can be partners in rural development.[2]

Thus, an effective interaction with the government is a key area for RSPs to focus on. While respondents expressed satisfaction with the pace of linkages being established with other sectors (donors, development NGOs, the private sector), they noted a substantive lack of interaction with government line departments. This process needs to be institutionalized so that RSPs and LSOs can tap into what is available – naming and shaming could be among the arsenal of tools available to them. As indicated earlier, service delivery is primarily the responsibility of the government. Organized communities will make the reception of these services more effective, but some pump-priming will also be needed to get them flowing in the short and medium term.

We found during our fieldwork that RSPs were in the process of sensitizing men to women-specific issues and had succeeded to a considerable extent; patriarchal/cultural biases inevitably creep in when men are in the majority. In this regard, the LSO management bodies (executive body, general body) need to become more gender-balanced in order to minimize these biases. A very positive finding of our fieldwork documented in Chapter 4 was that the outstanding women managed LSOs outranked all LSOs in terms of their development work.

A comparative institutional analysis in Chapter 5 evaluated the work of an RSP (National Rural Support Program) with two government line departments, Local Government and Rural Development Department (LGRDD) and Public Health Engineering Department (PHED). In principle, due to donor urging, the project rules and implementation procedures of the government departments now also endorse participation and are very similar to those of NRSP. The real question, therefore, is why they were less successful in realizing this than NRSP.

We found that one critical difference is in the way NRSP and the government projects approached social capital construction. The NRSP social mobilizer orientation was more often a genuine concern for mobilizing the community which is very painstaking work. The government project concern was with form and not substance. Thus, the LGRDD and PHED officials were generally satisfied with the formation of a community organization (CO) or a water committee. It did not seem to matter that this was done by working with the local notables in the community and that the general body of the community had little or no say in the decision-making.

One should not downplay the complex political realities in a rural setting. It is much easier to approach a community via the local notables. However, we found that doing so is likely to mean that the local notables will appropriate the major benefits of the scheme and that the community as a whole will not own or support it. We found this to be the case even when the NRSP social mobilizers' approach to the community was mediated by the local notables. All five out of the fifteen NRSP schemes that the field observers found to be non-sustainable had local notables dominating decision-making, appropriating the major benefits from the scheme and hence alienating the general body of the community. The only one of the five PHED schemes that was clearly found to be sustainable had a mobilized community with exposure to several of the most prominent capacity-building NGOs in the country. In three of the four LGRDD schemes found to be sustainable, an individual activist essentially played the role of an effective social mobilizer.

Of course, one could argue that some communities have a greater proclivity toward becoming mobilized. This may well be true. The more interesting policy issue is that NRSP staff managed to mobilize communities in three different provinces under very different social and economic conditions. This achievement was particularly noteworthy in Sindh where the communities were highly ethnically and class differentiated. For us, this represented a strong endorsement of the concept of social capital construction. What is it that makes the NRSP more effective? An important part of the answer is skills in social capital construction that comes from training and the motivation to apply those skills.

There is an important lesson to be learnt from the LGRDD experience in AJK. It appears that the field officers were able to impart what they had internalized. The concept of community self-help that they internalized was that the community should make cash contributions, carry pipes, lay the pipes, and build the tanks. While the community clearly had an incentive to do all this considering their need for water and considering that they solicited the schemes in the first place, it is still not a small achievement to get this kind of contribution from communities generally believed to be entirely dependent on the state. However, the important point is that if LGRDD field staff took the communities this far, they could have taken them further.

This also applies to PHED which was effective in establishing water committees and having them implement a tariff system. We found that the government projects field staff indicated a capacity for social mobilization. The problem was that they had limited expectations from the community and therefore got limited results.

While NRSP's performance was far superior to that of the government line departments, we don't believe that development NGOs are a panacea. This is because they confront inherent limitations of coverage even though the scale RSPs have achieved in Pakistan is impressive (Chapter 3). Many of their special advantages may be derived from nimbly operating on a smaller scale. Ultimately, one can probably only conceive of NGOs like NRSP as development partners. Their more important role is that of being path breakers.

We show that development NGOs, while limited in scope, may have important lessons to teach about delivering social services. Since their method of doing business is much more effective than that of the government line departments, one needs to find a way of making the government line departments function more like the development NGOs. Government personnel need to be trained and be given the right incentive structure to use this training.

Training in social capital construction is now not a scarce service in Pakistan. The right incentive structure can emerge from bonuses tied to results-based assessment done internally by the line departments and by outside evaluators. Interviews with government field staff revealed the lack of satisfaction with low salaries. Compared to LGRDD and PHED, NRSP field staff were paid a competitive salary, were better trained, and were expected to work hard.

Another public policy lesson for line departments emerged from our study. As long as they used village local notables as the entry point for communication with communities, they risked alienating the communities. A more effective strategy, and of course a much more difficult one, would be to ascertain who is generally trusted by the community and work with such individuals as activists and leaders like the RSPs do.

In Chapter 6 we discuss the denial of community rights in forests that customary law provided but that statutory law and practice negated. Communities still have some rights on paper, but are without the legal, institutional, or political means to avail of these rights to the fullest. Well-defined resource rights and entitlements, and the mechanisms to exercise these rights, would provide communities with a cushion. When resource rights are not secure and there are delays in royalty payments, livelihoods are threatened. In the Dir valleys in North Pakistan, this led to incidents of spontaneous and violent collective action. Such incidents have not however elicited meaningful policy changes. The government seems to have viewed resource-related conflicts as isolated events, rather than as a symptom of a much broader injustice.

To be successful, spontaneous collective action requires indigenous social capital, both bonding and linking—since several ethnic groups are involved. However, the spontaneous Dir collective action is a case of anger boiling over, collective action, some remediation and then the dissolution of collective action. By contrast, Sarhad Awami Forestry Ittehad (SAFI) collective action had its origin in the same anger over social injustice, but with the assistance of a development NGO (SUNGI), the collective action was sustained into an ongoing campaign with far reaching effect. This is a lesson for both communities and for development NGOs that want to help.

SAFI's financial standing however remains weak. The organization's effectiveness and geographical spread could increase considerably if its leaders could find a way to make it financially sustainable. An interesting challenge SAFI has faced has been donor-funding constraints. The context for success needs to be defined clearly. In other words, SAFI's process achievements can be identified more easily than the specific outcomes it was able to accomplish through these process measures. When expected outcomes are complex, as in the case of forestry reforms, the process which can realize these expectations also needs to be more intensive.

Donors are results driven and have less patience for processes, especially when such processes are politically sensitive. This has created an interesting conundrum in the case of forestry reforms. The reforms did not make much headway because the key players—the donors and the

Forest Department (FD)—excluded communities from the consultations. The resulting dominance of form over substance is not what the donors intended in the first place. However, this becomes an unfortunate reality; one which SAFI attempted to change through grassroots consultations and policy advocacy.

In other words, SAFI sought to give tangible shape to a reform agenda, which the donors had contributed to articulating. However, these donors were less willing to finance the means for achieving reform objectives. Thus, the Asian Development Bank, the Swiss Development Corporation and the Dutch government committed/spent upward of USD 100 million in devising reform strategies. Easily twice that amount was spent on projects. This strikes a discordant note when one considers that donor funding for SAFI activities did not exceed US$50,000. It also underscores the need for SAFI, and other peoples' movements to develop a funding mechanism that focuses on internally generated means (partly via memberships) to achieve financial sustainability.

An element that is key to both policy and management is resource rights. If community property and tenure rights to forest resources are not clearly defined, the policy and management reform agenda will make little headway. It is imperative that organizations like SAFI launch an information-based advocacy campaign promoting the traditional/customary resource rights of communities. They also need to complement this with an information campaign demonstrating the viability of forest conservation in areas where such rights have been honored.

Perhaps the most important lesson from SAFI's experience is its ability to involve relevant stakeholders from across the board, striking the correct balance between confrontation and collaboration. In SAFI's case, relevant stakeholders apart from the FD include the media, politicians, and the civil society. Every peoples' movement must analyze the institutional context it functions in. The idea is to devise a strategy to co-opt key stakeholders to gain maximum leverage.

It is essential to bring women on board as active members. Although SAFI highlighted gender issues and involved women in SAFI's major events, due to tribal mindsets women are not formally part of SAFI. This is a major deficiency in its make-up. Considering the dependence of tribal women on forests and impacts of deforestation on them, one way for peoples' movements in the forestry sector could be to establish a designated wing of women members so that their concerns could be addressed effectively.

Linking social capital is the ideal base for doing the organizational work with activists assuming a catalytic role. As documented in Chapter 7, The Pakistan Fisherfolk Forum (PFF) built an informal membership-based association, with women a third of the membership, and successfully engaged in advocacy, activism, and social movement construction to protect the rights of its members in the face of ingress of foreign trawlers into their waters. This ingress is with the connivance of the Federal Government bent on export promotion despite very negative consequences for fishing stocks. This problem for poor fisherfolk is compounded by lax policy on pollution prevention and aggressive policy on dam construction that has resulted in salt water incursions due to a lack of fresh water flow. These sins of omission and commission have devasted traditional fisheries.

Spontaneous collective action is also evident in the case of the Okara peasant revolt documented in Chapter 8. The advice of "urban activists" was critical to building the organization and sustaining the struggle. Eventually, the peasants legally prevailed in turning back the military's attempt to displace a sharecropping with a rental contract. Indeed, their direct action eventually led to the military acknowledging that the Government of Punjab rather than the army was the true owner of the land.

By contrast, Khan and Akhtar (2014) documented the struggle for a just price for land by peasants in a peri-urban Bharia (Navy) town development scheme on the outskirts of Rawalpindi, the location of the army General Headquarters. The lack of organization meant that the collective action in the form of rallies and demonstrations dissipated. The developers, with the support of the military and police used brutal intimidation and divide and conquer tactics, killed the social movement and displaced the villagers by inducing them to accept sub-market prices. Had the collective action assumed an organizational form, it might have been possible to sustain the collective action as in Okara.

As with protecting resource rights, communities also display surprising levels of resilience and coping capacity in the face of natural disasters. We argue once again that building on what exists at the grassroots level will strengthen the capacity of communities to manage their resources and cope with natural disasters. Minimalist intervention that buttresses local institutions and integrates peoples' voices, wisdom and experience represents the best of spontaneous and induced collective action.

While it is tempting to end on an inspirational note, the narrative in Chapter 9 is more sobering and more likely to be closer to reality when there is no catalyst to formalize indigenous social capital. The infringements on common property resources of the poor in Allai resulted in an open access regime that resulted in heavily denuded forests and therefore the intensification of the impacts of a devastating earthquake. Rehabilitation and relief were again impeded by the capture of traditional institutions (structural social capital) that could have leveraged what was available in assistance. Even so, the social capital-driven mutual support among the poor for relief and rehabilitation was inspirational.

To sum up, in terms of the key themes of the book, it appears that spontaneous collective action based on indigenous social capital is likely to come into play for defensive purposes like protecting property rights or recovery from natural disaster. It is less likely to come into play proactively such as for rural development. For the latter, constructed social capital that induces collective action has been more in evidence. However, success in constructing social capital is more likely when it builds on and gives shape to indigenous social capital. This is a finding evident in the broader literature on social capital and rural development and one that we found support for in our qualitative research. Another important lesson that emerged from social capital construction was not using the easy way out and allowing local notables to mediate the social mobilization. This proved to be a way of ensuring elite capture.

Defensive or spontaneous collective action when social anger bubbles over can dissipate once the authorities redress some of the issues but it generally does not lead to lasting social reform. For those wanting to see lasting social justice reforms, spontaneous collective action can represent an opportunity. Organizing spontaneous social movements and giving them institutional structure, as for SAFI in social forestry (Chapter 6) and PFF in fisheries (Chapter 7), can produce more lasting social change.[3]

Notes

1. Evidence cited in Khan (2020, Chapter 8).
2. Continuity is essential and we pointed out in the introduction how a new political regime was willing to undermine the RSPs since their success was associated with an earlier rival political regime.
3. A good example of this in the USA is a cursory look at the conservative Tea Party compared to the progressive Occupy social movements. The former got embedded in the political process, won electoral victories, and continue to have resonance in conservative politics. The latter shunned the mainstream political process and initially dissipated. Subsequently, that social impulse manifested itself in electoral politics and is shaping democratic politics in a substantive way.

References

Khan, S.R. 2020. *Development Economics: A Critical Introduction.* New York: Routledge.

Khan, S.R. and A.S. Akhtar, with S. Bodla. 2014. *The Military and Development Denied in the Pakistani Punjab: An Eroding Social Consensus.* London: Anthem Press.

Index

S. R. Khan and S. R. Khan, *Social Capital and Collective Action in Pakistani Rural Development*, https://doi.org/10.1007/978-3-030-71450-5

R

S

The manufacturer's authorised representative in the EU is Springer Nature Customer Service Centre GmbH, Europaplatz 3, 69115 Heidelberg, Germany. If you have any concerns regarding our products, please contact ProductSafety@springernature.com

Printed and bound by CPI Group (UK) Ltd, Croydon, CR0 4YY

30/09/2026

02225700-0006